Air raids on
South-West Essex
in the Great War

Air raids on South-West Essex in the Great War

Looking for Zeppelins at Leyton

Alan Simpson

Pen & Sword
AVIATION

First published in Great Britain in 2015 by
PEN & SWORD AVIATION
an imprint of
Pen & Sword Books Ltd
47 Church Street
Barnsley
South Yorkshire
S70 2AS

ISBN 978-1-47383-412-5

Typeset by Concept, Huddersfield, West Yorkshire, HD4 5JL.
Printed and bound in England by CPI Group (UK) Ltd, Croydon CR0 4YY.

Pen & Sword Books Ltd incorporates the imprints of Pen & Sword Archaeology, Atlas, Aviation, Battleground, Discovery, Family History, History, Maritime, Military, Naval, Politics, Railways, Select, Social History, Transport, True Crime, and Claymore Press, Frontline Books, Leo Cooper, Praetorian Press, Remember When, Seaforth Publishing and Wharncliffe.

For a complete list of Pen & Sword titles please contact
PEN & SWORD BOOKS LIMITED
47 Church Street, Barnsley, South Yorkshire, S70 2AS, England
E-mail: enquiries@pen-and-sword.co.uk
Website: www.pen-and-sword.co.uk

Contents

Foreword

A quarter of a century before the Blitz of 1940, the inhabitants of south-west Essex were terrorized by another aerial menace – gigantic airships. For nearly three years, German Zeppelins flew above their homes *en route* to unleashing hundreds of high explosive and incendiary bombs on London. In three of these raids, bombs were dropped on Leyton and many others fell elsewhere in south-west Essex. These early air raids are now largely forgotten in local memory, perhaps because of the much greater death toll and damage in the Second World War, but for the inhabitants of the time the attacks were unprecedented, unexpected and lethal.

This was the first strategic bombing campaign in history and the Zeppelin was the original 'stealth bomber'. Cruising under cover of darkness at an altitude so high as to be barely audible, Zeppelins would cross the North Sea from bases in Germany or Belgium and terrorize parts of Britain. This was a novel and unwelcome means of waging war, one that provoked a degree of panic and resentment and dispelled much of Britain's sense of island security. Although the raiders, demonized as 'baby killers' or 'sky pirates' for causing indiscriminate civilian casualties, did not crush British morale, they did disrupt war production and they succeeded in diverting personnel, arms and aircraft from where they were needed on the Western Front. Most importantly, the raids changed the face of warfare forever by bringing the whole nation into the front line.

When Britain declared war on Germany in August 1914, few residents of Leyton would have anticipated death and destruction falling on them from the night sky. Nor would they have expected their houses to be blasted into ruin amid the roar of exploding bombs and the firing of guns, while in the intervals between the explosions the air overhead would be full of the drone of huge airships. But, earlier than any other inland town in Britain, Leyton became a scene of war, and some 1,300 houses were damaged, 18 citizens killed and 82 wounded by bombing in three airship raids. Then, in 1917, a greater menace was to appear in the skies over south-west Essex – Gothas and Giants – two- and four-engine bombers that came by day and night.

As the war progressed, a proper defence system for the capital was built up and, during what has been termed the 'First Battle of Britain' or the 'First

Blitz', a complex network was installed - much of it in south-west Essex. This system finally prevailed and, with the exception of radar, was much the same as that which was to serve Britain in 1940: in fact, some of the anti-aircraft guns in use in 1940 were the very *same* guns used in 1918. Almost every part of this system had to be invented, at the same time as the aerial threat moved from hundreds of pounds of bombs in a raid to thousands, and from Zeppelins to Gothas and Giants. And whereas London's defences consisted of very few aircraft in early 1915, some 200 aircraft – eleven full squadrons – were available by the end of the war.

In the years since the Great War a wealth of literature has been published on London's first air raids and about the defence network that grew up around the metropolis. What happened in the capital's eastern suburbs and the nearby Essex countryside has received less coverage. This book attempts to put that right by looking at the area which, in 1914, was part of the county of Essex, but now comprises the London boroughs of Waltham Forest, Redbridge, Havering, Newham, and Barking & Dagenham. Working from a range of contemporary letters, diaries and newspaper reports, many from local sources, and focussing in particular on Leyton and Ilford[1], I have examined what happened before and after the raiders reached the capital, although I have strayed across the rivers Lea and Thames and gone further afield on a few occasions. This is not intended to be a 'bomb by bomb' account of every raid on south-west Essex, nor have I looked in any detail at the effect of the raids on the metropolis itself, as others have done that before me. To set the story in its wider context, however, I have included some material about the defence of the London area generally and reports from combatants on both sides.

Acknowledgements

I am particularly grateful to Georgina Green for permitting me to make extensive use of quotes from her 1987 book *Keepers, Cockneys and Kitchen Maids: Memories of Epping Forest 1900–1925*. The first-hand accounts she recorded there of people living locally during the Great War are invaluable and without them this story would be much the poorer. Gerald Ellins' permission to quote from the contemporary letters of his grandmother, Winifred Freeman, is much appreciated too. David Boote's transcriptions of entries in Leyton school logbooks inspired me to devote a chapter here to the effects of the air raids on school attendance.

I would also like to record my thanks to: Helen Mavin, Imperial War Museum, Photograph Archive; Mehzebin Adam, Imperial War Museum, Assistant Curator; Catherine Cooper, Fleet Air Arm Museum; Belinda Day and Venit Mehta, Royal Air Force Museum; Jo Parker and Gary Heales, Vestry House Museum, London Borough of Waltham Forest; and Dawn Ann Galer, Information & Heritage Service, London Borough of Redbridge, all of whom were of great assistance in pointing me in the direction of obscure photographs and granting permission to use copyright material in their institutions' collections. A final 'thank you' goes to my brother, Philip, for reading through the text and passing on his comments. In spite of the above help, any errors are entirely mine – if you would like to bring them to my attention, please do so through the publisher.

Abbreviations

AA	Anti-aircraft
AG	Aktiengesellschaft
BE	Bleriot Experimental
BOGOHL	Bombengeschwader der Obersten Heersleitung
DELAG	Deutsche Luftschiffahrts-AG
DH	De Havilland
DORA	Defence of the Realm Act
DSO	Distinguished Service Order
GER	Great Eastern Railway
GmbH	Gesellschaft mit beschränkter Haftung
HAC	Honorable Artillery Company
HE	High explosive
HQ	Headquarters
KAGOHL	Kampfgeschwader der Obersten Heersleitung
KC	King's Counsel
L	Luftschiff
LADA	London Air Defence Area
LCC	London County Council
LZ	Luftschiff-Zeppelin
MC	Military Cross
MM	Military Medal
MOS	Metropolitan Observation Service
MP	Member of Parliament
MR	Midland Railway
NC	Non-commissioned officer
NLR	North London Railway
PL	Parseval
RAF	Royal Air Force
RDC	Royal Defence Corps
RE	Royal Engineers
RFA	Royal Field Artillery
RFC	Royal Flying Corps
RGA	Royal Garrison Artillery

RNAS	Royal Naval Air Service
RNVR	Royal Naval Volunteer Reserve
ROC	Royal Observer Corps
SL	Schütte-Lanz
TDS	Training Depot Station
TNT	Trinitrotoluene
UDC	Urban District Council
VC	Victoria Cross

Chapter 1

'Peril from above'

The bombardment of cities from the air was a *leitmotif* of novelists in the years before the Great War, and the spectre of bombs falling on London was a regular theme. At this time, the world's most powerful airships were all German. Each was as long as a battleship, could stay aloft for hours and could carry a dozen men and several tons of bombs. No other country had anything as impressive, nor did any aeroplane have remotely the same performance. Equally important, this was a time when Anglo-German antagonism was at its height. In his 1908 novel *War in the Air*, H.G. Wells vividly described German airships bombing faraway New York; and one of the most popular plays on the London stage in 1909 was Guy du Maurier's *An Englishman's Home*, which dramatized an invasion of Britain by a thinly-disguised Germany.[1] Alarmist warnings began to appear in newspapers too, like this one from *The Daily Mail*:

OUR PERIL FROM ABOVE

Are so many of us indifferent still because we do not understand? Do we realize, from what we read in the daily press, that a foreign Power – and a Power regarded as a potential enemy – has perfected an aircraft which will fly, at the speed of an express train, for several days and nights without alighting? Do we realize that this machine – evolved at immense cost and after years of patient labour – is at last a practical warcraft, with a powerful, duplicate engine plant, a crew of specially trained navigators and an installation of wireless telegraphy which will flash a message several hundred miles? Do we realize that such aircraft, if launched against us with hostile intent, could steal across the North Sea at night, and rain down tons of incendiary and explosive bombs upon vital points of our coastline, and on London itself? Do we realize that, even after ceaseless warning, we lie practically defenceless against this peril, which grows from day to day?

In 1910, the Aerial League,[2] one of several independent voices urging greater preparedness in military aviation, produced a pamphlet which saw the nerve centres of Britain as imperilled. By 1913, dozens of mysterious airships were being reported from all over the British Isles. The reality of these phantom airships, or 'scareships', can be ruled out in nearly all cases, but it was widely believed that they could only be Zeppelins. In part, this was because it was thought that only Germany was able to undertake airship flights to Britain, but it was also assumed that only Germany would want to carry out such missions.

That the British press obsessed so much about the danger posed by German aerial supremacy is probably due to the persistence of the effects of earlier scares and panics about German spies, German invasions and German dreadnoughts.[3] The dreadnought crisis ('We want eight and we won't wait' was a newspaper headline of the time) had taken place in 1909, and since then certain sections of the press had been obsessed with hunting German spies, who were apparently everywhere.[4] In 1910, *The Sketch* ran a series of cartoons by William Heath Robinson about spies in England, including one showing them dangling from trees in Epping Forest.[5] German periodicals boasted that the Zeppelin would give the British what was coming to them, so it seemed plausible that Germany was sending over its new weapons by night to spy on Britain, or even to practice navigation and bombing techniques for a future war. And Conservative newspapers did not hesitate to use the 'fact' of German aerial espionage as a cudgel with which to beat the Liberal Government for its slow progress in forming an air force.[6] Despite this feeling, there was little belief in British Government or military circles that air attacks on civilians would soon become an integral part of modern warfare; for many the real threat posed by aerial warfare seemed less menacing than the literary one.

The outbreak of the First World War quickly altered these perceptions. In Germany, Major Wilhelm Siegert assembled the innocuous sounding Brieftauben Abteilung (Carrier Pigeon Unit) and mounted the first token raid on Britain's Channel ports on 21 December 1914, when a Friedrichshafen FF29 sea-plane dropped two bombs in the sea near the Admiralty Pier at Dover. A further sea-plane raid on Dover followed on Christmas Eve, when a bomb was dropped in the garden of a house, enabling *The Times* to report that 'the threatened German air raid has to some extent become an accomplished fact'. The 'carrier pigeons' were not to achieve a great deal with their raids, but these pin-pricks were to be followed by much more deadly attacks over the next four years. And some of these raids were to have devastating effects on the rapidly growing south-west corner of the county of Essex.

The late-nineteenth and early-twentieth century expansion of metropolitan Essex was perhaps the most remarkable feature of the county's recent history. By the 1890s, Barking and Ilford were joined in continuous growth to East Ham; by 1900, West Ham, East Ham, Walthamstow and Leyton had all been linked to London's growing suburbs. Between 1891 and 1911, Leyton's population grew from 63,000 to 125,000 and Ilford's from 11,000 to 78,000.

THE Daily Mail MAP
OF
ZEPPELIN AND AEROPLANE BOMBS ON LONDON.

Reprinted from "The Daily Mail," January 31, 1919.

This map was given away by *The Daily Mail* in 1919 and shows where some of the bombs fell in London and the surrounding area. The north-east quarter of the map, beyond the London County Boundary dotted line, shows part of the metropolitan Essex area. (*Author's collection*)

By 1911, almost every acre of land in West Ham and East Ham had disappeared under development: three wards in West Ham – Tidal Basin, Canning Town and Plaistow – each had a population of more than 30,000, making them larger than most of the county's municipal boroughs; and East Ham was England's eleventh-largest town. By 1914, some 700,000 people, more than half the population of Essex, were concentrated in less than ten per cent of the county's area. Yet despite this rapid growth, there was still agricultural land to be found in parts of that ten per cent, as rural as anywhere in the deepest Essex countryside.

Chapter 2

'Our nerves are on edge'

Zeppelin design

A Zeppelin was a type of large rigid airship pioneered by the German Count Ferdinand von Zeppelin at the end of the nineteenth century. It was based on designs he had outlined in 1874 and detailed in 1893. His plans were reviewed by a committee in 1894, but little interest was shown so the Count was left on his own to bring his idea to fruition.

The first Zeppelin flight took place on 2 July 1900 over Lake Constance. It lasted only eighteen minutes before Luftschiff-Zeppelin LZ1 was forced to land on the lake. It was largely due to support by aviation enthusiasts that von Zeppelin's idea got a further chance and would be developed into a reasonably reliable technology. Only then could the airships be profitably used for civilian aviation and sold to the military.

Before the First World War, a total of twenty-one Zeppelin airships (LZ5 to LZ25) had been manufactured. In 1909, LZ6 became the first Zeppelin to be used for commercial passenger transport. The world's first airline, the newly founded Deutsche Luftschiffahrts AG (DELAG), offered scheduled flights and had bought seven Zeppelins by 1914, by which time German airships had flown over 100,000 miles and carried 37,000 civilian passengers.

The German military, realizing the airship's potential for warfare, ordered several, the first entering service in March 1909, three years before the formation of the Royal Flying Corps (RFC) in Britain. At the outbreak of war, Zeppelins were used almost immediately, offensively bombing the Belgian cities of Liege and Antwerp on the nights of 6/7 August and 25/26 August 1914 respectively, killing several citizens in their homes.

The basic form of early Zeppelins was a long cylinder with tapered ends and complex multi-plane fins. During the Great War, following improvements by the rival firm Schütte-Lanz Luftschiffbau, the design was changed to a streamlined shape and cruciform fins used by almost all airships ever since. Within this outer envelope, up to nineteen separate balloons, also known as 'cells' or 'gasbags', contained lighter-than-air hydrogen gas. For most rigid airships the gasbags were made of many sheets of skin from the intestines of cows. About 200,000 were needed for a typical First World War Zeppelin.

The sheets were joined together and folded into impermeable layers. Crews included a sail-maker to repair small tears and holes in the gasbags.

The most important feature of Zeppelin's design was a rigid skeleton of aluminium or wood, made of rings, longitudinal girders and steel wires. This meant that the aircraft could be much larger than non-rigid airships (which relied on a slight over-pressure within the single gasbag to maintain their shape). This enabled Zeppelins to lift heavier loads and be fitted with increasingly powerful engines. Catwalks along the skeleton allowed crew members to move through the airship, and a vertical ladder gave access to the outside through the top of the hull.

Forward thrust was provided by internal combustion engines mounted in cowlings connected to the skeleton. A Zeppelin was steered by adjusting and selectively reversing engine thrust and by using rudder and elevator fins. A comparatively small compartment for crew was built into the bottom of the frame, but in large Zeppelins this was not the entire habitable space; they often carried crew internally too.

By 1914, state-of-the-art Zeppelins had lengths of 500 feet and volumes of nearly 900,000 cubic feet, enabling them to carry loads of around 9 tons. They were typically powered by three Maybach diesel engines of around 400–550hp each, reaching speeds of up to 50mph.

There were two types of ship operated by the air forces of both the German army and navy as two entirely separate divisions. The first was the Schütte-Lanz airship, which had a wooden frame. These machines were operated by the army. The other type was the aluminium-framed Zeppelin which found favour with the navy. At the beginning of the war the German army had nine machines (including three DELAG craft requisitioned from civilian ownership), the navy had four. All the craft were identified with the pre-war prefix LZ and a number; to avoid confusion between craft with the same number it is customary to use the prefix LZ for army craft and just L for navy craft (the Schütte-Lanz and Parseval types are sometimes identified with the respective prefixes SL and PL).

There were major differences in doctrine between the two services: the army emphasized bombing from a low level and close support of ground forces, while the navy had trained for reconnaissance and it was these fliers who carried out most of the airship bombing raids over Great Britain. Initially, the main use of Zeppelins was in reconnaissance over the North Sea and the Baltic, where the endurance of the airships led German warships to a number of Allied vessels. Zeppelin patrolling had priority over any other airship activity and during the war around 1,200 scouting flights were made. The German navy had some fifteen Zeppelins in commission in 1915 and was able

This was just one of a multitude of German propaganda postcards featuring Zeppelins. (*Author's collection*)

to have two or more patrolling continuously at any one time, almost regardless of weather. They prevented British ships from approaching Germany, spotted when and where the British were laying mines and later aided in the destruction of those mines.

Navigation

Flying a Zeppelin from Germany (or from occupied Belgium, where Germany also had airship bases) to London was not easy. The complicated systems of the Zeppelins were prone to breakdown, meaning many missions had to be aborted. Also, although Zeppelins could fly in almost any weather conditions, they were very much at its mercy. Cloud cover made navigation a nightmare, but moonless nights also had advantages since the defenders could not spot Zeppelins approaching in the darkness. Unexpected storms could damage airships or cause them to drift off course. Even when everything worked and the weather was clear, finding London was still a challenge.

The raiders lifted off from their seaside bases in the early afternoon, crossed the English coast at dusk, arrived over their targets around midnight, then attacked and headed for home before daybreak. They flew at an altitude out of range of AA guns and safe from the fragile and underpowered British fighters that rose to challenge them. Once over their target, the Zeppelin crews dropped parachute flares temporarily to blind the gunners below, or flew into a cloud or fog bank to hide from their pursuers.

Navigation was crude at best and, with no real navigational instruments, Zeppelin crews were forced to find their way by using maps and recognizing landmarks on the ground. They relied on railway tracks, the lights of towns, or the sheen of rivers, lakes and reservoirs to guide them to their targets. The only instruments in the command gondola other than ship controls were a liquid compass, an altimeter, a thermometer and an airspeed meter. To determine their location, the commanders had to use dead-reckoning, relying on what landmarks were visible from high altitude, and an inaccurate system of radio bearings, in which the airship would call for bearings and various stations in Germany would measure and compare the direction of the radio waves and estimate the vessel's location. When raids on Britain started, the German navy's High Command established radio stations at Nordholtz and Borkum to direct and help the Zeppelins. Not only did this crude system have a margin of error of several miles, but it also helped the British track the Zeppelins by listening to the German frequencies.

Because of these navigational difficulties, German airships found the targets they were aiming for only about ten per cent of the time. Although night-time raids were intended to target only cities and some military sites on the east coast and around the Thames estuary, after blackouts became widespread many bombs fell at random on Essex and East Anglia; German bombs were wasted on empty fields, minor villages or the sea. Even when the airships did manage to get over an industrial city, it was impossible for them to aim their bombs at specific buildings and most landed on streets, or strategically unimportant residential areas. The Germans had no way of knowing just how inaccurate their navigation was, and a high confidence in the efficacy of the raids was sustained in large part by the reports of the commanders, which always insisted that a valuable target was bombed.

Zeppelin crews

Flying a Zeppelin was more like sailing a ship than piloting an aeroplane. The captain stood, binoculars around his neck, with the watch officer and control-surface operators in the command gondola. There they maintained the airship's altitude and course with two nautical-style steering wheels. The captain gave orders through an intercom-like speaker tube to mechanics in the pair of gondolas that housed the Maybach engines, as well as to crewmen manning the bombs and ballast, or to lookouts and machine-gunners atop the ship.

For the Zeppelin crews, exhilaration and fear went hand in hand. Recalling a 1915 bombing run over London in a magazine article published thirteen years later, Lieutenant-Commander Joachim Breithaupt described flying high above the darkened city as he followed the winding River Thames to his target:

> We watched the beams of the searchlights slashing into the sky like unsheathed swords looking for our airship ... The ship rocked when a round came close and shrapnel filled the sky. How could the enemy fail to hit the huge target that was my airship? One hit from the incendiary shells and we would go up in flames with no chance of escape. No Zeppelin carried parachutes, for it had been decided every extra ounce of payload would be given to bombs.

Zeppelin duty was often a miserable assignment. The cold weather was the biggest enemy of the Zeppelin's crew, who often endured temperatures way below freezing, down to −22°F in some cases and airship crews frequently suffered frostbite. They had to wear greatcoats over their uniforms, and it was not until 1917 that they were provided with fur-lined jackets. Another problem was the altitude. At 15,000–17,000 feet the air becomes rarefied, and blood cells in the body may not receive enough oxygen, causing a series of physical problems. Some of the more sophisticated Zeppelins later carried oxygen for the crew. Otto Mieth, watch officer aboard airship L48, wrote in his memoir that, at 15,000 feet, 'We shivered even in our heavy clothing and we breathed with such difficulty in spite of our oxygen flasks that several members of the crew became unconscious'. The mechanics were the lucky ones as they were somewhat warmed by the engines, but had to suffer the noise and shaking of the clattering Maybachs, and the exhaust fumes, combined with the petrol and oil, mixed to produce intoxicating gasses. Provisions were very scarce. Thermoses of hot chocolate, a bottle of schnapps and sandwiches were the only sustenance taken during the raids. The off-duty crew could relax and sleep in hammocks fastened to the girders at the keel of the airship.

As the Zeppelins got bigger so did the crews manning them. At different times crew numbers were changed according to the circumstances: the largest numbered about twenty-two men, others were fifteen or sometimes fewer. The mechanics originally were expected to man the guns when under attack, but this proved impractical so extra gunners were carried. The later airships had two engines in one gondola instead of each engine in its own gondola, thereby saving one mechanic. As the British defences improved, the Zeppelins were forced to fly at higher altitudes, and to achieve this it was necessary to reduce weight and they eventually had to do away with defensive armament and gunners.

The men who flew these canvas ships filled with explosive hydrogen gas faced many difficulties and dangers. Despite the lessons learned from the accidents of the early years of the Zeppelin, and the resulting technological innovations, the airships were still rather flimsy. Severe storms or winds could tear an airship apart or push it above 'pressure height', causing hydrogen to be automatically 'valved' or released. Losing the lifting power of the escaping hydrogen, the ship would become too heavy to remain airborne, leading to a crash. Engine failures were common and, if an airship lost too many engines, it might not be able to make it home: one engine down was usually manageable, or repairable, but most Zeppelins turned back immediately if a second engine failed.

If the temperature was too cold, the airship would ice up, become heavy and lose altitude. The solution was to release water ballast or bombs, but sometimes this was not enough and the airship would crash. High temperatures were equally dangerous, causing the hydrogen to super-heat and dramatically increase its lifting power, thus making the airship rise rapidly. The way to combat this was to valve gas, but when the remaining gas cooled down again, the airship would be short of gas and would then face the problem of being too heavy.

When the British introduced explosive bullets against the Zeppelins, the advantage in aerial combat swung to the pilots of the RFC and RNAS. With the realization that they were now extremely vulnerable, German aircrew began to dwell on the last great question – if your Zeppelin is on fire and there is no hope of survival, do you jump to your death or burn in the wreckage? When Commander Heinrich Mathy was asked this question, he replied 'I won't know until it happens'.[1] Elsewhere one of his crew confessed the earlier cheerfulness had disappeared:

> We discuss our heavy losses ... Our nerves are on edge, and even the most energetic and determined cannot shake off the gloomy atmosphere ... It is only a question of time before we join the rest. Everyone admits that he feels it ... If anyone says that he was not haunted by visions of burning airships, then he would be a braggart.

Photographed from Zeppelin L12, Zeppelins L13, L10 and L11 are shown on their way to bomb England. L10 caused severe damage in Leyton during a raid on the night of 17/18 August 1915. (*Imperial War Museum. Ref. Q 58452*)

Even if parachutes had been available to Zeppelin crews, it would have been impossible for those manning the guns on the top platform to jump from their position – the huge curve of the Zeppelin hull would have prevented a clean jump without going through the airship's skin or snagging the parachute. Moreover, those elsewhere in the Zeppelin might well have felt it morally impossible to jump while leaving their colleagues trapped on the top platform.

Zeppelin bombs

Zeppelin bombs were approximately pear-shaped and suspended by a bolt within a bomb bay until released. They weighed from 12½kg to 300kg, the heavier bombs looking somewhat like a submarine torpedo. In an emergency, they could be released in order to ascend rapidly. Other bombs dropped included high explosive (HE) bombs, like small grenades, weighing about 2½kg each – the damage they could inflict on well-built houses was slight, but the serrated casing of the bomb could cause serious casualties when exploded.

Zeppelins also dropped incendiaries, which looked like lanterns and were simple metal canisters filled with a thermite core (a magnesium compound) surrounded by resin, and wound tightly with a layer of tarred rope with a fuse inside; incendiaries rarely exploded as they were used in conjunction with other bombs or shells.

The remains of incendiary bombs dropped from a Zeppelin. (*Author's collection*)

Chapter 3

'The Zeppelins were able to escape'

Organization

In August 1914, no British gun existed that was capable of hitting a Zeppelin flying at 10,000 feet or higher, and the country's military resources were incapable of providing any proper defence against aerial attack on towns and cities. However, as the war progressed, a defence system for London emerged and a complex network was installed around the capital, combining search-lights, AA guns, fighters, barrage balloons, observer and listening posts, and a direct-line telephone communication network.

Britain declared war with full knowledge that it was inviting Zeppelin attacks, and everyone knew that London would be the prime target. However, little was known about what to expect from such raids and little preparation was made for them. There was no recognizable organization for AA work, no agreed procedures for fire-control and nothing in the way of an early-warning system. Moreover, no arm of the services was properly equipped to take charge of air defence in general. Air power was divided between the army's RFC and the navy's RNAS. In the first weeks of the war, most of the military aircraft still on British soil belonged to the RNAS as much of the RFC had moved to France. In the early twentieth century, defending Britain was the job of the navy and not the army; so, poorly equipped as it was for the role, the RNAS was given charge of Britain's air defence. This arrangement meant that the defence was overseen by the First Lord of the Admiralty, Winston Churchill.[1] Churchill had taken considerable interest in both heavier-than-air and lighter-than-air craft before the war and was particularly concerned about defence against Zeppelins.

When the Zeppelins did come, London's early defences were of little use. The guns could not fire a shell high enough to reach the raiders and the air-craft took a long time to reach Zeppelin altitudes and had little offensive capa-bility even when they did. The deaths and injuries of 171 civilians in London following two consecutive raids in September 1915 ensured that the Govern-ment was made aware of its failure to prevent air raids and to ensure the safety of the public. This was fuelled by negative announcements from the War Office regarding the possible destruction of airships during raids, such as,

'Anti-aircraft guns were in action … Air patrols were active, but owing to the difficult atmospheric conditions the Zeppelins were able to escape'.

The Admiralty made the first organizational change on 14 September 1915, when Admiral Sir Percy Scott was recalled from retirement to command London's AA gun defences. Scott was chosen because of his outstanding work in naval gunnery before the war. In his opinion, 'The defence of London by aircraft begins over the Zeppelin sheds and the defence by gunfire begins at the coast'. He demanded more AA guns and searchlights, but said that only aeroplanes could halt the raiders. Much of the improvement in AA guns and ammunition was initiated during Scott's short tenure (five months and six days) in this position.

Despite Scott's appointment, the navy was acting as only a stop-gap authority over home air defence because of the army's early inability to assume this role. It was understood that responsibility for air defence would pass to the army when the War Office was ready to assume it. This occurred, with respect to London's air defences, in February 1916 (and in April 1916, the army's responsibility was extended to all of England) so HQ moved from the Admiralty to Horse Guards. The army immediately showed the importance it attached to this charge by making Field Marshal Lord French,[2] then Commander-in-Chief, Home Forces (and previously Commander-in-Chief, British Forces, on the Western Front), responsible for the air defences.

Zeppelins were raiding British cities and were not being intercepted, despite the existence of a substantial defence establishment. It was not that they could not be intercepted, but that they could not be intercepted consistently; shooting them down was another matter entirely. In his new role, French faced two major problems. The first problem was one of command, control, communications and intelligence. Information about incoming Zeppelins and their locations usually was not timely or accurate, making it hard for fighters to find them in the dark and most squadrons were based near the coast, meaning that the enemy was usually past the defences by the time the alarm was raised. The second problem was that because the targets of the raiders were difficult to determine – the Zeppelin crews themselves often did not know where they were and dropped their bombs almost at random – as a precaution alerts had to be given and lights blacked-out over large areas of the country. This disrupted sleep and domestic production far more than was necessary.

French brought in new measures to meet the Zeppelin threat. A new organization, Home Defence, was created and more fighter bases were established inland; from these, aircraft operated individually, flying along pre-set patrol lines hunting for Zeppelins caught in the searchlights as they approached London. A searchlight belt was also created twenty-five miles from the coast stretching from Sussex to Northumberland; and a sound locator system was deployed in an attempt to increase detections of the Zeppelins at night.

On 31 July 1917, in response to the Gotha bomber threat, the London Air Defence Area (LADA) was activated and Major-General Edward Bailey Ashmore[3] was appointed its commander. His task was to devise an improved system of detection, communication and control for London's defences. To achieve this, groups of AA guns, searchlights and observation posts were established between the coast and London with telephone links between themselves and central control in London. An important component of detection was the establishment of the Metropolitan Observation Service (MOS).

LADA was divided into three sub-commands giving support to the posts in central London manned by the Royal Naval Volunteer Reserve (RNVR): Western – from Watford to Croydon and Bromley, and from Windsor to Grove Park; Northern – with AA guns between Ware and Chingford; and Eastern – from Rainham and Romford across the Thames to Dartford and Sidcup. These were each commanded by a Lieutenant-Colonel acting under the orders of the Anti-Aircraft Defence Commander at Horse Guards. All three were run on similar lines with an HQ from which an elaborate system of telephones radiated to all parts of the district. The operations room at sub-command HQ was large, and around it were arranged several telephone boxes. These were divided into two categories – those for the receipt of information coming in to HQ, and those from which orders and information were sent out to the gun stations. Each box communicated with three gun stations, and each gun station collected its own messages from its attached searchlight stations and observation posts.

Each gun station was under the charge of an officer, and manned by a sergeant, a corporal, and between sixteen and eighteen men, according to the particular type of height-finding and other instruments with which it was equipped. The searchlight stations were each under charge of a non-commissioned officer (NCO), with six to eight men according to the various types of engines by which the electric current was supplied for the searchlights. This force was divided into four companies – two consisting of Royal Garrison Artillery (RGA) gunners who manned the guns, and two of Royal Engineers (RE) who manned the searchlight stations. In Essex, these AA units were formed mostly from men of the Essex territorials serving in the Essex & Suffolk Royal Garrison Artillery, and the Essex (Fortress) Royal Engineers.

Lieutenant-Commander Alfred Rawlinson[4] later wrote:

> Of the artillery rank and file it is difficult to speak as a whole, for they comprised so many different classes. Some, however, were excellent, and others

equally the reverse, many being unable to read, and some even being unable to 'hear'. In fact, a more curious medley was probably never brought together, and the wonder is that they were ever able to carry out any such elaborate system of defence as that which we were called upon to operate with any degree of success at all.

The personnel of the engineer companies contained a high proportion of very intelligent men. The capacity of their NCOs, also, was far in advance of the average of those of the RGA. The results of this were that in many cases the condition and efficiency of the searchlight stations, which were under the command of NCOs of the RE, compared most favourably with the conditions obtaining at many gun-stations manned by the RGA. This fact became of great importance during raids, as, in the first place, the searchlight stations vastly outnumbered the gun-stations, and, secondly, the stations of the 'advanced lights', being situated 'farther out', always obtained the first information of the actual attack. This first information was always of the greatest importance as indicating the vital points of 'altitude', 'direction' and 'strength'; and many times have I been most thankful for the confidence which it was possible to repose in the intelligent observation and correct transmission of the facts by NCOs of the RE in charge of the 'advanced lights'.

The telephone system adopted was that the searchlight stations each communicated with the gun station to which they were attached, and the gun stations then communicated with sub-command HQ. Each gun station was also connected with at least two observation posts. These were situated in opposite directions at considerable distances from the guns, in order to 'observe' the bursts of the shells and to 'spot', i.e. to advise the gun as to the position of the bursts in relation to the target, which could not be truly observed from the gun position itself.

Separate operational zones were allocated to aeroplanes and guns so that the two did not clash with each other, thereby enabling the fighters to attack enemy formations broken up by the AA fire. In September 1917, defences were again improved. Step patrols for aeroplanes were introduced (now four machines flew as a team at different levels), and AA batteries, lights and listening posts were better co-ordinated. New 90cm and 120cm searchlights, and their sound locators, were linked directly to the guns to provide early warning. Guns now fired barrages, rather than shots at individual bombers: barrages were virtual lines in the sky along which a number of guns could be brought to bear.

Late 1917 saw LADA's armament state as:

Inner Artillery Zone	55 guns	113 searchlights
Middle ring and coastal belt	94 guns	77 searchlights
Medway and Dover	53 guns	83 searchlights
Harwich	13 guns	33 searchlights
Mobile brigades	34 guns	17 searchlights

By the second half of 1918, the capital was defended by 304 guns. In late summer 1918, the completed defences included:

- AA fire zones: barriers from Folkestone to Margate, from Romney Marsh to north of Canterbury, and from Sheerness north across the River Blackwater; an outer ring around London from Chatham through Chelmsford, Ware, St Albans, Staines, Guildford, and Redhill; an inner ring as far south as Croydon and as far north as Cuffley;
- fighter patrol lines: Beakesbourne to the north, Throwley to the north, Goldhanger to the north and south, Rochford and Stow Maries to the north, Detling to the south, and between the outer and inner fire zones patrol lines from Biggin Hill, Suttons Farm, Hainault Farm, and North Weald; and
- balloon aprons in a reversed 'C' shape to the east and wrapping around London.

Searchlights

Searchlights were the most visible of the defensive measures taken, but they were as much about finding and temporarily blinding the Zeppelin crews and hindering accurate navigation as they were about pin-pointing the airships for the AA guns to shoot down. The brilliant beam of light that a searchlight produced was not from a bulb, but by electricity jumping from a positive carbon rod to a negative one causing a bright arc of light. During the time the arc was running, the carbon rods burned down and needed constant adjustment to keep the gap just right for the arc. Churchill had seen the need for many more searchlights right at the start of the war and he requested thirty to forty of these on 4 September 1914. At that time, only 60cm projectors were in production and the maximum height possible for these was some 6,500 feet. Under optimum conditions these models could illuminate the Zeppelins, but optimum conditions were not common.

The first Zeppelin raid on London occurred on the night of 31 May/1 June 1915. By that time, the air defences of London had grown to include twelve acetylene gas-powered searchlights manned initially by 120 special constables; but it was still not enough. The inexperience of the police led to a number of illuminated clouds being mistaken for attacking airships. At this early stage in the war, the co-ordination of AA guns and searchlights was poor. Moonlit nights were particularly difficult as moonlight neutralized the effects of the searchlights, lessening their range and making it difficult to pick out the enemy airships. Damp and rain severely diminished their efficiency, and fog and smoke could virtually block off their light completely.

In late 1915, Admiral Scott proposed two defensive rings for London: an inner circle of searchlights, and, for the area to the north-east of London, an outer circle of gun stations and searchlights. As part of this plan, in November 1915, an RE officer arrived at the Ilford UDC tramways depot in Ley Street with papers authorizing the requisitioning of two tramcars for use as mobile searchlight units. The depot staff carried out the conversions, removing all the upper-deck seats and fitting a 120cm searchlight at top-floor level at one end. The other end was occupied by a sheet-steel shelter for the searchlight operators. All lower-deck windows were boarded up and a generator was added inside one end, which took its power from the overhead supply line. The other end of the saloon was used as a mess and was kept locked during

A sketch by the late Leonard Thomson of one of the Ilford tramcars converted to carry a searchlight. (*Redbridge Museum/Redbridge Information & Heritage 2015. Ref. p14945*)

Ilford's searchlight tramcars were positioned outside the police stations at Barkingside and Chadwell Heath each evening. This postcard pre-dates the First World War, but shows a regular tram in a location at Barkingside later used by the searchlight trams. (*Author's collection*)

the day. Every day a food wagon called at the depot with rations for the RE team who operated the light. Every third day an ammunition wagon turned up and the soldiers would unlock and enter the saloon. As the depot staff were not permitted to enter the saloons, all maintenance work had to be carried out from underneath the vehicles. In this way Ilford tramcar No. 14 became the first searchlight vehicle and No. 16 the second (there was another such unit at Croydon, and six in the northern and western areas of London). The Ilford tramcars took up their stations each night; one at Barkingside and the other at Chadwell Heath, both outside the police stations where telephone communication was available.

After the Ilford units had been at work for some time, a fault developed in one of the generators causing the light to dim out. The War Office sent a replacement, which was fitted, the faulty generator being left lying in the depot. The officer in charge was tactfully approached as to its future, but he suggested that the War Office was too busy to worry about one faulty generator. So the tramway staff corrected the fault, and set it up and used it to

This postcard shows the location later used by Ilford's other searchlight tram – outside Chadwell Heath police station. (*Author's collection*)

charge their 'Edison' tower wagon, which up to then had been charged at the adjacent electricity works.[5]

By September 1916, London was defended to the north-east by searchlights at locations including Victoria Park, Homerton (at the Clapton Orient Football Club ground), Higham Hill, Chingford (by the Jubilee Retreat), Buckhurst Hill, Loughton, Theydon Bois (in Coopersale Lane), Epping (Lindsey Street), North Weald (airfield), Stapleford Tawney, Stapleford Abbotts, Chigwell Row, Lambourne End, Dog Kennel Hill (beside the seventeenth fairway of Hainault Forest golf course), Noak Hill, Chadwell Heath, Barkingside (these two on board the converted tramcars), Harold Wood, Upminster, Becontree Heath, Wanstead, West Ham, Barking, North Woolwich and Beckton. The Lambourne End location was the subject of an experiment carried out by the War Office involving a large searchlight of 150cm, fitted with a gold-plated reflector, giving an amber beam. It was intended to pierce mist and low cloud. By flying an aeroplane above, it was confirmed that penetration was made but, unfortunately, eyes at ground level could not follow the beam through.

These two small photographs come from a personal album compiled by Frank Heap, a member of No. 6 London Anti-Aircraft Company's searchlight team. He was based at Little Heath, near Cuffley, on the night William Leefe Robinson brought down L21. These photographs show 60cm searchlights and were taken when his team was at Noak Hill, near Romford, in 1918. (*Author's collection*)

This photograph also comes from Frank Heap's personal album. Looking very much posed, it shows three searchlights at Noak Hill, near Romford, in 1918. (*Author's collection*)

Further out in Essex, Charles Perfect, the vicar's warden at St Andrew's church, Hornchurch, recalled:

> ... it was not long before our neighbourhood was surrounded by a cordon of powerful searchlights, which were always a source of interest. Often we were treated to a veritable pyrotechnic display, when those great beams of light were sweeping the skies for enemy airships; and when, as occasionally happened, they discovered what they were searching for, we were privileged to witness most marvellous sights.
>
> Early in the evenings it was the custom for the searchlights to appear for a short period, and the absence of such displays on a dark night was a fairly sure indication that a raid was anticipated, and that, later on, the searchlights would burst out to some purpose. In these circumstances we all watched with interest, and not a little anxiety, for the silent signals in the sky ...

By 1916, the searchlights in use were of no fewer than five different makes. They were also of different sizes, and the electric current was produced by different engines. These engines required different periods of time in which to start up, and each suffered from its own peculiar trouble during the sustained running which became necessary during raids. The beam varied in the different models, so that an intimate knowledge of them all was necessary to control their use in order to obtain the best results.

Anti-aircraft guns

Churchill had realized early in the war that the number of AA guns available was too few to cover London. If a Zeppelin had appeared over the capital on an autumn night in 1914, protection would probably have been better provided by the lighting restrictions. In a directive of 5 September 1914, Churchill instructed that the priority for gun placement should be given only to the most vulnerable military targets, so the majority of the weapons were assigned to Chatham, Dover and Portsmouth. London had to make do, at least at first, with a limited arsenal. This arsenal was manned by the RNVR Anti-Aircraft Corps and comprised: one 4-inch gun, four 3-inch guns and twenty-eight 1-pounder pom-poms. The larger guns were stationed in Hyde Park, and the rest in a ring covering the central portion of London. In naval terms, 3-inch and 4-inch guns were pea-shooters; hundreds were fitted as standard to ships before the war. The pom-poms were also of very little value. They were a cheap option brought in early and had two disadvantages: there were very few of them; and their ammunition had to be made in small, special batches at Woolwich Arsenal. This ammunition was solid and would cause almost no damage to aircraft or airships unless it hit an engine or something similarly important – if it did not, it fell back to earth as a solid projectile. Their importance would have been more as a morale-booster for Londoners, who would hear the rapid firing during a raid, than as a serious defensive option.

With its RNAS armoured car squadrons as a basis, in early 1915, the Admiralty set up the RNVR Anti-Aircraft Mobile Brigade. Mounted on pairs of two- or three-ton Austin lorries, at first the guns used by these units were something of a compromise: with no AA guns, pom-poms or 6-pounders available, their fast vehicles carried small 0.303in Lewis guns and 0.45in machine-guns on high-angle mountings, together with a supply of acetylene searchlights. A typical section comprised a searchlight vehicle with an acetylene lamp mounted on a pedestal in the centre of the flat bed of the lorry and a similar vehicle mounting the guns in the same fashion. These mobile guns would respond to air raid warnings by taking up pre-determined positions to supplement the permanent static guns. If the warning was very short, an emergency position on Hampstead Heath was used.

First World War AA gunnery was *ad hoc* and techniques had to be developed on the ground. What was desperately needed was a gun with a high muzzle velocity to reduce the flight time of the shells to their targets. Even when AA guns were supplied with longer ranges, they were generally incapable of reaching a Zeppelin's cruising height, and were fired more to quell public disquiet than to shoot down the raiders. Churchill called for increased production of AA weapons, but the production increase did not result in a sufficient supply by the time of the first Zeppelin raids in 1915. As the attacks continued and civilian casualties and damage to both morale and property grew, attempts were made to increase the effectiveness of the AA response.

When the Government appointed Sir Percy Scott to the overall command of AA defence in September 1915, London was defended by twelve true AA guns at fixed points. Scott had a competent assistant in Lieutenant-Commander Alfred Rawlinson, who had been involved earlier in the organization of the air defences of Paris. Making use of his connections in France, Rawlinson travelled to Paris in September 1915 and returned to London with a French motor AA gun and its attendant ammunition vehicle. Based on a 35hp De Dion-Bouton or Panhard chassis, this consisted of a gun truck, with armoured radiator and bonnet, mounting a 75mm gun behind an armoured shield on a turntable at the rear. The vehicle, powered by a V8 engine, was quite capable of moving at over 50mph in pursuit of its quarry. The establishment was complemented by four Tilling-Stevens petrol-electric lorries mounting searchlights, plus the necessary ammunition carriers and staff cars. The ammunition wagon, or auto-caisson, was the same basic design with a body formed of ammunition lockers and extra seats for the crew.

As the French nation's need for its own equipment grew, so the supply of De Dion auto-cannons was limited to four, with just one ammunition wagon. A British equivalent was devised, consisting of a 30cwt Lancia IZ (later Peerless) chassis. Totally unarmoured, it was equipped with a drop-side body and a turntable-mounted Vickers 3-pounder gun. Eight of these were supplied. Heavier firepower came in the form of a 3-inch gun on a high-elevation mount fitted to the rear of a 3-ton Daimler lorry with special stabilizing outriggers.

When in action, this flying column was based at the RNAS depot at the Talbot works in Ladbroke Grove. Late in 1915, the stables of Kenwood House, Hampstead, were made available and here the whole force could be

(Opposite) Two illustrations of a mobile 75mm auto cannon brought over from France by Lieutenant-Commander Alfred Rawlinson and used for anti-aircraft defence. Such vehicles could travel at over 50mph in pursuit of their aerial quarry. *(Author's collection)*

accommodated. On receiving the alarm, the convoy would race along Oxford Street at high speed with headlights on and bell ringing, before arriving at the Honorable Artillery Company's (HAC) ground at Moorgate, which provided a suitable place for deployment – along with other locations to the east of London including Higham Hill, Wanstead Flats and Beckton. Unfortunately, these guns usually arrived at their destination long after the airship had left the reported area, but Rawlinson had few doubts about the effectiveness of his unit. He reported that it was:

> ... impossible to mistake the sentiments of the people, and I have often seen poor women with streaming eyes, holding up their children to see the guns as we passed, making it easy for us to realise the relief which it must have been to these poor defenceless people to see that at any rate some sort of defence was being provided for them.

In late 1915, more gun stations were built as part of Admiral Scott's plan. One of these was on Wanstead Flats; the Clerk to the Corporation of the City of London[6] receiving the following confidential letter from the Admiralty dated 26 October 1915:

> Sir,
> I am commanded by Lords Commissioners of the Admiralty to inform you that it has been found necessary for the defence of London to establish an Anti-aircraft Station (Gun and Searchlight) and to erect huts for the accommodation of the crew who will work the Station on Wanstead Flats.
>   2. I enclose a notice from a Competent Naval Authority as to the taking over of the land required under the powers of the Defence of the Realm (Consolidation) Regulations 1914.
>   3. My Lords will be glad if all possible assistance may be rendered to the representatives of the Office of Works, and the General Post Office who will carry out the work.
>   I am, Sir, Your obedient Servant,
>   O. Murray.

Other such AA stations included Monkhams Hall (near Waltham Abbey), Thameshaven, Purfleet and Woolwich Arsenal. Monkhams Hall commanded splendid views over London and was ideally placed as a site for an AA gun; it probably guarded specific installations such as waterworks, electric power plants, gasworks, and munitions factories of the Lea Valley.

By 13 November 1915, London was defended by twenty-four AA guns, nine of them mobile. The static guns were not without success, most notably when Zeppelin L15 was shot down in the Thames estuary by AA fire from the

Static anti-aircraft guns at Highbury Fields, manned by RNVR personnel. (*Author's collection*)

1/3rd (Purfleet) Company, Essex & Suffolk RGA on the night of 31 March/ 1 April 1916 (for which the gun crew were presented with gold medals by the Lord Mayor of London). The shooting was witnessed from Hornchurch by Charles Perfect, who recalled:

On the night of March 31st, 1916, we experienced a real impression of war in the air. At 9.30 o'clock there was no indication whatever of a raid, no searchlights were visible, and no warning had been given, but suddenly, just about 10 o'clock, we were startled by a succession of most violent explosions, and it was evident that bombs were being dropped at no very great distance. At that moment the searchlights disclosed a Zeppelin, which was heading away from London, and appeared to be unloading her cargo of bombs. Her tail was distinctly seen to dip, and it was thought that she had been hit, and a loud cheer went up all round in the hope and expectation of seeing her descend to earth. She, however, got away, but the following morning, Zeppelin L15 was discovered in the sea off the Kentish Knock, and this was doubtless our visitor of the previous night ... The actual spot where the bombs fell was Wennington, only four miles from us, where over twenty incendiary and explosive bombs fell in open fields within a very small area, quite close to a farm, but providentially no one was injured, and very little material damage was caused.

With the creation of the Home Defence organization in 1916, London's AA defences were re-arranged to thwart the Zeppelins' bombing operations. By June 1916, London had sixty-four guns and, by September 1916, the barrier to the north-east of London included guns at Purfleet, Tunnel Farm, Belhus Park, Newmans, Monkhams Hall, Enfield Lock, Temple House, Rainham, Romford, Chadwell Heath, Lambourne End, Kelvedon Hatch, Pole Hill, Theydon Bois, Epping, North Woolwich, Beckton, West Ham, Wanstead Flats, Clapton and Victoria Park. By early 1918, the gun barrier extended right around London. Many of these guns were mounted on timber towers, or convenient existing buildings. Others were given purpose-built concrete emplacements. At most gun sites, any accommodation provided was in temporary Boarden huts constructed out of corrugated iron and timber, as the preferred method in built-up areas was to billet crews in private houses, or else locate them in central points like Kenwood. The only brick-built structures would often have been the magazines.

At Pole Hill[7] in Chingford, the gun was mounted below the crest of the hill and shells were brought up to the gun on rails from the end of Mornington Road, a windlass with a wire cable being used for this purpose. The crew resided in a long hut and filled in their spare time by cultivating part of the field as allotments for vegetables. Dick Richards was a young boy living in Queen's Walk, near Pole Hill, during the war and he later remembered the AA gun there:

> When the gun on Pole Hill was fired, all the ornaments and things on our mantelpiece used to rattle and it really frightened us children. I remember that the shells for the gun were dumped at the bottom of Pole Hill and then they were hauled up by three or four of the gun crew, who actually lived up on the hill. They had a barracks there ... During the war the ammunition was kept in a reinforced concrete building and the shells were carried over to the gun when needed. It was arranged that all the guns around London would fire at the same time over a certain part of London, say Tower Bridge, and make a barrage, in the hope that the exploding shrapnel would damage any enemy aircraft or Zeppelins.

Once a target was identified, the officer in charge of the AA battery would estimate the target's height. Meanwhile, one of the gun team would have 'laid'

This photograph shows the anti-aircraft gun on Pole Hill, Chingford. The gun was mounted on a timber tower and accommodation for the crew was provided in temporary huts. Shells were brought up to the gun from the end of Mornington Road. (*Vestry House Museum, London Borough of Waltham Forest*)

on the target with a height fuse indicator – a useful piece of equipment carrying a scale marked in heights of horizontal lines and in curves which denoted fuse lengths. The officer estimated the horizontal and vertical deflections, which, in turn, were shouted to the gun-layer and man in charge of the height fuse indicator. The latter transferred vertical deflection to his instrument, and then read off the required fuse length; this information was passed to the ammunition team members. For a target approaching diagonally from left to right, a typical order would be 'Up four, right two, fuse ten inches'.

When an AA shell had exploded, its shrapnel continued along the shell's trajectory in a cone; HE shells sent out fragments as a globe. For shrapnel to be effective the target would have to be on the shell's trajectory and the fuse accurate enough before the shell reached it. HE would work even with a near-miss. HE also created air pockets that could severely shake a plane, causing structural damage, and although it might not bring it down it would require eventual repair before it could safely fly again. This could vary from re-rigging to the replacement of major wing components; the comparatively large-winged Gothas were more vulnerable to this.

At the height of the Gotha raids in the winter of 1917/18, the Germans' change from day to night sorties again showed up the AA guns' inability to defend London. Thirteen-pounder guns fired box-barrages, covering heights from 5,000–10,000 feet, often with an expenditure of 20,000 rounds per raid. If Gothas were seen approaching London from the south-east, several guns would receive the order 'Ace of Spades' and would then swing to pre-determined settings to set up a barrier of fire for the raiders to fly into. If they flew on instead towards the Isle of Dogs, the order 'Robin Hood' would then be sent, and a new barrier would be fired, probably drawing on some of the same

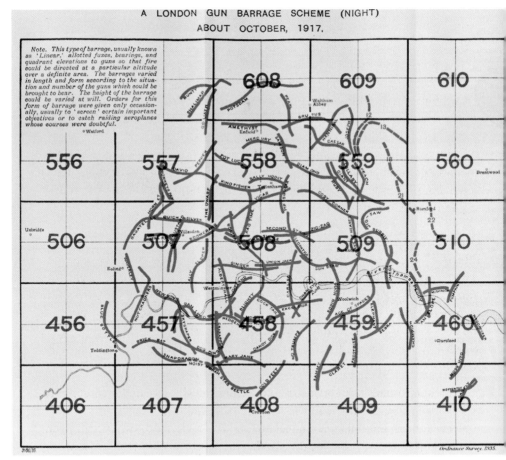

A map from October 1917 showing the names and locations of anti-aircraft barrages fired to protect London. (*Author's collection*)

guns, but with others joining in too.[8] Exhausted gun crews became temporarily blinded and deafened by the continuous salvos of gunfire. Hands suffering burns from red-hot gun barrels were another hazard. Deterring an attacker from dropping its bombs in an intended area by throwing up an impressive barrage was just as much a victory as shooting it down – results could not be scored solely on aircraft shot down.

By early 1918, AA guns around London could expect a life of 1,500 rounds and, with 13-pounders needed for the navy, as well as in France, supplies were often in a critical state. On many raids the cost of shells fired (each 13-pdr shell cost about £2) often exceeded the material damage done by the raiders.

After the war, London's anti-aircraft defences were quickly removed. In March 1920, *Flight* magazine reported that:

> The London County Council has been informed by the War Department that orders have been issued for the clearance of all anti-aircraft stations. The present position in the metropolitan area is as follows:- The stations at Archbishop's Park, Battersea Park, Blackheath, Bostall Heath, Clapham Common, Clissold Park, Deptford Park, Eaglesfield, Finsbury Park, Hainault Forest, Hampstead Heath, Highbury Fields, Meath Gardens, Parliament Hill, Ruskin Park, Streatham Common, Victoria Park, Wandsworth Common, and Wormwood Scrubbs have been dismantled and cleared of buildings, except in the case of Eaglesfield, where the huts and fence remain. Concrete work and debris still remain in every case. The station at Plumstead Common is being used as a stores depot.

Observation posts

Effective defence requires advanced warning based on accurate observation techniques. Following the German seizure of much of Belgium, the Admiralty decided that London needed eyes searching the sky for enemy aircraft making the passage between the Belgian coast and the Isle of Thanet – the half-way point to London. One such observation post was established at North Foreland, on the Kent coast near Ramsgate, staffed by members of the RNVR. Their instructions were:

- To keep a constant and sharp look out in the sky for any kind of aircraft from one hour before sunrise to one hour after sunset.
- To report immediately by telephone to Admiralty any aircraft seen, giving necessary description whether airship, aeroplane or balloon.
- Direction from which the aircraft seen is coming and direction in which proceeding.

- If an aeroplane, state whether biplane or monoplane, also whether seaplane or landplane, and any marks or numbers that can be distinguished.
- If an airship, the colour, type and number of cars.
- If making your first report, do not wait for a minute description, only state whether airship, aeroplane etc, with direction of flight. The fuller details can be sent in another message when established.

In London, the Admiralty initially assigned the responsibility to watch for enemy air incursions to the Metropolitan Police who were instructed to telephone to the Admiralty reports of any aircraft seen or heard within sixty miles of London. Individuals making aircraft reports were asked a detailed series of questions to determine the location, direction of travel, and description of the aircraft. In the days when telephones were not universal, locating one and forwarding a report was not a rapid process. Even when a report was received in a timely manner, the warning information had to flow through the civilian telephone system, making fighter interception or co-ordinated AA fire unlikely.

In 1915, the area covered by reports was extended to East Anglia, Northamptonshire, Oxfordshire, Hampshire and the Isle of Wight (and later still the whole of England and Wales). The Admiralty was then supposed to spread the alarm to Scotland Yard, to transport officials, to the Speaker of the House of Commons and to the AA gun and searchlight crews. In April 1915, the War Office took a hand in this and asked Chief Constables of country forces to send similar messages to them, and a system of interchange of air intelligence was also arranged between those Chief Constables.

In the later stages of the war, the number of airship raids decreased as raids by fixed-wing bombers grew. In response to this new threat, LADA was tasked with devising an improved system of detection, communication and control. The system, MOS, encompassed a network of approximately 200 observation posts and observers across the Metropolitan Police area, a few only in the west, but many in and near north-east, east and south-east London. Suitable high places were found, such as fire brigade towers, belfries, and the roofs of high buildings. On winter nights, observers felt their positions keenly: 'I used to be thankful when I got up', said one inspecting officer, 'but even more thankful when I got down'. These posts were connected to warning controls commanded by AA defence commanders with direct connections into the telephone trunk system. Controls issued air raid warnings to districts.

Leyton was in the Metropolitan Police J Division, as was nearby Buckhurst Hill where there was a useful observation post in the tower of St James' Congregational church in Palmerston Road. At the outset there was only an

An early view of Claybury asylum. The 170-feet high water tower on the left served as an observation post during the war, its top being nearly 400 feet above sea level. The wooden fence in the foreground extended for two and a half miles around the hospital estate. (*Redbridge Museum/ Redbridge Information & Heritage 2015. Ref. p3214*)

evening watch, but after the first daylight raid by aircraft, on 13 June 1917, the post was manned continuously. During raids the six men on the open top took their chance of being hit by shrapnel, which repeatedly fell upon and damaged the church roof – the watchers there were amongst the most ardent in welcoming the issue of steel helmets. At nearby Claybury a post was set up in the asylum's 170-feet high water tower, the top of which was nearly 400 feet above sea-level and gave a fine view of the Thames flats and across the river to Woolwich.[9] Here too a day and night watch was maintained, and the post was specially commended on several occasions for its smart detection of enemy aircraft.

The work of the Hainault post in K Division kept thirty-four officers and men employed. Robert Stroud[10] made available a tower at his residence for observation work, and this proved most useful as it was on a route often used by German aircraft bound for London. The post was manned night and day.

In N Division, the work was centred on High Beach (Palmers Bridge) and Edmonton, two observation stations where a continuous look-out was maintained. Miles of telephone cable, strung between the trees and telegraph poles, were erected in Epping Forest. One of the men who helped man the High Beach post was the writer Arthur Morrison.[11]

The following extract is from a contemporary account by Special Constable Hunter, one of the squad at an observation post at the top of the tower

at Severndroog Castle, Shooter's Hill in Kent. The account relates to one of
the later night raids by Gotha aircraft.

At ten o'clock our Sergeant pays us a visit. He brings the latest war-news
and checks the entries in our log-book. As we chat in a dreamy sort of way,
we hear a shout from the man on duty at the top, 'Aerodrome lights up.' He
has seen the landing lights of the aerodrome across the valley[12] and he
knows it to be a bad sign. Before we can report, the telephone bell is ringing
and O.R. (Central Observation Station) is saying that hostile aircraft have
crossed the coast.

Warning maroons are soon bursting high over London, and our eyes are
searching the sky. Very soon, too, we see a vivid flash away to the north-
east, quickly followed by other flashes, and by the time that elapses before
the sound reaches us we know that it is gunfire twenty miles away. Soon
this is succeeded by flashes nearer us, and we realise that the enemy has
broken through the outer ring of London's defences.

Now hostile machines are approaching the city, and line after line of
guns open fire. The noise and the flashes are nearing the river. Suddenly
the searchlight near our tower breaks out, and the gun close by comes into
action. The firing becomes more and more intense. Shrapnel is falling on
the trees around us, and we are glad of the comfort of our tin-hats,
although we know that only our heads are protected.

Our gun follows the enemy up the river, and presently it is firing directly
overhead. We can feel the old tower shake at every report, and the shells
scream over us. We watch the heavens above the bursting point, in the
hope of seeing the enemy.

Now the searchlights for miles around are centred over the great city.
There evidently the Gothas are. A great V-shaped flash comes up from the
ground, followed by a crash, and we report, 'Bomb dropped 2791.' In a few
seconds we know the fire brigade will be on the spot where the bomb fell.

The guns are silent, more bombs drop, and we report them. Then a fire
breaks out and that is notified. (We heard afterwards that in eight seconds
the brigade was warned.)

The 'phone rings just at midnight and the Station Inspector asks if he
shall send up the relief. 'No', we say, 'we'll stick it out.' While the Inspector
is talking the guns begin to speak again. Away to the south-east the enemy
is making his escape.

Shells are bursting high in the sky. Once more the shrapnel is falling
around us. Occasionally there is a shriek, as a large piece of shell crashes
and clatters among the trees.

There is an interval of quiet, and two of our comrades who had been caught in the barrage on their way to the tower join us, smilingly remarking upon the perfect beauty of the night. Then there is joyous music in the air. The buglers are sounding the 'All Clear'.

It was the duty of an observation station to look out for approaching attackers and, once hostile aircraft were seen, to determine and report their position, for the information and guidance of those in charge at nearby airfields and at AA gun and searchlight stations. Reports were phoned to LADA HQ at Horse Guards in London, and artillery and aircraft controlled from there. Ashmore was concerned about the speed and accuracy of visual detection and reporting. Priority telephone calls could now reach LADA HQ in as little as three minutes, but more often took ten, although the quality of information was sometimes poor. The absence of reports did not necessarily mean that no enemy aircraft were operating near an observer post. To remedy this Ashmore directed organizational changes, standardization in procedures, and new equipment:

- MOS was expanded outwards from London to manage other observer posts eastwards towards the Kent and Essex coasts.
- Observer posts received plotting instruments that showed the direction of an aircraft and allowed elevation to be measured. Using this system reports from two or more posts could be triangulated to fix position.
- Twenty-six sub-controls were established to serve as filter centres, collecting reports, establishing positions, and forwarding tracking data to central control at Horse Guards.
- Paper as a means of managing reports was eliminated. Carefully selected special constables from LADA HQ, and some also from other divisions, were seconded from their units and formed a central operations unit located at the London County Council (LCC) building in Spring Gardens, where the LCC made several large rooms available. Here the seminal step was taken to create an operations table with a map on which reports would be displayed by symbols and moved by plotters. These symbols were rudimentary by later standards – a round counter for a hostile aircraft and a rectangular counter for a formation. On one side an arrow was displayed to indicate direction of travel; if the direction was unknown the blank side of the counter was uppermost. At each level, clocks (known as 'colour change clocks') were divided into four 15-minute periods, with the first five minutes coloured green, six to ten minutes red, and eleven to fifteen minutes yellow. Counters were coloured in the same

way, and to eliminate clutter only the last ten minutes of position reports were displayed.

- Grid maps were introduced to provide standard map references throughout the system.
- Central control had a plotting table surrounded by ten plotters linked to tellers at the sub-controls. The commander had a chair on a raised dais overlooking the table from which he directed communications with each sub-control.
- Recorders maintained a record of each track using green, red, and yellow coloured pencils.

The improvements resulted in reducing the detection to display on central control's map to thirty seconds on average. MOS met with success and the warnings were often enough to get the fighters up in time to halt low-level daylight raids, forcing the Germans to operate at night or above 10,000 feet.

Balloons

The success of London's aerial defence was judged not only on how many aircraft were brought down, but also by how high the enemy was forced to fly and if he had to take evasive action thereby reducing his bombing accuracy. As German night raiders took advantage of the darkness to fly at lower altitudes with an increased bomb load, a new form of defence was devised and produced: the balloon barrage or apron.

The concept of balloon aprons originated before the war with citizens such as engineer William Booth who wrote a pamphlet outlining his ideas on the subject. Booth's balloon apron included electronically detonated charges on suspended wires and a warning system. When he sent his idea to the Ministry of Munitions in 1916, officials rejected it because they said enemy aircraft would be able to see and avoid the balloons. Booth defended his idea, believing that 'aerial nets' would protect London at night. After the especially deadly airship raids of September 1916, Major-General Ashmore (later supported by General Smuts[13]) called for a balloon apron for London. British officials travelled to Venice to see the apron bobbing over the city, and on their return to London they planned a series of balloon aprons.

Barrage balloons were sausage-shaped with fins. Made of rubberized cotton and as large as 70,000 cubic feet when filled with hydrogen, the balloons could withstand being tethered in strong winds. An apron consisted of three balloons 1,000 yards apart, anchored to the ground and linked by 500-foot cables. Every 25 yards, 1,000-foot steel wires hung vertically from these adjoining cables. The balloons would hover 7,000–10,000 feet above the ground. Barrage balloons were most effective at forcing attackers to fly at predictable and uniform heights. AA guns could then concentrate fire on enemy planes above the balloons. The presence of balloons also prevented accurate bombing. Coinciding with the introduction of Gotha bombers, the balloon aprons prevented these aircraft from inflicting as much damage as they would have done without these measures.

Balloon aprons were created on sites in vital parts of LADA and, on 20 September 1917, No. 7 Balloon Wing officially became a unit of LADA with a training centre at *The King's Oak* pub at High Beach[14] and its HQ at *The Royal Forest* hotel, Chingford. The Wing comprised three squadrons and ten aprons: No. 1 Squadron's HQ was at Longbridge Farm, Barking; and No. 2's at 'Banavie', Woodford Green. In early October 1917, the first two aprons were set up: one at Creekmouth (Barking), and one on Leyton Flats (Snaresbrook). Ultimately there would be a fifty-mile barrage of ten aprons covering the eastern and north-eastern approaches to London. Locally these were No. 1 Balloon Apron with its HQ at Eastbury House, Barking; No. 2 at Parsloes Park, Chadwell Heath; No. 3 at Gale Street, Barking; No. 4

On 20 September 1917, No. 7 Balloon Wing officially became a unit of LADA with a training centre at *The King's Oak* pub at High Beach. (*Author's collection*)

A balloon apron in the London defences. (*Author's collection*)

at 'Great Gearies', Barkingside; No. 5 at Salisbury Hall Farm, Chingford; No. 6 at Hazlebury Road, Edmonton; No. 7 at 'Fairlight', Snaresbrook; and No. 8 at 'Knighton', Manor Park. No. 3 Squadron's HQ and two aprons were south of the River Thames at Shooter's Hill, Abbey Wood and Bexleyheath.

One problem of establishing balloon aprons on Epping Forest land was the public's right of access. In 1918, the Royal Air Force (RAF)[15] complained that it was experiencing problems in keeping the public clear of the balloons. As well as a personal danger to the public, it was felt there was also the possibility that the balloons would be set on fire. As a temporary measure, before the sites were fenced off, policemen were detailed to patrol in their vicinity.

Sometimes when the balloons were sent up for practice, up to twenty of them could be seen from Leyton. That they were to serve some purpose in the general defence of London against aeroplane attack was recognized by most residents. Few, however, knew of the apron of thin steel wires suspended from and between the balloons. One who did was Winifred Adams, nine years old when the war started, and living in College Place, Snaresbrook, where her parents ran a grocery and sweet shop. She recalled the balloon apron nearby:

> There were three barrage balloons on Leyton Flats. One was stationed by where the car park is on Snaresbrook Road now, west of Eagle Pond; another one was at the back of the Green Man; and the third was halfway between those two. We called them 'pigs' because they were sausage shaped with ears. Sometimes when they were down they'd let the gas out and it did make a stink! They were moored to the ground on a mound which was the same shape as the balloon, but I don't think they ever actually rested on the ground. They would just sway in the wind, and then once they were let up into the sky they were controlled by the air currents. There were soldiers to man them, lodging at Buxton House. They could let the balloons up and bring them down with winches, and then the three balloons were linked together with chains. They made a sort of net which the German aircraft couldn't get through. There were numbers of barrage balloons linked together like that in various places round London so that it made a sort of 'lace-curtain' effect. The German crews couldn't see the chains between the balloons and their propellers got caught up. That was the theory, but I don't think it ever happened, much to our disappointment.

Despite Winifred's belief, some enemy aircraft were damaged by these aprons, although the damage was limited. The apron at Chingford had two wires torn away when hit by a German plane and, on its way into London on the night of 16/17 February 1918, the Giant commanded by Oberleutnant von Seydlitz-Gerstenberg struck the apron between the Royal Docks and Woolwich. His combat report stated:

> The aircraft was first pulled to starboard, then port and finally side-slipped out of control to the port side. The first pilot, Lt. Götte, immediately throttled-down all engines, then opened up the throttles on only one side, whereby the aircraft regained equilibrium once again after having fallen 300 metres. The impact of the balloon apron was so severe that the starboard mechanic fell against the glowing exhaust stacks,[16] which severely burned his hands, and the port aileron control cables sprang from their roller guides. The aircraft itself remained intact with the exception of minor damage to the leading edge of the starboard wing, propeller and mid-fuselage section.

Despite this shock to the crew and damage to the aircraft, the bomber was able to continue its mission.

Airfields ...

For the first months of the war there were no airfields in south-west Essex from which aircraft could have flown had German raiders come. Then, in late December 1914, the Admiralty identified a site at Chingford for four aircraft, although this did not come into use until April 1915 when aircraft and staff were transferred from Hendon. The site opened as a Preliminary Aeroplane School and second-class landing ground, becoming No. 207 Training Depot Station (TDS), the main training station for pilots of the RNAS. Ivor Novello, composer of such songs as 'Keep the Home Fires Burning', was a Lieutenant flying instructor at Chingford.

The site did not find favour with some of the pilots stationed there, one describing it as 'a strip of fogbound and soggy meadowland at Ponders End between a reservoir and a sewage farm'. Others recalled the smallness of the airfield, surrounded by a reservoir, streams and swamps. The adjacent King George reservoir was used as a landmark for landing, although several young fliers plunged to their deaths there after misjudging their landing approaches – crashed aircraft were also found in Epping Forest by the forest keepers.

A couple of months earlier, in October 1914, the RNAS had earmarked Hainault Farm, to the east of Hainault Road in the rural northern fringes of Ilford[17] and owned by Mr W. Poulter, as a day landing ground for future development. It passed the site over to the RFC in February 1915, but the RFC was short of men and aircraft and was unable to use the site until October 1915. Portable canvas hangars were then erected for two ex-RNAS aircraft that were initially to operate from there, as well as two RE sheds. The

17. 11. 16

This aerial view shows the RNAS airfield at Chingford on 17 November 1916. The airfield was referred to by one pilot as 'a strip of fogbound and soggy meadowland at Ponders End between a reservoir and a sewage farm'. Part of the King George reservoir is visible at the top of the photograph. (*Fleet Air Arm Museum. Ref. AIRSTATIONS/044*)

farmhouse on the opposite side of the road, which was unoccupied and un-furnished at the time, was used to billet the pilots. The arrival of the first small group of RFC personnel at Hainault Farm did not go unnoticed, and news that aeroplanes were there spread quickly. Arthur Scarborough, of Seven Kings, recalled that the novelty of seeing aircraft on the ground tempted schoolboys to play truant in case the 'airybuzzers' departed as swiftly as they had arrived. More permanent buildings were erected, including four aero-plane sheds, and the airfield eventually occupied 100 acres, in an area measur-ing 950 yards by 750 yards.

In the spring of 1916, the playing fields of Fairlop were chosen as the site for a sub-station to the expanding RNAS flying school at Chingford. The air-field was just 400 yards along Forest Road from the RFC airfield at Hainault Farm to the south-east. Although fifteen feet lower than Hainault Farm, the well-drained playing fields were an excellent choice for an airfield,[18] com-pared with the mud at Hainault Farm. RNAS Fairlop occupied 110 acres on a site measuring 900 yards by 600 yards. On 20 July 1918, it was re-designated as No. 54 TDS. Despite its TDS status, this was never more than a temporary airfield with limited accommodation for both men and machines – although it

This is a view of the RFC's early days at Hainault Farm, in late 1915/early 1916. The airfield lacks any permanent buildings – the barn-like structures in the centre are probably two temporary canvas hangars. Tents provide accommodation for the ground crew, with the pilots billeted in the farmhouse at the extreme left. (*Fleet Air Arm Museum. Ref. JMBGSL07692*)

Two of four more permanent aeroplane sheds erected by the RFC at Hainault Farm airfield. (*Fleet Air Arm Museum. Ref. JMBGSL07691*)

did have nine hangars. A small detached site on the southern side of Forest Road was intended for huts in anticipation of the 1918/19 winter, but these were never built.

Nellie Smith, of Dagenham, recalled her childhood days playing with friends in the goods yard at Hainault railway station,[19] just to the north-west of Fairlop airfield. Her memories included hearing instructions shouted above throttled-back aero engines and the whine of wind in the wires as aircraft skimmed the station roof coming down to land at Fairlop.

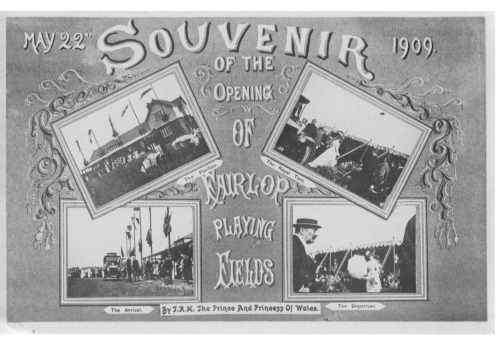

Fairlop Playing Fields were opened by the Prince and Princess of Wales on 22 May 1909. During the war the playing fields became part of the RNAS airfield at Fairlop. (*Author's collection*)

A Sopwith Pup, Sopwith Camel, Sopwith Triplane and Avro 504, probably of RNAS No. 54 Training Depot Station, on the ground at Fairlop. (*Imperial War Museum. Ref. HU 67899*)

Three advanced pupils in Sopwith Camels of RNAS No. 54 Training Depot Station in formation above some Avro and Curtiss training machines at Fairlop in 1918. (*Imperial War Museum. Ref. Q 33808*)

Suttons Farm at Hornchurch, owned by Tom Crawford in 1915, was also taken over by the RFC in October 1915 and, like Hainault Farm, was soon the site of canvas hangars and temporary accommodation for two BE2c aircraft. The airfield opened with just eight men in total, including the two pilots. A telephone was installed in the farmhouse and another in *The White Hart*, two places where the first personnel were billeted. Small tents on the airfield were used by staff on duty. The airfield site comprised 105 acres, 800 yards by 750 yards.

On 16 February 1916, the War Office took over control of London's air defences, which it began to reorganize. A new organization, Home Defence, was formed with a spread of thirty airfields – some new and some existing – and eleven squadrons from Dover to Edinburgh. Home Defence squadrons included a number of experienced pilots from France who were either in England on 'rest' or between operational periods. These were occasionally 'war weary' and in urgent need of a break, or sometimes comprised whole

The Henry Hughes factory in New North Road, Hainault, during or soon after the war. Opened in 1917, the factory made navigational aids for the RFC. Visible on the hill in the distance is a small part of Claybury asylum. (*Courtesy of Redbridge Museum/Redbridge Information & Heritage 2015. Ref. p8717*)

squadrons back from France when increased German incursions over England made this necessary. Among the Home Defence airfields was a handful in south-west Essex: Hainault Farm, Suttons Farm and North Weald; further out into Essex were Rochford, Stow Maries[20] and Goldhanger.

Whereas the airfields at Hainault Farm and Suttons Farm were already in existence at the time Home Defence was created, that at North Weald was new. The airfield there was declared operational in spring 1916, its grassed site occupying 136 acres, with approximate dimensions of 900 yards by 850 yards. By August 1916, North Weald was home to A Flight of No. 39 (Home Defence) Squadron; the squadron was widely dispersed, with B Flight at Suttons Farm, C Flight at Hainault Farm and its HQ at Woodford Green[21].

... and aircraft

In August 1914, aircraft defences in Britain were minimal. All the most modern aircraft were in France and those left for home defence were outclassed by German airships with their superior speed, rate of climb and operational ceilings – it took British fighters up to an hour to reach the height of the airships. In the autumn of 1914, the RFC had 116 aeroplanes in Britain; the RNAS had fifty better aeroplanes available.

The two services co-operated only minimally and there were inter-service rivalries. The RNAS would engage enemy craft approaching the coast and defend dockyards and naval facilities, while the RFC would only operate over the hinterland when the attackers had crossed the coastline. Soldiers manned AA guns in ports, while naval guns ringed London to defend the capital. In the early days of the war it was the RNAS that dictated Britain's aerial strategy, not the RFC, as demands upon the RFC by the army overseas made it impossible for the service to provide an organized air defence. However, the Royal Navy was also finding the burden of home defence, in particular of London, thirty miles from the coast and at most risk, growing more difficult as the U-boat campaign increased.

With the creation of Home Defence in 1916, the number of aircraft available varied: in February 1916, there were only eight squadrons and fewer than half the number of aircraft expected. By June the number of squadrons had fallen to six and only No. 39 Squadron was at full strength, with twenty-four aircraft.

From 1916 onwards, the RFC's obsolete aircraft types gradually disappeared, to be replaced by a reasonably modern, but not particularly suitable, aircraft – the BE2c. This was a variant of the BE2 series and the one produced in greater numbers than any other. The specification had been laid down to produce a safe military airplane inherently stable and free of difficult handling characteristics. The BE2c exceeded this requirement and delivered a platform so stable it could not manoeuvre rapidly against enemy aircraft. This made it unsuitable for front-line operation, but its stability lent itself to night flying and training. However, the performance of the engine and the high-drag airframe performance were mediocre so the open unused front cockpits of Home Defence versions were faired over with aluminium sheet or thin plywood to eliminate a little drag. Other modifications were introduced too. The British & Colonial Aeroplane Company built ten specially modified BE2cs for Home Defence duties. These were single-seaters, classified as BE12, and the space normally occupied by the front seat contained an extra petrol tank to increase endurance for anti-Zeppelin work. Until the Germans began to use the Gotha biplanes in place of airships, the BE2c and BE12 were the standard British Home Defence fighters. They are seldom credited with successes of any kind, but they did perform well on Home Defence duties.

On 24 July 1917, the officers and men at Hainault Farm were informed that they were no longer serving with No. 39 Squadron, but were now an independent unit, No. 44 Squadron, the first of three additional Home Defence squadrons being formed to counter the daylight Gotha bombing raids. One of its commanding officers at this time was Major Arthur Harris.[22] No. 44 Squadron was to remain at Hainault Farm for the duration of the war and afterwards until it moved briefly to North Weald in July 1919 before being disbanded in December 1919. The squadron's initial equipment was Sopwith 1½ Strutters, but most of these were soon replaced by Sopwith Camels. The Camel was difficult to handle, but to an experienced pilot it provided un-matched manoeuvrability. A superlative fighter, the Camel was credited with shooting down more enemy aircraft than any other Allied fighter of the war.

Nineteen-year-old Cecil Lewis[23] wrote:

> I was made a Flight-Commander and posted to No. 44 Squadron stationed at Hainault Farm, just out beyond Ilford in Essex. The squadron was quartered in an old farmhouse by the aerodrome. It was not particularly comfortable; but as Hainault was within three-quarters of an hour of the West End, pilots spent most of their nights in town.[24]

Sopwith F1 Camels of No. 44 (Home Defence) Squadron, lined up at Hainault Farm with attendant mechanics, 1917–18. Some of these aircraft have been specially converted for night-fighting, with the cockpits moved aft and twin Lewis guns, mounted over the upper wing in place of the Vickers machine guns on the nose. (*Imperial War Museum. Ref. HU 75730*)

Sopwith F1 Camel single-seat fighter aircraft of No. 44 (Home Defence) Squadron at Hainault Farm airfield. (*Imperial War Museum. Ref. Q 67903*)

 We were equipped with Sopwith Camels, the latest single-seater scout, fitted with a 110hp Clerget engine and two Vickers guns. The machine was new to me, so for the first few days after my arrival at Hainault I spent a good deal of time in the air getting used to it.

 Each squadron had a telephone operator constantly on duty. When raid warnings came through, he pressed a Morse key close to hand sounding three large Klaxon horns set up on the roof of the men's quarters and the officers' Mess. The men swarmed into the sheds and rushed out the machines, the pilots struggled into their kit and warmed up their engines. If the raid warning was followed by the action signal, machines were off the ground within a minute.

 In August 1917, the rest of No. 39 Squadron concentrated at North Weald, being replaced at Suttons Farm by No. 46 Squadron temporarily in the UK from the Western Front to boost Home Defence numbers, then No. 78 Squadron followed by No. 189 Night Training Squadron and finally No. 51

An informal group of five officer pilots of No. 44 (Home Defence) Squadron standing in front of a Sopwith F1 Camel at Hainault Farm airfield in 1918. In the middle is captain R.N. Hall. (*Redbridge Museum/Redbridge Information & Heritage 2015. Ref. p152*)

Squadron. At North Weald, the squadron started re-equipping with the Bristol F2B Fighter. The squadron now had a first-class aircraft. The two-seat 'Brisfit' possessed a single-seat fighter's combat manoeuvrability, good structural strength and a fighter-like performance; it had already proved itself over the Western Front. Moreover, it had the bonus of a rear gun defence/offence when required, something unavailable to any single-seat fighter.

It was while here that one young pilot had a trying experience. The night-flying aircraft carried wing-tip flares, which could be started electrically by the pilots to light up the ground in case of emergency landing. While he was high up on patrol, near Epping Forest, this pilot accidentally lit his flares, thought his machine was on fire and landed near the forest in something of a hurry. It was some time before he confessed what had happened, and the authorities searched Epping Forest for days looking for a hypothetical Gotha fallen in flames.

Mechanics of No. 44 (Home Defence) Squadron grouped in front of a Sopwith F1 Camel fitted with a twin Lewis gun mounting at Hainault Farm airfield. (*Redbridge Museum/Redbridge Information & Heritage 2015. Ref. p151*)

In November 1918, No. 39 Squadron began to move to France, but with the signing of the Armistice the move was not completed and the squadron was disbanded.

Weapons

The lack of an interrupter gear between propeller and machine-guns in early fighters meant the usual technique of attempting to down a Zeppelin was to drop bombs on it. Initially the War Office believed that the Zeppelins' inner hydrogen-filled bags were surrounded by an envelope filled with inert gas and that any rupture of the bags by machine-gun fire would produce an innocent mixture of the two gases that would fail to ignite. Thus it was considered that the only way an airship could be brought down by machine-gun fire was if it was filled so full of holes that it lost a large proportion of its gas through leaks, and thereby its buoyancy.

At the outbreak of the war, two sizes of bomb were available for use against Zeppelins: the Hales bomb, in 10lb and 20lb varieties. Introduced specifically for the RNAS by F. Martin Hale, an expert in explosives, the Hales bomb was manufactured by the Powder Company at Faversham, Kent. During the early part of the war it was used extensively by the RNAS and, from 1915, by the RFC. The 20lb bomb actually weighed 18½lbs and contained 4½lbs of amatol explosive (a mixture of trinitrotoluene (TNT) and ammonium nitrate). Its length was 23¼ inches and the greatest diameter 5 inches. It consisted of a steel, pear-shaped body, with a flanged aluminium holder for the tail fins and fusing mechanism and was armed by a small propelled device aft of the tail fins rotated by wind pressure during the fall. How a pilot was expected to drop a bomb on an airship which could fly up to 10,000 feet higher than his own aircraft is not clear.

The Ranken aerial dart was developed for use against Zeppelins by Engineer Lieutenant-Commander Francis Ranken. It was initially used as a RNAS weapon, but was also adopted by the RFC in 1916. It consisted of a tinplate tube with a cast-iron pointed nose at one end, and a plug and three spring-loaded arms at the other. The arms were kept closed in storage by means of a cap, either tin or rubber, which acted as a buffer when the dart was in its dropping tube. Ranken darts measured some 5½ inches long and weighing 13 ounces. The three sprung arms were designed to catch in airship fabric once this had been pierced by the cast-iron nose. It was a non-explosive device, but its filling sent back a shower of sparks, fired by the jerk of their lodging in the fabric to ignite the volatile mixture of air and escaping hydrogen. They were carried in metal cases of fifty and dropped in groups of three from 60 feet above the target. They were supported in their fall by a small rubber parachute. Apart from the difficulties of effective aim from above – British aircraft could rarely climb high enough for the pilots to use the dart – the darts were no less dangerous to the population on the ground than the Zeppelin bombs themselves.

The idea for an explosive bullet originated in 1914 when the War Office rejected a design by an Australian, John Pomeroy. In 1915, the War Office reconsidered the idea, with two additional developments: an explosive bullet created by Royal Navy Commander F.A. Brock; and a phosphorous bullet created by F.J. Buckingham. The three bullets were combined to create Brock-Pomeroy-Buckingham machine-gun ammunition to tear through a Zeppelin's skin. If these bullets hit the framework of the airship and detonated, they almost invariably ignited the hydrogen. These bullets caused so much grief to Zeppelin crews that the Germans called them 'the invention of the devil'.

Home Defence fighters ultimately bore a variety of weapons, but standard armament for a BE2c flown as a single-seater was laid down officially as a Lewis gun and four bombs or a box of Ranken darts; for a BE12 it was a Lewis gun, a box of Ranken darts and ten Le Prieur rockets.[25] On a BE2c or BE12 the Lewis gun was usually a single fixed upward-firing gun mounted ahead of the pilot.

A number of Home Defence Sopwith Camels were extensively modified as night fighters, with over-wing Lewis guns added and the cockpit being moved rearwards so the pilot could easily reload the guns. This modification allowed the guns to be fired without affecting the night vision of the pilots.

Flying at night

The main role of the local Home Defence squadrons was to defend London from German attacks approaching over south-west Essex. This was the regular route to the capital for bombers when they had crossed the North Sea. The RFC's chief activity to date had been day reconnaissance without any need to fly at night. Now the pilots had to master the techniques of flying at night without radio[26] or adequate landing aids.

At the same time as No. 39 Squadron was formed, the first scheme for night training began and night-flying equipment and anti-Zeppelin armament began to be standardized. An instructional course in flying at night started in early 1916 at Hounslow. Established pilots had to complete a programme, which included five night flights and a small amount of armament instruction.

Flying at night took a high degree of courage and there was virtually no assistance from the ground once an aircraft was airborne. Pilots found it impossible to see the airships, even at a distance of 200 yards. If it was not too dark a night, their darker bulk might be spotted by the keen-eyed and pilots could be guided towards their prey by searchlights and bursts from AA fire. When close to an enemy airship, the glow from its exhausts might give away its position; otherwise it was fly, search and hope that luck was on your side. Attacks took place in the dark, in aircraft with minimal modified instrumentation and lighting, at altitudes of 10,000–15,000 feet and with no oxygen supply. The BE2c and BE12 aircraft were at their maximum ceiling, and the blast from an exploding airship might have blown the attacking aircraft out of control. Furthermore, the airships were armed with machine-guns, which regularly opened fire on the pilots during their attacks.

Nights were generally dark enough to make it an extremely dangerous environment to be in, sitting in a fairly frail aircraft, in an open cockpit, without a parachute, and only the pilot's individual skills to aid him. Life was much easier on moonlit nights than on those without a moon; easier for the bombers too as it made it simpler to navigate and find targets. Taking off was straightforward, but landing back on some grass airstrip seemingly in the middle of nowhere was quite another (even with the addition of under-wing flares to aid landing). There was a high risk of crashing on landing, assuming the pilot could even find the nearest airfield in the dark. Occasionally search-lights might give an indication of direction, or the pilot may have some knowledge of where these lights were situated, always assuming he had not become totally lost in the gloom and often cloudy sky.

Chapter 4

'Take cover'

Air raid warnings

The chance of a bomb falling on any individual or his home was very small. A writer to *The Hampstead Times* in February 1918 calculated that:

> Taking the area of London as 100 square miles, a bomb affecting an area of 60 square yards in diameter and, assuming the enemy could drop 22 bombs a month all year round, the War would have to last 32 years for it to be likely for a bomb to fall in one's own circle. The chance of a direct hit on one's own roof of 10 square yards would need 894 years. If people realised such facts as these, there would be no more panic.

Air raid warnings in the early years of the First World War were highly variable. In fact, a contentious question of the time was whether there should be public warnings at all. The result was a patchwork of different regulations in different areas, and under different local authorities who dithered over whether it was advisable to give warnings at all, since they could lead to unnecessary anxiety. It was possible for civilians not to know there was an air raid alert on at all, particularly if they were already asleep. In London, Scotland Yard was alerted by telephone when Admiralty coastal observation stations detected Zeppelins heading for the capital; the London Fire Brigade and Woolwich Arsenal were then alerted and some private warnings were given by telephone to hospitals, important firms, prominent politicians and others, but this 'system' was largely hit and miss.

At Ilford, notice of an approaching air raid was given to residents in the Ley Street area by extinguishing the red lantern outside the fire station there. At a meeting in June 1915, Leyton UDC considered whether warnings should be given by a steam siren on the electricity station in Cathall Road. However, the police objected to such a warning for fear it would cause panic in the neighbourhood. The council therefore resolved to take no action. More than two years later, the council was still resisting calls for a siren: in October 1917, the Leyton Emergency Corps reported on its work in recent air raids, requesting the council to provide 'a loud and distinctive syren' on the electricity works or other suitable place. The council declined and resolved to give warning by the

Ilford fire station. Notice of an approaching air raid was given to residents in the Ley Street area by the extinguishing of the red lantern outside the fire station. (*Author's collection*)

firing of maroons from Leytonstone fire station. As late as January 1918 the council was still receiving requests, this time from the Birkbeck Estate Patrol, for a siren to give warning, and it still declined to do so, relying on the firing of maroons. By the end of the war some authorities had provided sirens, but it was not until early 1918 that the one in Romford was permitted to be used after midnight.

In July 1917, an official system in three stages was instituted: warnings (first stage); mobilization (second stage); and the 'Take cover' order (third stage). Subsequently, eighty-six official warnings went out in the Metropolitan Police area, in fifty-eight of which there was a general order to mobilize. Mobilization meant, in anticipation of the 'Take cover' order, policemen manning local shelters. On a number of other occasions commanders and station chiefs were called to posts if it looked likely that quick mobilization was considered probable.

For daytime raids policemen walked or rode bicycles through the streets, blowing their whistles or ringing their bells, sometimes carrying billboards bearing the notice 'Air raid – take cover'. Warning of an impending night-time air raid was given by the firing of maroons, which exploded with a loud report. Hilda Bazalgette, in Leytonstone, recalled:

> When there was an air raid it was announced by maroons, two or three enormous explosions which sounded violent and made us jump out of our skins. Sometimes we went down into our cellar, or sometimes we sat in the middle of the ground floor of the house. My grandmother had a carpet laid in her cellar, and an armchair placed in the middle so that she could take refuge there in the raids.

Leyton resident Jack Milford's earliest recollections included air raid warnings being 'carried out by Boy Scouts with their bugles'. It was the role of the bugler officer at police stations to take charge of the buglers, keep them in order and see that they remained under cover while bombs were falling. Then, when the command was given, it was his duty to get pairs of buglers into waiting cars, each of which sped off on its appointed round, to sound the 'All clear' within a few minutes. When it was all over, the buglers were driven to their respective homes, and returned to their parents.

Air raid precautions

In places where no public warnings were given, residents sometimes took matters into their own hands. As early as June 1915, a street patrol of fifty-five volunteers was keeping an eye on Rendlesham Road, Clapton, prepared to call out residents who had responded to a leaflet asking if they wanted to be alerted in the event of a raid. Other areas were similarly organized: in August 1915, *The Ilford Recorder* carried a series of letters about the Cranbrook Zeppelin Patrol, which had been inaugurated two months previously at a large public meeting in Ilford's Highlands Schools. In nearby Wanstead Park Road there were 340 houses with about 1,500 residents and from these a list of about sixty people had been drawn up comprising four patrols each night from 10.30pm to 2.00am. One correspondent, who lived in Wanstead Park Road, objected to a house-to-house collection of a minimum of 6*d* being made to cover the patrol's expenses as he considered the sum raised to be far in excess of anything likely to be incurred on 'printed matter and a few badges'.

Another example was in Poplar, mentioned in a letter in London's *Evening News* on 13 March 1935:

> On the brick wall at the side of our street door can still be seen faintly two large letters, 'P.P.', which stood for Poplar Patrol. Every Friday night it was my job to collect 3*d* from each house-hold that belonged to the 'P.P.' This

A contemporary illustration of a Boy Scout bugler sounding the 'All clear'. The earliest recollections of several residents in south-west Essex included the 'All clear' being carried out by Boy Scouts with their bugles. (*Author's collection*)

paid for rent, fire and refreshments for our small front room, where three men, each in his turn, used to sit up every night. In the event of a raid, as soon as they got the first warning they used to run and knock on every door where there was 'P.P.'

By subscribing 3d a week, any family in Poplar concerned about being caught in its beds when the Zeppelins came could be assured of a loud knock on the door.

In June 1915, the Commissioner of the Metropolitan Police issued official advice to civilians about what to do in an air raid:

In all probability if an air raid is made it will take place at a time when most people are in bed. The only intimation the public are likely to get will be the reports of the anti-aircraft guns or the noise of falling bombs.

The public are advised not to go into the street where they might be struck by falling missiles, moreover the streets being required for the passage of fire engines, etc., should not be obstructed by pedestrians.

In many houses there are no facilities for procuring water on the upper floors. It is suggested, therefore, that a supply of water and sand might be kept there so that any fire breaking out on a small scale can at once be dealt with. Everyone should know the position of the fire alarm post nearest to his house.

That same month, Leyton UDC authorized the council's surveyor to provide heaps of sand in various parts of the district, and three trucks to be placed at three police stations, plus poles and tripods for use as barricades after air raids.

During the raids, people were left largely to their own devices, being advised to take to cellars as the safest precaution, or to lie down if they were caught in the open. Other advice included avoiding top-floor rooms and placing mattresses on upper floors to cushion impact. Poster or leaflets, such as this one entitled 'Advice on air raids', were displayed or distributed to homes by some local authorities:

What to do before an Air Raid. Prepare your basement as follows:- Have some warm wraps, food, a bucket of water and candles stored there, also some strong tools such as hatchet, saw, hammer, chisels, crowbar or strong poker, etc., as debris might fall, and these will help you to get out. Drape with dark material all the windows of your lighted rooms – it is your duty to yourself and your neighbour and may save your district from a visit. Keep all inflammable materials such as oil lamps, paraffin, etc., in cellar. Make arrangements with a few neighbours to help each other. You will feel a lot more comfortable if you know that someone will be looking after you in case of an accident.

What to do during an Air Raid. Don't stand in the street or look out of the window. It may be exciting to see Aircraft but it's very dangerous. You have not only bombs from Aircraft to fear but shot and shell fired at the Aircraft. Bombs dropped from Aircraft in motion do not descend vertically so that safety is not secured by simply keeping out of the line of flight. If you are in the street ask for shelter in the nearest building. If you are in open country get into a ditch or other shelter. If you are in the house go to the basement. As soon as you get the warning of raid, extinguish your fire and turn off gas or electric light at the meter. Close all shutters, windows and doors but don't lock them. Don't shelter in Railway Stations and don't attempt to go there with the idea of getting away. Don't attempt to leave the district by the roads. Obey all instructions of the authorities. Don't shoot at an aircraft – leave that to the proper authorities.

What to do after an Air Raid. After a raid do all in your power to put out fires and assist the authorities in rescue work, etc. When doing rescue work in damaged buildings, do not carry naked lights or there may be an explosion. Do not touch unexploded bombs or shells and prevent others from doing so. Report the whereabouts of bombs to the authorities at once.

At Fairlop, completely against any advice, residents in the railway cottages in Forest Road would sometimes go over to the station and spend the time in the subway between the platforms there during raids.

In January 1915, *The Walthamstow Sentinel* reported: 'The local St John Ambulance Brigade are ready for any emergency in case of an air raid ... There is no need for alarm'. In Leyton there was also the municipal Leyton Emergency Corps to deal with issues of civil defence, particularly search and rescue. In July 1917, Leyton UDC agreed that the corps could use Canterbury Road School and Mayville Road School as concentration stations in case of daytime air raids; at night-time, boys stationed in the Town Hall would call out the corps. In March 1918, the council was requested to allow Mrs Noble, a convenience keeper near *The Green Man* and a member of the corps attached to No. 5 (Mayville Road School) Emergency Station, to leave her conveniences on receipt of an air raid warning so that she could attend her emergency post. The council agreed to her request.

Air raid shelters
On 13 June 1917, Gotha aircraft struck at London for the first time, yet even by September 1917 the Government saw no need to construct official air raid

The Leyton Emergency Corps was created to deal with issues of civil defence, particularly search and rescue. This 1919 photograph dates from just after the war and shows Section 5, based at Mayville Road School. (*Vestry House Museum, London Borough of Waltham Forest*)

shelters. General Smuts, in response to his colleagues in the War Cabinet, reported:

> It is generally agreed that the time has not come to construct dug-outs or special shelters and it is hoped that they will never become necessary. London has sufficient basements and underground cellars to accommodate the population against all immediate dangers. All that is necessary at the present stage is that, by means of the Press, the public be kept fully and continuously advised and warned by the Home Office to retire to houses and basements on the first sign of danger ... So far it cannot be said that the public have unduly ignored the notices and warnings issued to them.

As a result of the June raid, some authorities on the eastern side of London instituted their own air raid shelters and warning systems. Jack Milford recollected being taken by his mother 'down to the air raid shelters in the stables under the Lea Bridge Road arches'. In October 1917, Leyton UDC twice declined a suggestion from Mr A. Vennell Coster that air raid shelters be provided by excavating under public spaces. In the same month, the council gave instructions to caretakers to open schools to give shelter to persons in the streets during air raids and this was soon followed, on the advice of the London Air Raid Shelters Committee, by arranging to place sandbags at several schools used out of school hours as public shelters. Two months later, the council considered a letter from the Leyton Urban District Ratepayers' Association suggesting the strengthening of the cinder banks at Leyton Football Club's ground in Lea Bridge Road for the purposes of an air raid shelter. The council reported that the London Air Raid Shelters Committee had advised that, due to a lack of skilled labour and the need for a large amount of timber, it could not advise proceeding. In Barking, all first-floor windows of public buildings and schools were sandbagged, and all public buildings were made ready to shelter residents during an air raid.

Gas attacks

On 26 May 1915, there appeared in *The Times* an advertisement for the 'Life-saving Cavendish anti-gas inhaler' – in other words, a gas mask. This was an early attempt to combine the threats of aerial bombardment and chemical warfare:

> You can effectually avert the threatened peril to yourself and family from asphyxiating bombs dropped by the enemy's airships if you are provided with enough 'CAVENDISH INHALERS'.
>
> You cannot afford to make mistakes in this matter: it is vital. Pads and the like made with the best intentions, but without the necessary chemical knowledge, are only partly – and for a very short time – protective against slowly spreading vapour. They are of no use whatever when the gas is exploded and forced through every cranny into your home.
>
> Closing the lower windows and doors of your house is NOT a sufficient protection against the rush of gas driven in by high explosive. You need – for yourself and your family – absolute protection against actual contact with the fumes.

It claimed that one charge would work for half an hour, 'quite long enough for absolute security from danger' – a bargain for 5/6 post-free.

This advertisement was surprisingly early. It dated from just over a month after the first large-scale use of gas at the Second Battle of Ypres (22 April 1915). It was also a few days before the first Zeppelin raid on London

(31 May/1 June), and three weeks before the Commissioner of the Metropolitan Police issued official advice to civilians about what to do in an aerial gas attack (15 June); his advice also appeared in *The Times*:

> All windows and doors on the lower floor should be closed to prevent the admission of noxious gases. Any indication that poisonous gas is being used will be that a peculiar and irritating smell may be noticed following on the dropping of the bomb.
>
> Many inquiries have been made as to the best respirator. To this question there is no really satisfactory answer, as until the specific poison used is known an antidote cannot be indicated. There are many forms of respirator on the market for which special advantages are claimed, but the Commissioner is advised by competent experts that in all probability a pad of cotton-waste contained in gauze to tie round the head and saturated with a strong solution of washing powder would be effective as a filtering medium for noxious gases, and could be improvised at home at trifling cost. It should be damped when required for use and must be large enough to protect the nose as well as the mouth, the gauze being so adjusted as to protect the eyes.

Lighting restrictions

Lighting restrictions had been introduced on 11 September 1914, but not until a raid had occurred were they more rigorously enforced. Regulations made under the Defence of the Realm Act (DORA) meant that it was up to local authorities to decide what to do, such as imposing a blackout, which often amounted to the dimming of lights just before an attack. But there was still uncertainty: some street lights could be left unlit, while others could be dimmed or shaded; it was also forbidden to shine torches into the sky. In Walthamstow, some street lights had their glass painted green; in homes, blinds or blackout curtains were to be used; and in Woodford, at the Ray Lodge Congregational church, members put covers that looked like inverted dustbins over their gas lights.

On 21 May 1915, under the heading 'The Zeppelin Raids. Grave Warning to Ilford Residents', *The Ilford Recorder* carried the following notice:

> We are officially requested to warn the public of Ilford that the exhibition of lights during the night is highly dangerous, and especially after midnight. It is known that in the recent air raid on Southend the Zeppelins were directly guided by a strong light on the sea front. Ilford is on the direct route from the North Sea to the City. If all lights are extinguished throughout the town, the danger from explosive and incendiary bombs will

be considerably minimised. But if lights are displayed – even a solitary beacon here and there would be sufficient – Ilford will almost certainly be raided. Should any householders ignore the warning, either through carelessness, or from pro-German sympathies, it will be the duty of their neighbours to inform the police at once, and the offenders will be strongly dealt with.

Persistent offenders were liable to six months in gaol or £100 fine. Ilford's residents took little heed of the newspaper's warning, however, for, on 4 June, four days after the first air raid on London, an article entitled 'The Lesson of the Zeppelin Raid' appeared in the paper:

The chief topic in Ilford this week is the air raid that is officially reported to have been made on certain parts of London during Monday night. For obvious reasons the exact localities visited, and details of the damage, have not been permitted to transpire, and although a good deal is known to us, we are precluded from passing on this information to our readers. Suffice it that Ilford probably narrowly escaped serious mischief, and that the town may be far less immune when the bomb-droppers come this way again. The lesson for all of us is to exercise a rigid supervision over our lights. An aggregation of houses such as there is in Ilford is indistinguishable, at the safe altitudes traversed by the murderous airships, from wooded or pastoral open country but for the lights that illumine it.

We understand that the public street lamps are henceforth to be extinguished at midnight. They ought to be put out at least an hour earlier. Monday's raid was in progress by eleven o'clock, and had the aerial craft shaped their course across Ilford they would have had an ideal target below them. It may be urged that a fair volume of vehicular traffic ebbs and flows along the High-road until after the midnight hour, and that darkened streets would very likely lead to serious accidents. But with the special care that drivers are bound to exercise under such circumstances, these dangers can be reduced to a minimum. And in any event they are much less serious in their consequences than a concerted Zeppelin raid is likely to be. Therefore it is to be hoped the authorities will decide forthwith to shut off the public lights at half-past ten, or at latest by eleven. Their responsibility will then have ended.

Unfortunately there are many private people in Ilford who appeared to be quite unconscious of the aerial menace, for, with the vanishment of the public lights, numberless beacons become clearly visible in all parts of the town, some of them shining on into the morning hours. These would guide an approaching enemy as surely as the public lamps. It is difficult to

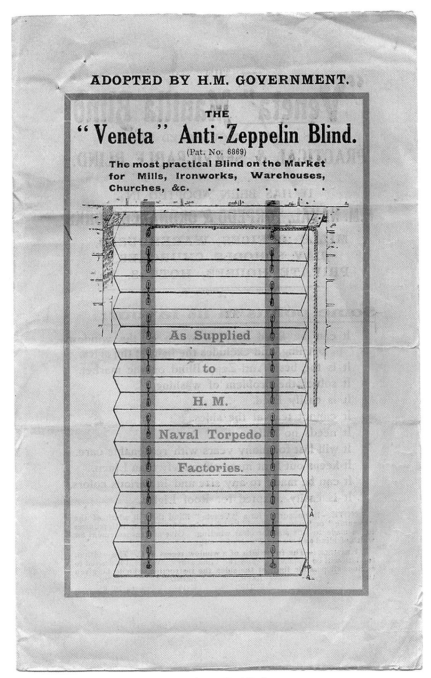

An advertisement for the 'Veneta' anti-Zeppelin blind. (*Author's collection*)

find adequate language in which to stigmatise the almost criminal folly that permits lights to blaze from windows and from the fanlights of doors across the street without, when at any moment the enemy in the clouds may be searching for just such indications of life and bricks-and-mortar on which to shower his bombs. If the foolish people who thus suicidally court danger have no care for themselves, at least they ought to show some consideration for their neighbours. All artificial illumination that is needed in the home after these long mid-summer days have waned should be scrupulously screened from the outer world. Thereby a very real and ever-present peril may be considerably lessened, and perhaps altogether averted.

On 3 June 1915, three days after the town's first air raid, Leyton UDC's Baths & Washhouses Committee reported that the police considered the lighting in the swimming baths to be excessive and likely to prove a danger in case of further air raids – the lighting should be considerably decreased or the baths should be closed earlier. The Committee approved a quote of £17.15*s* for 'colouring with "Nightshade"' (i.e. painting black) the tops of the lantern lights and the glass in the roof of the first and second class swimming baths; they also agreed to fix large shades over the lamps in the baths. Later that month, the council's Highways & Lighting Committee resolved that street lamps should be darkened, but that the streets must remain sufficiently lit for the safe passage of traffic.

In January 1916, following an air raid on the Midlands, a public outcry for an official warning system was ignored, but the London lighting regulations were extended to the Midlands and the West Country. Clocks were also stopped from chiming, as the sound was thought to guide the Zeppelins. It was not until the summer of 1916, however, that a total blackout was imposed.

Transport

Motor vehicle headlights were ordered to be covered at night, but that posed a danger to pedestrians. In Barking, in 1916, James Bones of Westbury Road was killed when hit by a bus in the dark, the driver claiming that he did not see Mr Bones. In Ilford, some of the roadside kerbs were painted white to help motorists see where they were going. The brightness of lights inside trams, buses and trains was also reduced, and they were usually extinguished during a raid. In the case of the railways, the policy until about the middle of 1916 was to extinguish lights and stop work in stations and goods yards on receipt of a warning and to stop trains running in the danger zone. Then, in order to reduce disruption to traffic, instructions were issued that trains were to run at reduced speeds and that in stations and goods yards lighting should be reduced to the absolute minimum consistent with the carrying on of railway working.

Quite early in the war, the Great Eastern Railway (GER)[1] adopted an air raid reporting system to protect not only its rail network but its employees and passengers too. This was successful and was later used as a model reporting system throughout the country. By means of the company's telephone and telegraph system, the GER Military Office at Liverpool Street station was sent reports of enemy action near any GER station. For this purpose, the GER system was split into reporting areas, each with a unique number (in 1917, Leyton and Leytonstone stations were in Area 43). The reported sightings were telegraphed through to the railway's Military Office and recorded on a large map of the company's operating area, which when translated gave an idea of how a raid was progressing and the areas likely to be affected. Through the Railway Executive[2] this information was transmitted to the Admiralty, and later the War Office.

The system worked in the following way: *Report from Leytonstone 11.30pm one Zeppelin moving north-east.* A white-headed pin with the time 11.30pm would be put on the map at Leytonstone. As that Zeppelin moved and further sightings were reported, a red-headed pin would be stuck on the map at the relevant reporting station. If there was more than one Zeppelin in the raid, a differently coloured pin would be used too. If bombs were dropped, another appropriate symbol was put on the map. If the Zeppelin was shot down, officials would put an airship-shaped piece of paper on the map.

In September 1916, Walthamstow UDC had resolved:

That the Tramway Manager be directed to reduce the service of cars as much as possible immediately an official intimation is received from the Fire Brigade, or otherwise of a possible air raid, and on receipt of the Field Marshal's notification, that the remainder of the cars be at once returned to the Depot at reduced speed, and immediately the searchlights are thrown into the sky the drivers to at once stop and remain stationary, placing lights in front and rear of cars until notice to resume normal conditions comes through.

Leyton UDC had also considered the matter of trams running during air raids and came to the same conclusion as Walthamstow; it had also received a petition of 1,878 signatures in favour of stopping running. The council therefore resolved to make representations to the Commander-in-Chief, Home Forces, that it was desirable that railway traffic, motor omnibuses, trams and other vehicular traffic should be stopped when warning was received of impending hostile raids. However, the military authorities would not allow trams to be stopped on the road during air raids and they threatened to prosecute managers, motormen and tramways committees. In October 1916, the council issued a notice reminding tramways staff of the requirements of DORA, i.e. trams should be kept running, but at no more than six miles per hour.

Fire brigades
Scotland Yard issued instructions for controlling fire. The majority of bombs dropped by Zeppelins on London were incendiaries, but although these caused material loss, loss of life was comparatively light from fires. The distinctive Harrow Green fire station in Leytonstone opened in July 1914 (an earlier fire station had existed there since 1881) and, when bombs began falling, it provided much reassurance to nearby residents and quickly became a local landmark. The other fire station in the district was in Church Road, Leyton. The firemen's responsibilities included rescuing survivors following a bombing attack and the men's efforts were instrumental in restricting fire damage and casualties.

In June 1915, Leyton UDC authorized the purchase of various pipes, hoses and respirators for the fire brigade. The council also approved twelve auxiliary firemen for the brigade, and for the brigade to be paid 10/- per night whenever it was called out to an air raid. Two years later the council appointed an Air Raid Sub-Committee and one of its first actions was to arrange the purchase of a motor ambulance for use by the fire brigade.

In January 1917, Ilford UDC received a report from its Fire Brigade Committee:

> That the thanks of the Council be given to Corporal E.A. Goddard and Privates W. Kent and D.F. MacIntosh, members of the Scouts Defence Corps, each of whom has made over 100 attendances for all-night duty at the Central Fire Station, and that a copy of the resolution, under the seal of the Council, be presented to each of the scouts named.

The scouts and their scoutmaster subsequently attended a council meeting and received their sealed resolutions. Seven more scouts received similar presentations from the council that year, but sadly D.F. MacIntosh, who had since joined the armed forces, was later killed in action in France and the council expressed its regret and sympathy.

In Leyton too, Boy Scouts were based at fire stations during the day and, when the fire brigade received warning, one would run to each school and inform the head teacher. He would then return to the fire station and later run

The fire station at Harrow Green, Leytonstone. The brigade is posed outside 'ready' for an air raid. (*Author's collection*)

back to the school with news of the 'All clear'. However, Leyton's scouts were not as well behaved as those in Ilford for, in September 1917, the council reported that they were damaging the fixtures and fittings at the fire stations and so should be withdrawn, with new arrangements made for warning schools of air raids.

In December 1918, after the war was over, Leyton UDC's Highways & Lighting Committee received the following report from the captain of the fire brigade:

It will be interesting for you to know that for the past four years the Brigade have kept strict duty at their stations, and on several occasions have received Air Raid calls, sixty-nine in all and Air Raid fire calls.

They were the means of saving four persons in Bakers Avenue, Leyton, and preventing damage to St. Augustine's Church and adjoining properties from fire by incendiary bombs, besides attending several minor disasters.

On the occasion of one Air Raid the Brigade had a narrow escape of a serious accident. A tree had been blown down in Knotts Green Road and a man killed, the members being stopped just in time by a bus employee who was presented by the members of the Brigade with a suitable gift for his action. During the times mentioned the Officers and men have had a very trying and anxious time.

The Brigade have mustered full strength on every occasion.

The committee responded by placing on record its appreciation of the valuable services rendered to the district by the brigade under exacting conditions, and recommending to the council that a certificate and medal be awarded to each member of the brigade.

Special Constabulary

Wherever bombs fell, amongst the first on the scene were the special constables, often with rescue equipment. The Home Office allowed forces to recruit a substantial number of extra constables or police reserves to replace those who enlisted and to bolster police generally during the war. These recruits came from local men, some in reserved occupations and so wholly or temporarily exempt from military duty, others not yet volunteers or conscripts for the armed forces. Public response was good: Ilford could muster 225 special constables by November 1914; Goodmayes and Chadwell Heath supplied a further forty; in Buckhurst Hill more than fifty men were recruited. Their duties were the same as those of regular police officers, with the addition of wartime responsibilities, especially the development of an efficient air raid and civil defence organization. They were empowered to stop and challenge anyone of whom they were suspicious, and were instructed:

> ... to take notice of all passers-by and stop and question all who look like foreigners or suspicious persons, and if the Special Constable suspects them to be either German or Austrian to demand their permits ... and unless produced to detain the suspects.

A vague directive of 15 September 1914 also allowed them to challenge 'any evilly disposed people'. Special constables were initially sworn in for a year. Their uniform consisted only of an armlet – sergeants and corporals had an 'S' or 'C' embroidered on them. Training was minimal: constables were drilled twice a week by corporals, and once a fortnight by a police sergeant. The Special Constabulary was one of the unsung heroes of the war. At Hornchurch, Charles Perfect recalled:

> During the four and a half years of their service the public saw very little of the Special Constables, except, perhaps, when a careless householder happened to be showing too much light, and then he was promptly

acquainted of the fact by one of them, and duly warned of the consequences. Their measured tread was, however, often heard in the dead of night. Often, too, they were out in strong force awaiting the consummation of a first warning of approaching enemy aircraft, and ready either to take up their air raid posts, or, in the event of a threatened raid not maturing, the order to resume normal conditions, in which case those not on actual patrol duty would be free to go back to their homes and beds, and the general residents would be unaware that anything out of the ordinary had happened.

At Ilford, however, special constables enforced the blackout with such vigour that residents complained that the severe lighting restrictions increased burglary in the town.

'Friendly' fire

What goes up will sometimes come down, and AA shells did so in alarming numbers. The more AA fire was thrown skyward, the more the raiders were deterred and the safer an area became from German bombs; but, equally, the greater became the hazard from falling shells and shrapnel. Some AA shells exploded too low and the shrapnel caused both damage and alarm on the ground.[3] Frequently the gunfire was terrific and it became a common amusement of the children to collect shell fragments on the morning after a raid. They often came to school with handfuls of trophies; splinters of steel or, greatest prize of all, the nose cap of a shell.

In early October 1917, *The Ilford Recorder* published a report of damage to the town caused by friendly gunfire during a raid on London on 29 September:

At 2 Argyle Road, the home of Capt Alexander Christal, an unexploded shell crashed through the roof and two floors, smashing a marble mantelpiece, damaging the drawing room before burying itself beneath the kitchen floor. Another unexploded shell ploughed into the playground of Downsall School. At 41 Grange Road a nose cap from a spent shell damaged the front door of the home of Mr C.J. Lewis.

Having stayed at her parents' house in Seven Kings for the weekend, Mrs Amey and her child returned home to 24 Grange Road on Monday morning to discover that a shell had fallen through the roof, front bedroom and into the parlour below, doing much damage. In the next road, Windsor, an unexploded shell also crashed through the roof of no. 94, missing the bed by inches and knocking the corner off a table in the lounge below, before passing through a wall to bury itself several feet in the back garden. Luckily Mr Berry and his family were in the front room and

escaped injury. 24 and 26 Clarendon Road, Seven Kings, were also damaged by a shell that fell in the road opposite. A house in Auckland Road
also suffered damage when a shell fragment ricocheted through a kitchen
window.

Government assistance

For air raid victims across Britain some assistance was available from the
National Relief Fund. The fund was a scheme for relieving financial distress
due to the war and had been launched largely in recognition that financial
responsibility for social distress arising directly from the war should not
devolve upon the poor law authorities. When war was declared in August
1914, the Prime Minister, Herbert Asquith,[4] put William Wedgewood Benn[5]
in charge of the fund. With the support of newspapers such as *The Daily
Telegraph* and *The Times*, Benn was able to raise over £1,000,000 in ten days.
The fund, with other voluntary sources, provided temporary assistance up to
June 1917 to civilians and their dependants disabled in air raids. The assistance covered allowances for replacement of essential furniture and other
necessary expenses, including the cost of medical or surgical treatment or
appliances.

In June 1917, the Prime Minister, David Lloyd George[6], announced that
the Government had decided to make *ex gratia* awards of a more permanent
nature where personal injury had resulted in death or permanent disable-
ment and where the disabled person or his dependants were otherwise not
provided for. Claims for assistance were investigated by local representative
committees under a Government committee, and the awards were made on
the general principles of the Workmen's Compensation Acts. Those awards
were made by the Treasury and administered through the Local Government
Board.

Insurance

There were also insurance policies available against air raid damage (and
coastal attack): one such was *The Daily Mail* policy; another type of policy was
underwritten by the mainstream insurance companies. It was also possible to
insure against injuries from Zeppelin raids. For example, for a premium of
10/- the London Guarantee and Accident Company offered insurance for the
duration of the war, paying out up to £500 for various injuries or death.

The government also issued insurance against air raid damage (especially
fire damage) that had formerly been left uncovered by private insurance. For
some years, fire insurers had limited their responsibility to fires from specified
causes in order to avoid the possibility, however remote, of being involved in

a loss too great for their resources. Among the causes usually omitted were fires started by any act of war; war-caused blast damage was also usually not covered. Local authorities took advantage of the government scheme: in July 1915, Leyton UDC recommended insuring its tramways depot, tramcars and electric power station against damage from enemy aircraft. The council's other properties were already covered for fire damage, but for an extra £630 they would be covered against air raids too.

Reporting

As the first raids occurred, the press and the government were in a quandary: should they highlight the attacks in order to condemn the killing of women and children, or keep such reports low-key for fear of fuelling public anxiety? DORA, enacted four days after hostilities began, gave the authorities power to stifle criticism of the war effort and included restrictions on the press. One of its regulations stated: 'No person shall by word of mouth or in writing spread reports likely to cause disaffection or alarm among any of His Majesty's forces or among the civilian population'. Its aim was to prevent publication of anything that could be interpreted as undermining the morale of the British people, forbidding the reporting of news liable to cause alarm and despondency.

The Admiralty issued D-Notice 217[7] in the early hours of 1 June 1915, stating that in the public interest, and to prevent publication of information useful to the enemy, 'nothing must appear in the press in regard to raids by enemy aircraft except the official statements issued by the Government'. Instructions to the press were that the exact localities affected were not to be named, nor the observed course of the airships to be described or shown in the press by way of maps, thus depriving the enemy of any confirmatory intelligence or any information to confirm the accuracy of its navigation. The briefest of reports was permitted – casualties could be enumerated, but only the minimum details in terms of damage.

Following the first raid over London, on 31 May/1 June 1915, *The Daily News* ran 'Zeppelin Raid over Outer London' as its main headline. A second reported raid on London brought concerted and immediate demands for security. As the government had starved the press of a regular flow of information from the Western Front, a generally patriotic press was desperate for stories. If news was not available to fill the columns of the daily papers – there were sixteen newspapers serving London alone – editors were liable to use the stories most readily accessible, namely those produced at home.

On 2 June 1915, a coroner's inquest was held into the deaths, on the night of 31 May/1 June,[8] of Henry Thomas Good and Caroline Good, of Stoke

Newington. The inquest format allowed the newspapers to report plenty of details:

> The coroner, the jury, and all in the Court leant forward eagerly when, stooping down, the constable picked up two incendiary bombs found in the basement of the house. One, he explained, had fallen through the roof and through the front rooms. The other had dropped through the roof and on to the staircase and had set fire to the stairs. The constable added that both were very heavy.
>
> The coroner remarked that they did not seem to be very finely finished, but apparently they were very effective. They contained an explosive called 'thermit,' which was invented some years ago. It gave off enormous heat, as much as 5,000 deg., and set everything on fire that it touched. It was a barbarous weapon.

Coroners were well aware that the eyes of the nation were upon them, and that they and their juries had a responsibility to avoid damaging morale. The report continued:

> It is not desirable, he added, to make much commotion about this matter. We do not want alarm to spread around the Metropolis, which has, up to the present, taken these acts very quietly and cooly, although we all stand in danger. It does not seem desirable to go into these matters very deeply, for the simple reason that it can do no possible good. In a case of this sort where it is impossible to get hold of the culprits, there is no good purpose to be served by it.

Coroners also knew that they had a unique opportunity to mould public opinion and even official policy. They could express popular outrage at the barbaric Huns:

> The aeroplanes and Zeppelin airships of the Germans had created a new sphere for military genius to act in defence and attack. While armed airships, it was an entirely new and barbarous practice to use them as weapons of aggression against defenceless civilians in their beds in the undefended suburbs of our cities, seaside and health resorts, and country villages. Apparently there was a great deal of danger in attacking fortified places, so the German airships did not go to them.

They could also make recommendations on how best to thwart the raiders:

> The coroner said there seemed to be only one argument that was of any avail. The more men that could be got to enlist the better it would be for the country.

The jury returned the verdict that the deceased 'had died from shock, suffocation, and burns on 31 May owing to an explosion and consequent fires created by bombs no doubt dropped by a hostile airship'. That was about as far as the jury could go in assigning blame, as its members had no direct evidence as to who the murderer was, but everyone present knew that an agent of the hostile German army murdered the Goods.

Death was not always the direct result of bombing. Thomas W. Parkin, coroner for St Pancras, recalled a family that had moved from Leyton to St Pancras:

> The north-east of London was one of the first to be attacked and at Leyton lived a father and mother with two girls in their teens. They were the sole occupants of a house close to where a bomb fell. The younger daughter, who was having a warm bath at the time, hurriedly left the house inadequately clad and, in the chill of the night air, contracted a cold which developed into pneumonia, from which she died a few days later.

Propaganda

Zeppelins featured in British propaganda in newspapers and on posters. The Publicity Department at London's Central Recruiting Depot wasted little time in using the airship's menace to help stimulate recruitment for the war effort. In February 1915, during the month which followed England's first raid, it published a poster with the strap line 'It is far better to face the bullets than to be killed at home by a bomb'. At this time the capital had not yet been attacked, but by picturing an airship caught in searchlights over London's unarmed and civilian-populated areas, it showed that the capital would be the raiders' primary objective. That said, the poster would have perhaps also shown London because this would have represented Britain and thus unified the nation. Reflecting the belief that the raids were barbaric, it was hoped that this stance would make men more determined to enlist in the war. Although it is not known how much of an affect this particular poster had on civilians, it was reported throughout 1915 that in the days following raids on London there was an increase in men enlisting.

By September 1915 a 'business as usual' cartoon was in print two weeks after London's third and fourth raids. Showing a traditional British family-run grocery in complete ruins and totally uninhabitable, the elderly owner was writing on the external walls of the grocery 'Business as usual during alterations'. This confirmed what the press had depicted about the population of London remaining '… cool and free of panic.' Constantly portraying the unwillingness of Londoners to fall victim to this terrorism, as *The Times* stated following London's fourth raid, had Germany conducted the war decently then civilians might never have fully awakened from their slumbers until it was over; Germany's decision to wake them with their bombs was consequently 'the costliest of all their psychological mistakes'.

Humorous postcards soon appeared. One, with the caption 'Looking for Zeppelins at Leyton', shows citizens in various forms of night-wear and other clothing sitting on roof-tops scanning the skies with telescopes and binoculars for enemy airships. Sent by Leyton resident 'Jeanie' to her sister 'Jessie', the message on the back reads:

> I thought you would like to see how the folks at Leyton are scared on Zepp nights, for that's how we have been all this week. We heard the Leyton guns for the first time last Tuesday night firing at a Zepp about five miles away. We could see it quite plain. It was awful, the terrific reports from the guns. Tell Mother I'll write her after the raids are over if we are all spared, for you never know. We haven't been to bed until 1 o'clock in the morning all the week.

This humorous British postcard was one of many poking fun at the Zeppelin raiders. The locations were interchangeable, but the images were often similar. (*Author's collection*)

Similar cards included Enfield and Ponders End in their titles; others headed 'Looking for aircraft at Woolwich' and 'Looking for Gothas at Manor Park' were also produced. Following the successful shooting down of several Zeppelins in September 1916, triumphal postcards also began to be published, depicting the plight of the fallen craft or celebrating the bravery of the RFC pilots.

Posters of British and German aeroplane silhouettes were also issued so that people could differentiate between enemy and friendly aircraft, giving advice on what to do and whom to contact in the event of an air raid.

Chapter 5

'Knocking the chimneys down'

Riots . . .

In January 1915, *The Essex County Telegraph* poured scorn on those it thought were over-reacting to the threat of air raids with an editorial headlined 'Silly Zeppelin Scare in Essex'. However, this danger soon turned into a reality as Kaiser Wilhelm II, experiencing mounting military and public pressure to sanction Zeppelin raids on Britain, approved their possibility on 9 January 1915.[1] The first such raid was made on the night of Tuesday 19/Wednesday 20 January, on King's Lynn and Great Yarmouth on the Norfolk coast. Essex itself was bombed for the first time on Sunday 9/Monday 10 May when Southend-on-Sea was the target. The airship, LZ38 commanded by Hauptmann Erich Linnarz, made two successful bombing runs over Southend dropping nearly 100 bombs, mainly incendiary, causing much damage and one death.

The official approval of Zeppelin raiding plans on England was given in this decree by the Kaiser on 12 February 1915:

1. His Majesty, the Kaiser, has expressed great hopes that the air war against England will be carried out with the greatest energy.
2. His Majesty has designated as attack targets: war material of every kind, military establishments, barracks, and also oil and petroleum tanks, and the London docks. No attack is to be made on the residential areas of London, or above all on royal palaces.

Although the order banned the bombing of civilians, because of the inaccuracy of the airships and the close integration in London of civilian houses near the targets, the decree, to all intents and purposes, permitted airships to unleash terror from the skies upon the population of the capital. The Zeppelins of 1915 could not accurately distinguish between military and civilian targets. The London docks, for example (as designated in the Kaiser's order), were only yards away from the houses of the East End.

During May, the German military pressed the Kaiser for a free hand over London, for they believed it would be a mistake to spare the capital as this would not be understood by the German nation, and would be regarded by England as weakness. The Kaiser did not yield to this pressure, but eventually extended the, so far theoretical, ambit of the London raids, allowing attacks anywhere east of the Tower of London. The capital was subsequently bombed by Zeppelins on nine occasions, and during three of these raids bombs fell on Leyton; in these and other raids bombs fell across a wide part of south-west Essex too.

There was already much anti-German feeling in the area for, following the torpedoing of the Cunard liner, *Lusitania*, in May 1915, there had been riots in several parts of east London and south-west Essex.[2] At Stratford, a mob of some 3,000 people had wrecked a baker's shop and thrown its contents into the street; there were twenty arrests. Evelyn Potter, a 15-year-old girl living in Stratford, was a witness to some of these events and recorded in her diary:

> Great riots everywhere in London. Girls coming from 'Longthorne' district [Silvertown] brought news of German owned shops being stoned and entered. They also said mobs were out. About the middle of our [dancing] display people heard banging and shouting outside. Doris Edwards wanted to go home but got as far as the gates and was forced back by the crowds. What they wanted, or thought, is not known. Mr Cyril Hodges and Mr Jennings addressed the people who seemed satisfied and went away. Mr Oliver, our caretaker, locked and bolted all the doors and none of us were allowed out until the end of the display. Rumours Schuarmoffels the bakers being looted, other shops smashed, a Zeppelin overhead, mobs everywhere etc. were flying about. On leaving school about 10.00pm (I came home with the Wrights) we were cautioned to form ourselves into parties and keep out of the mob's way, and in the middle of the road. We wished to see if the rumours were right, so we walked up Tennyson Road. Everyone was out of their doors. When we reached Schuarmoffels shop all the windows were smashed to atoms. Glass everywhere. Blinds torn, pieces of framework hanging out, and all the bread and cakes gone! Upstairs windows broken as well. When we arrived at the 'Princess Alice' all was comparatively quiet, but people were busy smashing Goebels windows. D'Armes, the florists on the bridge had its windows smashed. A small shop opposite was wrecked.

The Stratford Express condemned the rioters as cowards and opportunists, but was prepared to concede that German 'frightfulness' had pushed some people over the edge:

> At last however, the stolid Britisher appears to have been put off his usual imperturbability. The last straw has been added by the sinking of the *Lusitania*, and this latest phase of their barbarity has loosened the restraining

influences, and even the self-control of a certain section of the public, who have begun to take the question of reprisals into their own hands.

At West Ham, John Glasson, who claimed that he and his parents were 'true-born Britishers', had all four of his shops in Barking Road wrecked. He estimated the damage at £1,000; with the cost of his stolen goods taken into account, the mob had cost him £3,000–4,000. There were 110 arrests at West Ham. A mob at Upton Park smashed into a butcher's shop making off with the stock and three bicycles from a back room. Girls also tried to tear up the linoleum from the shop floor.

A horde of 2,000 people rampaged through East Ham looking for foreign-owned shops. At one, a pork butchers shop at the junction of High Street North and Harrow Road, run by Mr C. Goetz and his family, threatening crowds gathered outside the shop and threw stones, eventually shattering all the windows. The police were powerless to stop it, although thirty-eight people were arrested.

In Walthamstow, there were riotous scenes in the High Street, St James's Street and Hoe Street. Tradesmen known to be of German origin had their shop windows broken, premises smashed and the occupiers frightened into leaving. One local newspaper had a long description of the way the crowds reacted and the difficulty the police had in stopping the destruction. The report also noted that:

> The disturbance in Wood Street a few months ago has rid that district of German butchers, and there are other shops in Hoe Street and other parts of the town whose German occupiers have likewise been hounded out, although we should like to see the names effaced from the premises.

In Leyton, a Mr Schubert had to sell his baker's shop in Lea Bridge Road, three doors from *The Greyhound* pub, after it was stoned for being German-owned. There were fifteen arrests. Under a heading 'Excitement at Leyton', *The Stratford Express* reported:

> The window-smashing campaign extended to Leyton on Wednesday evening when mad scenes were witnessed in the High-road. A large number of special constables were called out to aid the uniform officers.
>
> The first premises to be attacked were Mr Smith's bakery, opposite the Town Hall. That gentleman, as is reported elsewhere, is this week mourning the loss of his son, who was killed at the Front.
>
> A stone hit the glass panel at the top of the principal window, but fortunately Captain D.M. Smith, JP, Chairman of the Urban Council, happened

to be coming out of the premises at the time, and he, addressing the crowd, told them he had known Mr Smith a great many years, and he was a respected citizen of the town and country.

In Leytonstone, a crowd of 2,000 gathered near *The Thatched House* pub and moved north to Harrow Road and Church Lane ransacking 'German-owned' property and smashing windows, including those of J. Buck, a baker, who was thought not to be naturalized. Mr Buck had put the following notice in the local press, but it failed to save his shop:

FOR THE INFORMATION OF THE PUBLIC

Mr. J.H. Buck, baker and confectioner, 568 and 570 High-road, Leytonstone desires it to be known that he was born at Aix-la-Chapelle on the Belgian frontier, Brussels. In 1887 he came to England and renounced his foreign rights and privileges. In 1891 he married an English lady and during 1910 was granted letters of naturalisation.

Mr Buck's bakery in Leytonstone High Road was a victim of the anti-German riots of May 1915. Buck was a naturalized Briton of Belgian origin and married to an Englishwoman, but this did not save his shop from attack. (*Vestry House Museum, London Borough of Waltham Forest*)

The crowds then attacked a German barber's shop and, after ransacking another shop, threw a piano from the premises into the street. Also in Leytonstone, Ellen Wengel was keen to assert her 'Britishness' in the press:

TO THE BRITISH PUBLIC

I, ELLEN WENGEL (née ELLEN BLIGH), bred and born in the County of Norfolk, England, and whose family are all born in Leytonstone, appeal to a generous public for fair treatment and support in carrying on my business as UMBRELLA MAKER, 817, HIGH ROAD, LEYTONSTONE, RE-COVERING AND REPAIRING A SPECIALITY.

N.B. The Toy and Fancy Shop at the end of Church Lane will be carried on by my daughters.

Anti-German rioting also took place at Manor Park and in Ilford, but not to such an extent at the latter. Here the police and specials were out in force when a crowd gathered on Ilford Hill opposite Mr Zissell's bakery; the rioters smashed windows, but the police were able to disperse them, assisted by a sudden downpour of rain. *The Ilford Recorder* reported:

Ilford has happily escaped the serious tide of anti-German turbulence and disorder that has flowed over neighbouring districts and the country generally, since the 'Lusitania' was torpedoed and sent to the bottom of the sea with its crowd of perfectly innocent non-combatants. As stated in last week's 'Recorder', the mob, some thousands strong, that laid waste a number of shops and a private house at Manor Park on Wednesday night, tried to invade Ilford, but Inspector Hamilton and his force of ordinary and special police kept the disorderly throng at bay.

Among the 300 specials who assisted the police so ably, were the following, all of whom gave evidence at East Ham Police Court next day against some of the perpetrators of the outrages – Sub-Inspector Lobb, Sergeant J.C.W. Kelllow, Sergeant King, Special Constables Osborne, Cutmore and Onion. On Thursday night stones were thrown at the Cauliflower Hotel, High-road, and smashed some of the windows. The same night, while Inspector Hamilton was directing the operations of the police at Manor Park, an attempt was made to pull him from his horse. Also a stone was hurled at him which cut his head, but, happily, not seriously. The special constables again rendered valuable service at Ilford Broadway in dispersing the crowds during the exodus of the Hippodrome audiences and other places of amusement.

Remarkable scenes were witnessed in Ilford High-road on Friday night. Early in the evening, two officers in khaki entered Mr Thres' restaurant to have tea. Several persons who were passing at the moment stopped, out of curiosity, in order to ascertain the officers' business, it being erroneously and quite unwarrantably thought by some people that Mr Thres was an alien, whereas he is an English native. The few inquisitive spectators soon became many, and the crowd swiftly grew like a snowball until the High-road was almost impassable. The police early came on the scene, followed by the special constables, and they did their best to disperse the throng, but without avail. All that could be done was to keep people on the move. It is highly probable that not a single individual had any thought of doing damage or injury to the premises in question or its occupants. The crowd simply acted on the quiescent Micawberist policy of waiting to see what would happen. Nothing happened, and there was no disorder or damage. It was, however, very hard upon a loyal citizen like Mr Thres that his place should have been the scene of such a senseless demonstration, and probably it seriously interfered with his business. The air was full of rumours on Saturday of a similar display being intended in the evening, though for what reason nobody seemed to know. The whole thing came to nothing, and long before eleven o'clock, the High-road throughout was more than normally quiet and deserted.

Some of the naturalised Germans in Ilford endured an agony of suspense on Friday, owing to the pilgrimage of pillage and passion that was known to be in progress elsewhere, and to the receipt of threatening messages. Many of the unhappy victims voluntarily sought the protection of the police. In one case an elderly and highly respectable tradesman, who has been naturalised and carrying on business in the town for more than forty years, cleared out his house and shop, and sent all his belongings to be stored at a furniture warehouse. He and his broken-hearted wife remained in the empty premises, having nowhere to go, and sobbed, one against the other, throughout the greater part of the day. Many similar experiences could be recorded.

The police carried out the internment duties, in accordance with the latest Government orders, with kindness and discretion. About twenty local aliens were sent away on Sunday, and another big batch on Monday.

More than a year later the matter of enemy aliens was vexing councillors in Ilford and, on 10 October 1916, Ilford UDC resolved: 'That this meeting hereby records the opinion that the presence in this country of so many thousands of enemy aliens constitutes a grave danger to the safety of all concerned, and therefore calls upon the Government at once to intern all enemy aliens, naturalized and otherwise, and calls for the removal from every branch of public service of all such enemy aliens'.

The *King of Prussia* public house, Stratford. During the war, the pub's name was changed from the Teutonic *King of Prussia* to the patriotic *King Edward VII*. (*Author's collection*)

Unsurprisingly, some residents of German ancestry anglicized their names: in Woodford, D. Oppenheimer became Openshaw and A. Langemann became A. Langham; in Leyton, A.M. Schloss became A.M. Castle, a Mr Hillebrecht became simply Mr Hill, C.A. Crompf became C.A. Normington and H.M. Scharm decided to become H. Millington. Even *The King of Prussia* public house in Stratford Broadway changed its name, becoming *The King Edward VII*.

... and raids: 31 May/1 June 1915

Zeppelins had dropped bombs on England on seven occasions before any raiders reached the Metropolitan Police area. In the tenth month of the war, London joined the counties of Norfolk, Northumberland, Essex, Suffolk and Kent, when it too became a victim of German airship raids. On the night of Monday 31 May/Tuesday 1 June, Hauptmann Erich Linnarz – allegedly believing he had stuck to the Kaiser's original conditions regarding the bombing of London – commanded army airship LZ38 on the first air raid on the capital.

Flying from its base at Brussels-Evere, after encountering a brief, south-westerly thunderstorm, LZ38 climbed to 10,000 feet and crossed the English coast near Margate at 9.42pm in fine weather with a light north to north-westerly wind. At this point aircraft from nearby RNAS Westgate were 'scrambled' to look for the Zeppelin. The following is an extract from a letter from Flight Sub-Lieutenant R.H. Mulock to his father back in Toronto:

> We were out for two hours last night and had the meanest time yet. Just black between ten and twelve, no horizon or stars and just enough haze so that we lost the coastline when over 7,000 feet. We were after a Zeppelin, but on account of the haze never saw it. I took the little fast machine and went up to 10,000 feet over the Essex coast, down to Dover and all around the sea at 90 miles per hour and no goggles. Then landed in the dark, or at least with the aid of gas flares, rolled onto the ground at 60 miles per hour and scared everyone as they said I could not fly this particular machine at night and keep right side up.

LZ38 then turned west and headed towards the Essex shore of the estuary. At 10.00pm, once over Shoeburyness, the airship followed a curving inland course from Southend over Billericay, Brentwood and Wanstead.

The Metropolitan Police were warned of an incoming raid around 11.00pm; a few minutes later small incendiary bombs began to fall. The first fell on a house at 16 Alkham Road, Stoke Newington; others were scattered around residential streets as the Zeppelin flew south over Stoke Newington and then Hoxton. Two incendiaries fell on Shoreditch Empire music hall and, as LZ38 turned to the south-east, explosive bombs were dropped on Spitalfields and a whisky distillery in Commercial Road. Turning north-east the remaining load was dropped on Whitechapel, Stepney, and Stratford.

Linnarz survived the war and later wrote of this first raid on London:

> Inside the gondola it was pitch dark save for the glowing pointers of the dials. The sliding shutters of the electric lamps with which each one of the crew was provided were drawn. There was tension as I leaned out of one of the gondola portholes and surveyed the lacework of lighted streets and squares. An icy wind lashed my face.
>
> I mounted the bombing platform. My finger hovered on the button that electrically operated the bombing apparatus.
>
> Then I pressed it. We waited. Minutes seemed to pass before, above the humming song of the engines, there rose a shattering roar.

Was it fancy that there also leaped from far below the faint cries of tortured souls?

I pressed again. A cascade of orange sparks shot upwards, and a billow of incandescent smoke drifted slowly away to reveal a red gash of raging fire on the face of the wounded city.

At Stratford, at 11.20pm, an incendiary bomb fell onto 26 Colgrave Road, passing through the bedroom of Peter Gillies and his wife. A neighbour reported:

I heard the droning of an aeroplane but I could not see anything. According to the noise it came lower and then I saw the bomb drop. It was simply a dark object and I saw it drop through the roof of number 26.

Finally, around 11.30pm, five bombs fell on Leytonstone: an HE bomb in Park Grove Road which did little damage, as did the others in Florence Road, Granleigh Road, Dyers Hall Road and New Fillebrook Road. The last bombs fell at 11.35pm and only three people in Leytonstone were slightly injured.

LZ38 then headed back home passing over the River Crouch at 12.30am on the return journey. Throughout the raid the airship was unseen and, due to its height, almost unheard, adding to the fear and uncertainty on the ground. A Metropolitan Police report on the raid dated 1 June stated that:

An aircraft, supposed to be a Zeppelin, the engines of which were distinctly heard, passed over Chigwell Row, Essex, shortly before 11.00pm on Monday, 31st ultimo, travelling in a westerly direction. It appears to have reached Dalston shortly after 11.00pm, dropped bombs, and returned via Leytonstone – where more bombs were dropped – Wanstead, Barkingside, and Chigwell Row, between which two last points it seems to have left the Division at about 11.30pm.

Police at Wanstead and Barkingside also report having heard an aircraft, which they could not with certainty describe, passing overhead an hour later, ie. at 12.30am 1st instant. Whether this last aircraft was hostile or not is unknown.

Back in Leytonstone, at 85 Park Grove Road, home of George Argent, a fitter's mate, the roof, front bedroom and landing had been damaged. No. 6 Florence Road was occupied by Charles W. Green and his 41-year-old wife, Rebecca. There three panes of glass in the front windows were broken and Rebecca was slightly injured in her left thigh and suffered from shock. Frederick John Foreman, aged 17, of 11 Florence Road was passing at the time and he was slightly injured on his left side. At 27 Florence Road, home of

James Mitchell, a private in the King's Royal Rifles, the roof and a ceiling were damaged.

At 71 Granleigh Road, occupied by Walter Pavett, a labourer, the brickwork at the side of the house was damaged, and six panes of glass in the front windows were broken. No. 69 Granleigh Road was home to George Young, a stoker; here a pillar and wall were damaged and two panes of glass in the front window broken. Aubrey Farbrother, a tailor's manager, lived at 66 Granleigh Road; four panes of glass in the ground and first floor windows were broken. No. 46 New Fillebrook Road was home to Albert Fisher, a clerk, whose roof, ceiling and front and back bedrooms were damaged.

At 47 Dyers Hall Road, home of Sandford Mason, an engineer, a wall and passage were damaged and one window on the ground floor was broken. At no. 49, occupied by Arthur Cohen, a salesman, three windows on the ground floor were broken. At 51 Dyers Hall Road, home of Richard Blackmore, a hosier, five windows and a fanlight in the ground and first floor windows were broken. No. 53 was occupied by William Rippengale, a linotypist; here five windows on the ground and first floors were broken. Next door, no. 55, was home to Elizabeth Deas, a widow, and she also had five windows on the ground and first floors broken.

On the other side of Dyers Hall Road, at no. 14, occupied by Arthur Clark, a pawnbroker's assistant, two windows on the ground floor were broken. Next door, at no. 16, home to Thomas Butters, a man of independent means, a pillar and stonework were damaged, and one window on the ground floor was broken. At no. 18, Thomas Gilbert, a traveller aged 35, was slightly injured in the head; two panes of glass in his front door were broken, with woodwork splintered and four windows on the ground floor broken. At 20 Dyers Hall Road, home of Clarence Garwood, a clerk, four windows on the ground and first floors were broken. No. 22 was occupied by William Woolnough, also a clerk, where two windows on the ground floor were broken.

Police arrived on the scene and controlled the crowds that assembled without difficulty; there was no sense of panic. Members of the Special Constabulary and of Leyton UDC were also present and remained until it was considered that all danger had passed. The Leyton Fire Brigade was also in attendance, but its services were not needed. The slight personal injuries were treated by family doctors in each case. The police subsequently found three brass detonators and three bags of grey material: a detonator and bag in Dyers Hall Road; a detonator and bag in Granleigh Road; a detonator in a bedroom at 85 Park Grove Road; and a bag in Florence Road. All of these were handed over to the military authorities.

In total, some 120 bombs were dropped during this raid, including ninety-one incendiaries, twenty-eight HE bombs and two 'grenades'. Seven people in London were killed, thirty-five were injured; forty-one fires were started, burning out seven properties, damage was priced at £18,596 by the London Fire Brigade. Except for two soldiers, all those injured were civilians. Germany was overjoyed: 'The City of London, the heart which pumps the life-blood into the arteries of the brutal huckster nation . . . has been sown with bombs by German airships' proclaimed the *Neueste Nachrichten* of Leipzig.

The RNAS had fifteen aircraft in the air from six airfields, including three from Chingford, looking for LZ38, but only one pilot (Flight Sub-Lieutenant A.W. Robinson, flying from Rochford), in an obsolete Bleriot monoplane, caught a glimpse of the Zeppelin in the moonlight before engine failure forced him to abandon the chase and land on the mud at Leigh-on-Sea. None of the others saw the Zeppelin and none succeeded in intercepting it, due mainly to the height at which LZ38 was flying. Two of the pilots from Chingford had narrow escapes. Towards the end of an uneventful patrol at 6,000 feet, Flight Lieutenant C.W.H. Pulford lost sight of the airfield, so he dropped a petrol bomb to act as a marker. When this failed to ignite, he continued his blind descent and hit the top of a tree, but was able to walk away from his wrecked aircraft. The other lucky pilot was Flight Lieutenant F.W. Merriam. Accompanied by an observer armed with a rifle and grenades, he had flown over central London for more than an hour when his instrument lights failed. He then lost his goggles but, almost blinded by oil from the engine and unable to see any flares, he still managed to 'pancake' his aircraft with no more damage than a bent axle. No ground-based guns fired and no searchlights found the airship. This marked failure by the capital's defences led to the British government implementing strong press restrictions on the reporting of air raids – D-Notice 217.

On 2 June, the Commissioner of the Metropolitan Police sent a confidential minute to the Home Office giving particulars of the raid and the course probably taken by the Zeppelin, also setting out steps that he considered essential with a view to providing some possible protection on the occasion of aerial attack. The Commissioner took the view that the GER lines might have been a guide to the Zeppelin as the GER's third class carriages were not provided with blinds so the lighted carriages would have been a noticeable feature from the sky. He also noted that searchlights and AA guns were not brought into use although the Zeppelin must have passed over the Clapton Orient football ground at Homerton where there was a searchlight and a 3-inch gun,[3] the explanation probably being that the airship was so high as to be invisible.

The Commissioner stated that aeroplanes could not be deemed effective protection at night because they could not ascend rapidly and when up could see little and hear nothing. He believed that their work would be made easier by the more efficient illumination of the airship and this meant providing more searchlights. He had previously drawn the attention of the Home Office to the lack of protection afforded by guns – he regarded the present protection as wholly inadequate. If there were a sufficient number of guns and searchlight stations, searchlights could be turned on with more chance of discovering the position of the airship whose presence would be indicated by the noise of its engine. A good searchlight under favourable atmospheric conditions could illuminate a target up to 10,000 feet.

The Commissioner also drew attention to the state of the personnel of the various fire brigades of which there were nearly forty in the wider London area. From nearly all of these he had received representations that their staffs had been dangerously reduced in strength owing to their men enlisting or taking employment at munitions factories. He urged that the working efficiency of fire brigades was a matter of the utmost importance and asked that recruiting officers be directed not to enlist firemen and munitions factories be asked not to employ them.

17/18 August 1915

On 11 July 1915, Kaiser Wilhelm lifted all constraints under which the German armed forces had operated. Zeppelins were now free to roam the skies and London's second raid saw airships drop more bombs on metropolitan Essex.

Navy airship L10, commanded by Oberleutnant Friedrich Wenke, bombed Walthamstow, Leyton and Leytonstone on the night of Tuesday 17/Wednesday 18 August, apparently mistaking the reservoirs of the Lea Valley for the River Thames, and subsequently dropping 107 bombs. L10 flew in over Waltham Abbey where a searchlight briefly caught it and the AA gun there fired two rounds. L10 then moved out of range and began to drop its bombs on Lloyd Park, Hoe Street, Bakers Avenue, Lea Bridge Road, Dunton Road, Farmer Road, Leyton High Road, Midland Road, Moyers Road, Grosvenor Road, Claude Road, Murchison Road, Albert Road, Twickenham Road, Oakdale Road, Ashville Road, Grove Green Road, Lincoln Street, Mayville Road, Southwell Grove Road and Wanstead Flats (very much following the route of the Tottenham to Forest Gate line of the Midland Railway (MR)). To those who saw the fallen brickwork and the splintered glass of the ruined houses the next day, it must have seemed almost unbelievable that only ten people were killed and forty-eight injured. Damage to property was estimated at £30,750 by the London Fire Brigade.

The first bomb, an incendiary, was dropped on Lloyd Park, Walthamstow, at 10.32pm. Then an HE bomb fell in Bakers Avenue, Leyton, demolishing four flats and shattering all the windows in the street: four men, two women and two children were injured. Three more HE bombs then fell close by in the grounds of the mid-nineteenth century Master Bakers' Almshouses in Lea Bridge Road, badly damaging the buildings of the tramway depot across the road, also causing a small fire and breaking the windows of seven shops: one man was slightly injured.

Harold Webster, who lived in Walthamstow, recalled:

I was just going out to post a letter for my sister, whose boy was out in France. I had just got to the gate when this thing went roaring over – the Zeppelin – and it sounded almost as if it was knocking the chimneys down. Then we heard the boom. One of the bombs fell near the Almshouses by the Bakers Arms. In those days the Zeppelins could do what they liked, even if a thousand shells were shot up at them, they never touched them, even though they were such huge things.

An HE bomb in Dunton Road badly damaged a house and broke the windows of many others; another HE bomb in Farmer Road caused severe damage to a house there.

Four HE bombs fell on and around the booking office at Leyton's MR station, destroying the ticket office and a billiard hall in the arches under the platform, and seriously damaging one house and breaking the windows in a large number of others plus those of the nearby Wesleyan church. A steam-roller was also badly damaged. Three men and one woman were killed; seven men, four women and three children were injured. Local resident Charles Nicholson later reported:

On the night of August 17th 1915, my father and I were in a billiards saloon under the arch of Leyton Station. The third bomb fell outside the saloon door which, like the front was all glass. My father and I were badly cut by the flying glass. On the opposite side of the road, a night-watchman was killed in his cabin.[4]

Two incendiary bombs fell in Grosvenor Road causing little damage. An HE bomb fell on 117 Claude Road, wrecking the house and killing a man, woman and girl and injuring a boy there. The same bomb broke the glass in the windows of 175 more houses in Claude Road, Morley Road and Norling-ton Road. At 117 Claude Road, Special Constable William Goodman was carrying out brave work and, for his actions there during this raid, he was awarded an Honorary Certificate by the Carnegie Hero Fund Trust.[5] Details held by the Trust record that:

> William Arthur Goodman, Special Constable, 86 Windsor Road, Leyton, on 17th August 1915, rescued a child from the ruins of a house which was demolished during a hostile air raid. Goodman, with the aid of a constable, entered the house by means of a ladder, and after crawling beneath rafters found the child under the debris of timber and brickwork. Soon after, that part of the house also collapsed. The child was only slightly hurt, but the dead bodies of his parents and sister were afterwards found under the ruins. The Carnegie Hero Fund Trustees awarded an Honorary Certificate and the sum of £10 to William Goodman.

In addition to the above awards, Goodman's name was entered in the Roll of Honour, an illustrated book that contains the names of over 6,000 people whose heroism has been recognized by the trustees since the foundation of the Carnegie Hero Fund Trust in the UK.

An incendiary bomb hit 181 Murchison Road, which resulted in broken windows. No. 57 Albert Road was hit by an incendiary bomb which caused a slight fire and badly damaged the house. Another incendiary bomb hit 78 Albert Road with the same result, but also slightly injured a woman and a child. No. 130 Albert Road was badly damaged by an HE bomb, but there were no injuries. An incendiary bomb hit 62 Twickenham Road, which started a small fire and badly damaged the property.

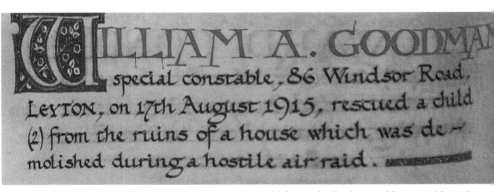

Special Constable William Goodman rescued a child from a badly damaged house at No. 117 Claude Road, Leytonstone following the raid on the night of 17/18 August 1915. He was awarded £10 and an Honorary Certificate by the Carnegie Hero Fund Trust for his actions and his name was inscribed in the Trust's Roll of Honour. (*Author's collection*)

No. 78 Oakdale Road was also badly damaged as were twenty-nine other houses in Oakdale Road, Ashville Road and Pearcroft Road. In addition, 123 houses in the same three roads had their windows broken and suffered other slight damage. These two bombs caused most of the casualties: two men were killed, and four men, eleven women and six children were injured. One of those killed was Joseph Hollington, a 34-year-old brewer's drayman and father of seven children living at 84 Ashville Road. Relatives later recorded that he had been killed when a bomb dropped outside his house, but that his body was not found until the front door, which his searchers had been walking over, was raised to find him lying beneath. His death was recorded as 'Through explosive bombs fired by enemy aircraft'. His widow, Edith, applied to Leyton UDC for financial assistance and, unable to look after seven children on her own, she put several of them into an orphanage.

The Zeppelin then crossed the GER line between Grove Green Road and Norman Road dropping an incendiary bomb on the tracks, but causing no damage. Two incendiaries were dropped on Lincoln Street, gutting St Augustine's church,[6] and another incendiary bomb in Mayville Road started a fire in a kitchen. Mayville Road was where Alfred Hitchcock and his sister Nellie attended school. Hitchcock sometimes spoke of attending school behind the family shop, a grocery store above which they lived in a modest flat in Leytonstone High Road. At least one episode from the war years left Alfred with a vivid memory of a Zeppelin raid. One night, he came home in the midst of an air raid on London. He arrived at the flat he shared with his mother and found the place in chaos, and his mother was desperately trying to put her clothes on over her nightgown. In his official biography, Hitchcock spoke of his mother's clumsy dressing and hiding under their kitchen table to escape. Hitchcock records his mother's 'struggling to get into her bloomers, always putting both her legs through the same opening, and saying her prayers, while outside the window, shrapnel was bursting around a search-lit Zeppelin'. This incident later inspired a humorous preamble to his film *Murder!*

An HE bomb fell on Southwell Grove Road demolishing much of nos 63 and 65 and breaking windows and causing damage in 132 other homes. One man, Mr Osborne at no. 63, was killed. Here the front of his house was almost entirely blown out, leaving the interior as a heap of piled-up building material and broken furniture beneath which lay his body; his hand had been torn off by the explosion and was found many yards away from the house. The explosion of the bomb was so freakish that a mantelpiece remained fixed to the wall above the wrecked fireplace and upon it stood the only undamaged thing in

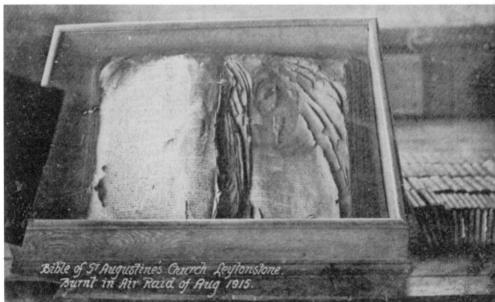

During the Zeppelin raid of 17/18 August 1915, L10 dropped two incendiary bombs on Lincoln Street, Leytonstone, gutting St Augustine's church and severely burning the bible there. (*Author's collection*)

the house – a little glass vase that one could have crushed between finger and thumb. His son, a soldier later home on leave, reported:

> On my way home on leave in answer to a telegram telling me of my father's death, I overheard a conversation about a raid on Leytonstone. Much to my surprise, it concerned my Dad. What a shock it was to me when I turned the corner of Southwell Grove Road and found that I had lost my home. Where was my mother? She had been saved by seeing a picture twice at the Premier Cinema. I found my pigeons alive after being under bricks, rafters and debris but had survived.

An HE bomb and two more incendiaries fell on Wanstead Flats, north of the railway and east of Montague Road, breaking the windows in seventy-three houses. Another HE bomb then fell near the model yacht pond on the Flats, breaking the windows in seventy-five more houses. Finally, at 10.43pm, six more incendiary bombs fell on the Flats causing no damage.

An undated, but contemporary, five-page letter from a young woman (signing off as 'Notabene') living at 43 Manor Road, Leyton, to a friend (Miss Finucane) working in the Admiralty gave details of what she had heard herself and since learnt from others about the casualties and damage to property caused by this Zeppelin raid and described her reaction to it. She wrote of:

> ... typing a letter to you from the office in a spare five minutes but we are going to bed a little earlier now of a night after the terrible raid and really when I get home I don't feel like writing.
>
> Jimmy got quite chatty over the raid, came and told me during the day each bit of fresh information he got. First of all it was one man killed in the Billiard Saloon in the Midland Road, then it got to 6. As a matter of fact it was the proprietors son. Mr Swann, a friend of Mr Mile next door to us, was there at the time. When they first heard the Zepp coming he (the one that was killed) said 'get under the table'. They all managed to get under but he was killed and Mr Swann who was only under the next table luckily escaped hurt.
>
> The loss of life round here is terrible. The papers say ten killed but it is more likely to be twenty or even more. I don't think it was the number of bombs that were dropped but the terrible size of them and the damage they did really does not bear thinking about. One bomb seems to have shattered all the houses for quite a distance around.
>
> You will remember the Midland Railway Station and how close it is to us, well all the windows there were broken, the bakers shop at the corner and also the little paper shop opposite had all the glass broken. A night

watchman at the corner of St. James lane was blown to pieces and also the steam roller he was guarding. The Wesleyan church, at the corner of St. James lane, was almost done for, when I say almost done for, a bomb dropped within about 3 yards of the entrance and broke all the coloured glass windows over the door, which they tell me are now bulging. I simply cannot go and see all the damage myself. They seemed to turn close to the Midland Station and then went to the tram terminus in Lea Bridge Road. This was set on fire and every window along the Lea Bridge Road just about there was completely broken. There was a hole made in the road large enough to bury a horse, and the tram lines were all twisted. They then went over Lea Bridge Road and passed over those Almhouses opposite, I believe I showed them to you, the Bakers Almhouses, (nearly all old Germans).

There is a small Avenue of Houses at the back of these houses and the road suffered terribly. Two houses were levelled to the ground. I tell you, it was terrific, and the row was something terrible. They passed right over Mr. Francis' house and he had the hardest matter to prevent Mrs. Francis' going into a fit. Ashfield Road Leyton, only a stones throw away, was terribly wrecked. Every house in the road suffered some damage and a great number have been condemned by the police as unfit for habitation. Dad went round that way yesterday and tells us the road is blocked as it is not safe for people to go along it. The offices by the tram works are just the same, mother saw these and says, (by the way they are letting people walk past these latter) the walls are very much damaged and all the stonework is falling off. I believe all this damage in Lea Bridge Road was done by one bomb, and the force of the explosion was so terrible that a piece of masonry was blown right up to the Kings Hall (where we went).

I really can't write any more about it, it was too awful. By the way St Augustines Church Leytonstone (Roman Catholic) was burnt right down before the fire-brigade could get to it. Our window cleaner tells us this and he lives quite near there. He says he was sitting in his kitchen and the first thing he knew was the clock falling off the mantelpiece on to his leg, which it cut badly and then when all the windows in the house went smash he said he thought it time to go out and look round.

'Notabene' continued with a few lines about mutual friends and acquaintances, some of whom had enlisted (one had been killed in the Dardanelles) or had become engaged. She then concluded:

I hope I never never have to tell you the same things again for it absolutely knocks one up to think of the terrible time we had. The bombs that they used this time were the worst they have ever used and they seem to have been made of shrapnel this time from the pieces of shrapnel which have been picked up all round about.

The raid was over in eleven minutes. There was some action from the AA guns at Beckton, West Ham and Victoria Park, but when over Leyton the Zeppelin was not seen by any gun crew, except that near Waltham Abbey. The RNAS had six aircraft from three airfields looking for L10 that night; two Caudron G3s crashed on landing after their search, in one of which Flight Sub-Lieutenant C.D. Morrison suffered severe burns to his hands and face when the Hale's bombs beneath his aircraft detonated as the machine touched down on the Chelmsford night landing ground at the end of his patrol. The Zeppelin suffered no damage in the raid. *The Walthamstow, Leyton & Chingford Guardian* reported that: 'Anti-aircraft guns were in action. Aeroplanes went up, but were unable to locate the airships'.

Significant destruction at an unspecified location in Leyton, possibly the four flats in Bakers Avenue demolished in the raid of 17/18 August 1915. (*Vestry House Museum, London Borough of Waltham Forest*)

COPY.

HARRIS AND CO.,
7, WILSON STREET,
SOUTH PLACE,
MOORGATE STREET,
LONDON.

DETAILS OF SETTLEMENT OF DAMAGE BY HOSTILE
AIRCRAFT TO THE TRAMWAYS SHEDS. LEA BRIDGE
ROAD, LEYTON.

	£. - s. - d.
CARS AND ARC LAMPS.(EXCLUDING ADVERTISING GLASSES).	805. - 0. - 0.
JOINERS & PAINTERS SHOP.	10. - 0. - 0.
DAMAGE TO BILLIARD TABLES ETC.	14. - 0. - 0.
ARMITURE ROOM, MACHINE SHOP & MACHINERY & STORES.	150. - 0. - 0.
TEMPORARY REPAIRS TO OFFICE & STABLES & LABOUR IN STRIPPING BROKEN GLASS THROUGHOUT DEPOT.	22. -15. - 3.
DAMAGE TO OFFICE FURNITURE & TICKET STORE.	20. - 0. - 0.
DAMAGE TO MAIN BUILDING (EXCLUDING GLASS & TEMPORARY REPAIRS TO SKYLIGHTS).	965. - 0. - 0.
DAMAGE TO OFFICE (EXCLUDING GLASS).	107. - 0. - 0.
GRANT TO TRAMWAYS MANAGER FOR PERSONAL TROUBLE & TIME INVOLVED IN CONNECTION WITH LOSS.	31. -10. - 0.
AMOUNT & VALUE OF GLASS TO BE RE-INSTATED BY WAR RISKS COMMITTEE AGREED AT £1200.	
	£2125. - 5. - 3.
HARRIS & CO'S FEES & CHARGES IN CONNECTION WITH LOSS. (REPRESENTING 5%).	170. - 0. - 0.
	£ 2295 - 5 - 3.

Paid to Eatons reglazing roof — 928. 4. 6

3223 . 9 . 9

Settled Feb. 1917

The bill for the repair of Leyton UDC tram depot in Lea Bridge Road. The depot was seriously damaged in the raid of 17/18 August 1915 and cost £3,223 to repair. (*Vestry House Museum, London Borough of Waltham Forest*)

Wenke reported that his craft had bombed an area between Blackfriars and London Bridge, much to the jubilation of the German press, whose readers passionately believed in the Zeppelin as a war-winning machine, predicting that Britain would have to sue for peace, rather than have her capital destroyed by aerial bombardment.

General Sir Francis Lloyd,[7] the General Officer Commanding (GOC) London District (and later the owner of Rolls Park at Chigwell), visited Leyton to see the damage and then went on to the West Ham Infirmary[8] to see the injured. The asylum at Claybury was also used to treat a number of members of the public suffering from shock and fear of the Zeppelin raids.

Two months later, on the night of 13/14 October, the most ambitious raid yet launched against London took place. Five Zeppelins set off, but only one, L15, commanded by Kapitänleutnant Joachim Breithaupt, reached central London, where it dropped thirty bombs between the Strand and Limehouse before departing over Ilford and Hainault. The airfields at Hainault Farm and Suttons Farm each sent up aircraft, but only one pilot, from Suttons Farm, positively saw the Zeppelin.

23/24 September 1916

Air raids on London continued into 1916, but things had changed since the raids of the previous year. Defensive aircraft no longer sat on the ground waiting; they now flew in relays and there was sometimes at least one already at the same height as a Zeppelin, ready to attack as soon as the pilot was able to see the airship.

On Sunday 2/Monday 3 April, under the command of Oberleutnant Ernst Lehmann, LZ90 reached Epping Forest and dropped sixty-five incendiary and twenty-five HE bombs on his approach to Waltham Abbey, including two HE bombs behind *The Wake Arms* public house and incendiaries near Honey Lane. These all caused only minimal damage to a farm, breaking roof tiles and windows and killing three hens. Just after midnight, the AA guns at Waltham Abbey fired a heavy bombardment and the Zeppelin turned for home. Seven RNAS aircraft had been up that night, but only one claimed to have seen LZ90.

On the night of Tuesday 25/Wednesday 26 April, LZ97 dropped bombs over south-west Essex. Arriving over West Mersea at about 10.00pm, the Zeppelin followed the course of the River Blackwater. Passing Chelmsford, it headed west until, at about 10.45pm, it dropped forty-seven incendiary bombs in a line from Fyfield to Chipping Ongar. Fifteen minutes later, after steering a south-westerly course and with the crew believing they were over

London, LZ97 began bombing again. Linnarz's second-in-command, Ober-leutnant Lampel, later recalled:

> [The commander's] hand is on the buttons and levers. 'Let go!' he cries. The first bomb has fallen on London! We lean over the side. What accursed long time it takes between release and impact while the bomb travels those thousands of feet! We fear that it has proved a 'dud' – until the explosion reassures us. Already we have frightened them; away goes the second, an incendiary bomb. It blazes up underneath and sets fire to something, thereby giving us a point by which to calculate our drift and ground speed.

But the crew had miscalculated, and this second batch of bombs fell over Fairlop Plain, between Forest Farm and Aldborough Hatch. Caught in the beams of the searchlight on the tramcar at Barkingside and fired on by an AA gun, one of its bombs narrowly missed Fairlop station, falling close by in Forest Road, causing a large crater and damaging some of the station cottages, but injuring no-one. The Zeppelin then followed a curving route southwards towards Newbury Park as searchlights flicked to and fro across the sky. LZ97 circled over Seven Kings before making its escape back towards the east, dropping two small bombs between Goodmayes and Chadwell Heath, destroying a wooden cottage, but causing no casualties.

However, the airship was not out of danger. The airfields at Hainault Farm and Suttons Farm were not far away and two aircraft took off from each in pursuit of LZ97. Captain Arthur Harris, then commanding B Flight at Suttons Farm, was first up and, at about 10.45pm and 7,000 feet, he saw the airship turning and climbing over Seven Kings at a height of about 14,000 feet. Harris climbed and attacked, but his gun jammed and LZ97 slipped away.

A little over a year since its second raid, Leyton was bombed for the third time, this time on the night of Saturday 23/Sunday 24 September by navy airship L31, commanded by Kapitänleutnant Heinrich Mathy. L31 had set off across the North Sea with eleven other Zeppelins to attack various targets in England. L31 approached London from the south, dropped a few bombs on Kenley and Mitcham and was picked up by a number of searchlights, which Mathy was able to blanket by dropping dazzling flares. He then dropped forty-one bombs in rapid succession over Streatham and Brixton before the airship crossed the River Thames. On reaching Leyton, L31 then dropped bombs on the GER's Temple Mills marshalling yard and, at 12.46am, ten bombs were dropped in the Lea Bridge Road area, killing eight people and injuring thirty-one. Nearly 200 buildings in Leyton were damaged, including a police station. L31 then headed home. Mist had risen and obscured the Zeppelin from any of the north-east London AA gun stations.

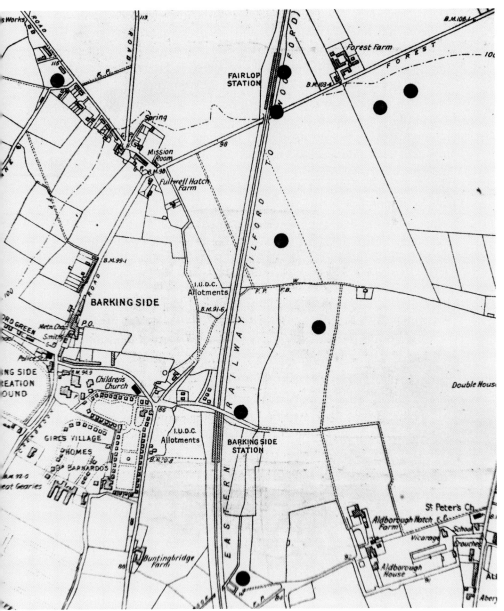

Here is an extract from a contemporary Ordnance Survey map of the Barkingside area (originally at a scale of 25″ to 1 mile). The small dark circles show where high explosive bombs were dropped alongside the railway line by Zeppelin LZ97 on the night of 25/26 April 1916, and where an anti-aircraft shell fell north-west of Fullwell Hatch during the first daylight raid by Gothas on 13 June 1917. (*Redbridge Museum/Redbridge Information & Heritage 2015*)

Damage at Temple Mills was minimal as the bomb fell on wasteland along-side the railway lines. A 50kg HE bomb was dropped on 'Richmond Villa' in Lea Bridge Road, another at no. 503, and a third near the junction with Russell Road. A 100kg HE bomb fell between Westerham Road and Bromley Road, a 50kg HE bomb at 831 High Road, Leyton, another 100kg HE bomb in St Hittier's Road, and a further 50kg HE bomb near the north-west corner of Leyton Green Road. A large 300kg HE bomb fell in Essex Road, near its junction with Lea Bridge Road, and the final two bombs, both 50kg HE bombs, fell each side of Halford Road.

It seems likely that Mathy had miscalculated his position, for in his report he claimed to have bombed Pimlico and Chelsea, then the City and Islington. Flying at 13,000 feet he may have mistaken Streatham/Brixton for Pimlico/Chelsea, with this confusion extended as he bombed Leyton.

Reporting restrictions precluded the press from naming districts where raids had taken place. *The Walthamstow, Leyton & Chingford Guardian* for 29 September 1916 reported that:

> Very considerable damage was done to property in a north-eastern suburb, but on Sunday morning shops were open with 'Business as usual' and 'Keep smiling' notices prominently displayed on the boarded-up window spaces.

It also reported that the Rt Hon Sir John Simon KC, MP[9] for the South-Western or Walthamstow Division of Essex paid a visit to the scenes of the Zeppelin raid in a north-eastern suburb on the Monday afternoon. As the only 'north-eastern suburb' to be bombed that night was Leyton and Sir John's constituency included Leyton, it must be to Leyton that the report refers. The report continued:

> In a district where eight persons were killed and about eighteen injured, there was evidence that the raider followed the tram route, and local indignation that had often been voiced that the flashes from the overhead wires of trams afforded a guide to the airships reached boiling point.

Lea Bridge Road was a tram route and the newspaper had previously reported local fears about flashes from trams making the area a target.[10] The newspaper report went on:

> Some of the bombs dropped in that district must have been of extraordinary explosive power, for the holes which they made in the earth were very deep and extensive in diameter. The majority of them, curiously enough, dropped on waste land, but in the vicinity of house and shop property, which suffered severely.

A Labour Exchange was badly shattered, as well as many houses and surrounding buildings, by a bomb which fell at the rear, whilst in another part of the locality the effect of a bursting bomb was to ruin a block of five houses, which were of recent date and inhabited. The side and front of a large corner building was demolished, the residents escaping injury, and the flying debris smashed the windows and damaged the masonry of a police station on the opposite corner [at the junction of Lea Bridge Road and Shrubland Road]. Not far away a bomb fell in the front garden of a large house, and a retired baker and his wife who were standing in the doorway were killed. Another man was killed while gallantly escorting home two ladies, business colleagues. In another part a married couple also lost their lives while standing on their doorstep.

The 'retired baker and his wife' were George and Virginia Sexton of 'Richmond Villa' at 495 Lea Bridge Road. The couple were buried in St Mary's churchyard, Leyton, on 28 September. The bomb on 831 High Road completely destroyed the home of 48-year-old Dr Harold Everett Pace, but he and his family all escaped alive.[11] At a coroner's inquest after the raid, the jury emphasized the importance of remaining indoors during raids. A doctor who had attended a victim said that one woman who was injured about the legs was reported as being very brave, saying: 'Do not bother about me. Attend to the others who are more seriously injured'. The doctor suggested that if special constables knew how to control haemorrhage, and put up a badly fractured limb, lives would be saved. A police officer said they had a very efficient first aid squad, but they were attending other cases; he reported that the bombs fell at 12.42am, and the first body was removed to the hospital at one o'clock.

Winifred Freeman, a teacher employed by the LCC (and the daughter of Robert Saunders, headmaster of Fletching School, near Brighton), was living at 154 Colchester Road, Leyton, and wrote several letters to her parents and family during the Zeppelin and Gotha raids. None is dated, so it is not possible to say for certain to which raid she is referring, but in one, which may be about this raid (although the times of the bombs do not match with official reports) she wrote:

> You will see by this morning's paper we had our old Zeps over again & for about ½ hour I was in my usual condition of violent trembling. Our first alarm was bombs dropping & then it sounded like airship guns firing at the Zep, not like our big ground guns. Being more used to them now after the first shock, we did not fetch the children down but got everything ready &

stood by ready if it came nearer, which it didn't. We heard rumours they were at Crystal Palace & Sydenham, & then again another 'twas at White-chapel & Aldgate but no definite news as yet. I must own it does unnerve one, for the time being. Em & Elsie just came down & they had been up a good part of the night. The first bomb was heard about 8.30 & things settled down about 10.45, then 11.30 a second banging commenced but I did not hear that, tho all my neighbours were out & Em & family who had gone up to bed all came down again.

At a meeting on 28 September, Leyton UDC expressed its thanks to the Leyton Emergency Corps for its work during this air raid.

The navy's latest Zeppelin, L33, also flew over south-west Essex on the night of 23/24 September 1916. Commanded by Kapitänleutnant Alois Böcker, the airship passed over Upminster at about 11.30pm and dropped four incendiary bombs, followed by six HE bombs close to Suttons Farm airfield at 11.50pm. Unsuccessfully trying to work out his craft's position, Böcker dropped a parachute flare to the south of Chadwell Heath at 11.55pm then headed towards Wanstead, Beckton and West Ham. Here L33 was hit by an AA shell from the Beckton or Wanstead Flats battery, which exploded in the gas cell just behind the control gondola and caused a loss of hydrogen. In an attempt to gain height Böcker dropped nearly two dozen bombs on Bromley-by-Bow and Stratford. One of these fell on St Leonard's Street hitting W. Lusty's timber yard and wiping out a row of small houses, killing five and injuring twenty-four people. Mrs A.E. Park later recalled:

I was listening to the music of a late night party in St Leonard's Street (in fact neither myself nor my mother could sleep because of the noise) . . . About midnight there was an enormous crash and my mother and I were blown down the stairs . . . I saw the woman of the house where the party was being held standing by, whilst her daughter, terribly injured, was being extricated from the ruins.

A 50kg HE bomb grazed the wall of Spratt's dog biscuit factory and exploded. A 300kg HE and two 50kg HE bombs fell on the North London Railway (NLR) carriage depot, damaging a shed, a boiler house and some rolling stock; two men were injured. At 12.12am a 50kg HE was dropped on the Particular Baptist chapel in Botolph Road. This caused great damage to the chapel and also to sixteen shops and houses, slightly damaging another four; two people were injured. A direct hit by a 100kg HE bomb on *The Black Swan* pub at the corner of Devons Road and Bow Road killed five people, including two of the landlord's children, and injured four more. W.G. Roberts of the 4th Battalion, London Regiment, recalled:

> I was on hospital leave from France and I was going home on the evening of September 23rd, 1916. Reaching home, I warned my wife and family to take cover and, placing my kit-bag in the hall, went into the garden.
>
> The Zepp was moving in direct line with our house and was being held by the searchlights with shells bursting beneath her envelope. As she came on, I went in and joined my wife and two small daughters, who were very frightened. Suddenly, with an awful roar, which seemed to rock our house on its foundations, a bomb fell. Our front door burst open, and the front (iron) entrance gates were blown off and broken. Every window in the front was blown out.
>
> After making sure my family were safe, I went to Bow Road, where a large public house, *The Black Swan*, had been wrecked. Only the carcase of it was left standing, and a heavy pall of black dust hung over the ruins. I and others groped our way amongst the debris searching for any victims who might still be alive. Lifting some flooring, we discovered the wife of the licensee, Mrs Reynolds, lying in the cellar, where she had been blown by the bomb. It had struck the house dead in the middle, taking the floors to the basement.
>
> Firemen found a baby stuck in the rafters.

Nos 25–29 Devons Road were damaged and three people injured there; nos 4–22 Shepherd Street were also damaged and one person injured. The residents of Bromley-by-Bow subsequently subscribed to a testimonial for the men of the Brunswick Road fire station in recognition of their work on the night of this air raid.

An incendiary bomb fell on Bridefield Road damaging one house there, and a 100kg HE bomb that dropped on Cook's soap works in Stratford failed to explode. Two 50kg HE bombs were dropped on Marshgate Lane causing severe damage to the British Petroleum company works and a sewer there. Seven further 50kg HE bombs then fell on Stratford marshes, but caused no damage; but another was dropped on Judd's match factory, setting the building on fire and destroying much of the company's stock. The wounded Zeppelin then left the area, passing over Leytonstone, Woodford and then Buckhurst Hill at 12.19am before heading east across Essex.

The RNAS had thirteen aircraft from six airfields looking for Zeppelins on the night of 23/24 September. The RFC had twelve aircraft from seven airfields up, including five from No. 39 Squadron – two from North Weald, one from Suttons Farm, and two from Hainault Farm – but these were not

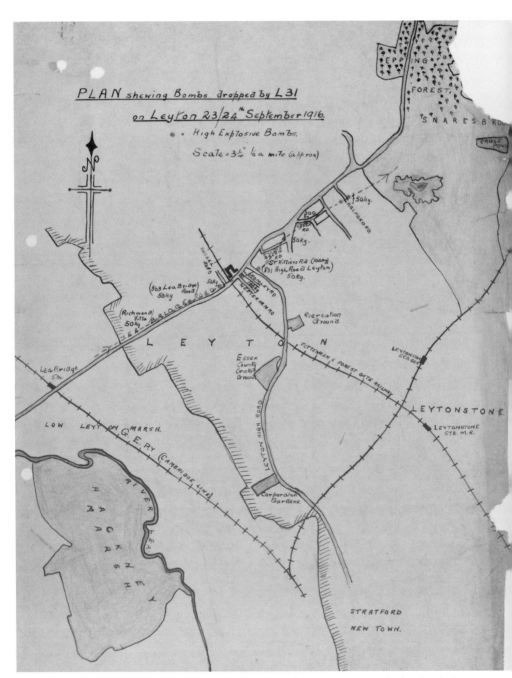

A map drawn by the Metropolitan Police showing the route over Lea Bridge Road, Leyton, taken by Zeppelin L31 during the raid of 23/24 September 1916. (*Author's collection*)

ordered up until L33 was only ten miles away so they had no prospect of intercepting it on its inbound journey.

One of those flying from Hainault Farm was 2nd Lieutenant Alfred de Bathe Brandon[12] in a BE2c, who saw L33 shortly after it had been hit, but promptly lost sight of it as it flew out of the searchlights. Brandon found the airship again near Kelvedon Hatch but, while preparing to attack, had problems of his own to overcome. His automatic petrol pump failed, which called for hand pumping, and this hampered him when cocking his gun. Then the gun came adrift from its mounting, and by the time this was sorted out he had overshot the airship. He turned to make another approach from the rear port side and fired a whole drum, seeing the Brock bullets bursting along the underside but with no result. He reloaded and began a second attack, but this time his gun jammed after nine rounds. Though not stated in official reports, it is likely that Brandon was carrying Le Prieur rockets or Ranken darts, because he next attempted to climb above L33 to attack, but lost sight of the airship against the ground.

That same night, at Claybury asylum, one of the hospital's employees was summonsed for building an eight-foot high bonfire in the grounds. The man responsible claimed that the fire had been burning for fifteen years. The magistrate dealing with the case fined the man £5 and said that there seemed to be lunatics outside the asylum who should perhaps be in it. However, at a meeting of Ilford UDC later that month, it was reported that the steward at Claybury had written to the council stating that, since the opening of the asylum, they had invariably disposed of the domestic refuse by burning, but that lately the military authorities had ordered them to put out the fire. Perhaps the summonsed man's claim was not so far-fetched after all.

(*Overleaf*) Unlike many generic Zeppelin postcards, this one can be given a date and location – or two locations. Correspondence in *Essex Countryside* magazine in the early 1960s revealed that the photograph was taken by Mr H. Scott-Orr of Woodford Green on 13 October 1915 (the night of the 'Theatreland' raid on London). It shows a Zeppelin approximately over Ilford and was taken from the upper room of a house at the corner of Mill Lane in Woodford Green. The spire is the Congregational church in Broomhill Road (pulled down after being destroyed in the Second World War). The chimney stack on the left of the picture belongs to an old house then occupied by Mr Kendon, the butcher, and pulled down in the early 1920s. The centre of the picture shows the outline of an avenue of trees which extended as far as Snakes Lane. The chimney stack on the right belongs to Ralph Kent, the grocer. Alternatively, Jack Farmer, a lifelong local resident, agreed that that the photograph was taken by Mr H. Scott-Orr, but recalled that he took it in the yard of Barnes the baker at Theydon Bois. In the foreground is the bakehouse chimney with its reinforcing ironwork, whilst in the background can be seen the spire of St Mary's church. The airship was picked up and held by a searchlight down Coopersale Lane at Theydon Bois. Jack Farmer stated that an original print of the photograph was still in the possession of the Barnes family in 1986. (*Author's collection*)

"THE RAIDER"
PUBLICATION SANCTIONED BY OFFICIAL PRESS BUREAU
(Copyright,)

Publishing Office
39 St. Andrew's Hill, E C

Chapter 6

'A big cigar in front of the moon'

A response felt by some local residents to the air raids was curiosity. This curiosity was seen during London's first raid when *The Evening Standard* reported that: 'The ineffectiveness of the German methods of terrorism is shown in the demeanour of the people of London today who are merely interested in discovering that the outskirts of their city have come into the arena of the war'. For others, such was the novelty of experiencing an air raid that it was not unusual for large numbers to remain outside to observe the sight of the bombing rather than taking cover. Winifred Adams, from Snaresbrook, vividly remembered the Zeppelins passing over:

> You could see the Zeppelins quite distinctly when they went by, especially if there was a moon up. They'd look like a big cigar in front of the moon, with a basket hanging down underneath. They'd drop their bombs from that. I remember one of the first air raids. I was staying with my grandmother in Dunedin Road, Leyton, and a bomb came down in the next garden to ours. It made a hole about three to four feet across and everyone came to see it. It could have done quite a bit of damage if it had hit a building because of the force with which it came down. When there was a Zeppelin raid you didn't get a siren warning, but a policeman used to come round knocking on the doors saying 'Lights out, lights out, raid on, keep in'. Later, if they thought of it, they came round and told us it was all clear. The raids weren't frequent and it was quite exciting really.

Hilda Bazalgette grew up in Old Fillebrook Road, Leytonstone, during the war and did not share Winifred Adams' point of view:

> When the Zeppelin raids started we were terrified. Nothing like that had ever happened before as aircraft hadn't been sufficiently developed for bombing raids then. You could hear the Zeppelins coming and then going for such a long time, with a z-z-z-z noise. I shall never forget that terrible sound, you didn't know whereabouts it was, but it just kept on and on. It didn't occur to me as a child that there were men in them, they were just great juggernauts overhead that were going to drop things on us.

At Hornchurch, Charles Perfect remembered:

> On one occasion the searchlights had been exceptionally active quite late in the evening, and we were therefore not surprised when, at about 11.30pm, we heard the deep booming of guns. On looking out of a window at the rear of our house towards London, we immediately saw a bright silvery object, in shape like a huge cigar, in the centre of the rays of a large number of searchlights, probably not less than two dozen. Here, then, was the Zeppelin, the much dreaded monster before our eyes, and only three or four miles away. It apparently knew not which way to turn, for whatever movement it made the searchlights held it fast, a clear target for the guns which were firing incessantly. After a little while it veered slightly to the south and then shot upwards, so that it looked to us almost perpendicular. It then came on a level keel again, with its nose pointing Londonwards, but the firing appeared to be getting too hot, for it gradually came right round, and then sailed away in a north-easterly direction. All this time the guns were blazing away, and they continued to do so until the huge airship got outside the range of the searchlights.

Local residents were also witness to the destruction of several airships shot down in 1916. Beryl Rickard's grandfather, Charles William Harsant, moved from Homerton to Matlock Road, Leyton, shortly after the Fillebrook Road sorting office opened in Leytonstone in 1912 as he had received a promotion. Beryl and her cousins were told that her grandparents saw the airship shot down at Cuffley.

Walthamstow resident, Harold Webster, remembered this too:

> I was about 16 at the time and was near the Bakers Arms, looking towards the south, watching the Zeppelins go over. We got one or two over most nights by then; usually they would drop their stuff and then go, but some-times they seemed to hang still in the sky for a long time before moving off, and the searchlights would try to locate them. That night, as we watched, we suddenly realized that all the windows on the other side of the street had turned blood-red. So we rushed across the road, looking back and then we saw it, all on fire with bits falling off in flames. It was fantastic the light it made.

Bill Hobson, a child living locally at the time, later recalled:

> The street where we lived was crowded with people who had seemingly decided to ignore the air raid warning which had been given some time earlier and there seemed to be plenty of people about, the majority staring expectantly at the sky. My mother was among them and, to protect me from

the cold which was penetrating, despite the fact that it was only the beginning of September, had wrapped me in a shawl, the greater length of which was wound around herself as well as me, the better to secure me in its folds.

'Look Billy', she said suddenly, turning my head as she spoke, the better to see what was going on above our heads. Uncomprehending what it was, I remember the sight of a flaming thing which had now begun to fall with increasing speed as it did so, lighting up the surrounding street objects, now being sharply picked out against the background of the darkened sky.

Out at Hornchurch, Charles Perfect recalled:

With many of our neighbours I had the unique experience of seeing the first Zeppelin brought down in flames. We had been watching the gun flashes and searchlights, which had by now – about 2.00am – receded in a north-westerly direction, when we suddenly saw a red flare light floating in the sky; gun fire ceased, and then in a few moments the whole neighbourhood was brilliantly lit up, and to our great delight and wonderment we saw the Zeppelin falling down in flames. We could hardly believe the evidence of our eyes, our wonder was so great, but our delight was intensified when we learned a little later that Lieut. Robinson, from our own aerodrome, was the plucky aviator who had accomplished the gallant deed.

Another eye-witness reported:

On Saturday night, as early as 10.30 the 'raid feeling' was in the air. It was pitch dark. All lights were out, and half a dozen searchlights persistently wavered round and round one spot in the eastern sky. Everything was quiet with that breathless, expectant quietness heralding a coming storm. At five minutes past two the air vibrated to the beat of distant engines. Searchlights roved the sky in scores. Suddenly, a light flickered on a long bright body and instantly there she was, at least 12,000 feet up, sailing due north, the centre of attraction for the whole outfit of lights.

In a moment the air was filled with the crash of guns, and shells screamed their passage towards their target. Slowly the airship turned on her course, drifted due north, 'crabbing' all the while as though temporarily disabled and drifting with the wind. I saw her quite plainly, end view and broadside on, and give as my opinion that she was a Shutte-Lanz.

The 'crabbing' lasted five minutes, and then she appeared to get under power and bore round until she was steering almost due west, making towards London. Guns were pounding at her incessantly, and from my point of vantage the shells appeared to burst all over her: under and over and at both ends. Suddenly every gun ceased as if by magic, and in the full blaze of the searchlights she sailed ahead. It was an ominous silence that seemed to tell something else was about to happen.

A flicker of flame appeared at her nose, died down, and then burst into bright light for a fifth of her length. It lit the sky with brilliant light that got more powerful as the flames ran along the envelope the entire length. For a few moments I saw her full outline as a burning mass, during which time she continued to travel forward. Slowly, very slowly she dipped, forming a graceful curve, and then stood end up. This was when, as the flames roared up from the front and joined those farther back, the brightest light was shown.

Where I stood, ten miles away, it lit the streets and woods until one could imagine it a sunset, for the flames were principally crimson. The slow speed at which she fell was amazing. I had expected, once she got nose down, to see her go at a terrible pace. But the mammoth appeared to be a huge mass of flame supported by a parachute. When yet 5,000 feet up, the light turned to a brilliant ruby, through crimson and pink to an incandescent white at the top, trailing pale yellow. At that moment there was a crackling as of exploding ammunition, or it might have been twisting girders or breaking timber. Then she disappeared behind the trees with a crash and a final flare flashed up. Cheers echoed throughout the whole of London – but in the district where I stood, we had another on our own, as three coloured lights sprang into being and hung motionless in the sky, for we knew them to be the guiding lights for the returning victorious airman.

Just across the border in Hertfordshire, the crew of the Temple House gun station in Theobalds Park were convinced that they had scored a direct hit on the airship. This conviction was evidently shared by the local civilian population, who organized and contributed to a fund to provide a gift to each of the men. Of 'their' success, the commander of the AA gun station at Temple House reported:

A sheet of flame was seen, and the outline of the airship was indistinguishable. In a few seconds a burning mass of wreckage dropped below our searchlight beam, the head of the ship leading and the tail part practically consumed. The nose of the craft could be seen quite clearly in the fire, the circular rings and longitudinal ribs showing black against the flames.

In Middlesex, the destruction of the Zeppelin was seen by Lieutenant-Colonel Nathaniel Newham Davis, commander of the 116th Company, Royal Defence Corps (RDC) at Alexandra Palace. He recalled:

On Sunday morning 3rd inst. the sounds of guns in the direction of London roused me. At 2.20am when I reached the Eastern entrance to

Alexandra Palace the enemy airship which had been shelled was out of sight behind some clouds to the East and the firing had ceased. At 2.25am either the clouds broke away or the airship broke through the clouds and she was plainly visible, the searchlights focussing on her at once. She seemed to be over Enfield, NNE from the Palace. She, at the distance of about 5–6 miles, looked to be about half the size of a spectacle case held at arm's length and she resembled a spectacle case in shape. Her colour in the searchlight rays was bright silver gilt. The shell fire ceased but there was the occasional boom of a dropped bomb. Men whose hearing is more acute than mine heard the sound of machine-gun fire. For many seconds the airship appeared to stand still and then at her stern a crimson patch appeared on the envelope. This spread with great rapidity, and the clouds and the mist which hung above the earth were suffused with a ruddy glare. The nose of the airship dipped and with flames rippling off from the whole envelope she glided at an easy angle towards the earth. Still burning, she disappeared into the mist, and the glare disappeared from the sky. From the moment of the attack by one of our aeroplanes to her disappearance not more than five or ten minutes elapsed.

The airship was Shütte-Lanz SL11, shot down on the night of Saturday 2/ Sunday 3 September by 2nd Lieutenant William Leefe Robinson[1] of No. 39 Squadron flying from Suttons Farm airfield; Robinson was awarded the Victoria Cross (VC) for his bravery. The airship crashed in a field behind *The Plough* inn at Cuffley, Hertfordshire. Some reports suggest that when SL11 exploded, the light was so bright it could be seen over a radius of sixty miles, from Reigate in the south to Cambridge in the north. Although not the first loss of a German airship, the destruction of SL11 represented the first successful shooting-down of one of the attackers to take place over British soil. The weather conditions were such that to all of the thousands of spectators it seemed as if the machine was directly overhead as they woke their children to witness an event that they would remember into old age.

Not everyone was caught up in the euphoria, however. Philip Dodgson, an officer serving overseas in 237 Brigade, Royal Field Artillery (RFA), on 29 September 1916, wrote in a letter home:

The British Nation seems to be quite unbalanced as far as Zeppelins are concerned. To a casual reader of the papers it would seem that the destruction of one Zeppelin was of more importance than everything else put together. I suppose it is natural as it is only by reason of the Zeppelins that large numbers realize there is a war at all. When it comes to spending hundreds of pounds on a memorial of the spot where the Zeppelin was

A postcard commemorating William Leefe Robinson's destruction of Shütte-Lanz SL11 on the night of 2/3 September 1916. The airship was originally claimed to be Zeppelin L21, possibly because a Shütte-Lanz was considered by some to be a lesser form of airship. Robinson had no connection with Ilford, having flown from Suttons Farm airfield at Hornchurch, but this card is one of many published to celebrate the airman's achievement. *(Author's collection)*

brought down it is getting rather absurd. It is bad enough giving the man who brings the thing down money, especially as he also got the VC. What about the airmen out here who run greater risks almost every day?

The fear of sharing the fate of SL11 might well have been in the minds of the crew of Zeppelin L32, which was also over Hertfordshire that same night. The airship's logbook recorded:

London on port bow. A great many searchlights. Tried to reach London. Several airships attacking London. Gunfire visible. A great fire which shone out with a reddish yellow light and lit up the surroundings within a large radius and then fell to the ground slowly. We could see the conflagration on the ground up to the limit of the range of visibility. The burning object was one of our airships that had been shot down.

Zeppelins in the night skies above Essex were visible from across the Thames estuary where spectators also took great delight in their destruction.

The night of Saturday 23/Sunday 24 September was a very successful one as both L32 and L33 were shot down over Essex: L32 by 2nd Lieutenant Frederick Sowrey[2] of No. 39 Squadron flying from Suttons Farm airfield; and L33 by AA fire. A report from *The East Kent Times* recorded the scene on the cliffs near Margate as crowds gathered hoping to watch the fate of the Zeppelins across the estuary:

On the night of Sat. 23 Sept. 1916 an alarm took place and for the first time the local inhabitants became aware of the fact that British aeroplanes were in the air with pilots ready and willing to give fight. People lined the cliffs and seafront, anxious not to miss a possible opportunity of seeing the realisation of their hope (the successful interception of a Zeppelin).

An 'East Kent Times' representative stood behind one little group and passed a most interesting half hour. 'I can hear it, Pa!'; the words, coming from a young lady of about eighteen summers, broke a silence which had lasted several seconds. 'Where?' was the immediate and concerted query from the rest of the party, whose hearing powers were at once strained to the utmost pitch. The night air was not broken by the sound of aircraft, however, but the father, after reprimanding the girl for what he termed her silliness, appended the question, 'Where did you hear it?' Dutifully, his daughter pointed to a vague part of the sky and again silence descended on the group, only to be broken by the piping voice of a small boy who reiterated the girl's remark that he could hear it. 'I think I can too', remarked the lady who was apparently the mother of the youngster and certainly by that time the sound of an engine could be heard. Nearer and nearer it approached. Louder and louder became the sound. 'Is it a Zeppelin, Dad?' eagerly enquired the irrepressible young lady in wondering tones. Father was too busy gazing skywards to reply, for the throbbing of a motor had by then increased until it had become a roar. Then he began to laugh with a heartiness so unexpected and infectious that the rest of the party joined in, and the tension was broken. 'A motor car!' he ejaculated – 'ha ha!' and again he roared with laughter.

When the mirth had subsided, the query 'What's that, Dad?' came from one of the boys in the group, and the youngster pointed to a distant light in the sky which, he was firmly convinced, was moving. 'It's only a star', was the answer, but so insistent was the boy that the father levelled a pair of glasses in the direction indicated, and then gave vent to an exclamation of profound astonishment. 'Bless my life, the boy's right. There is something moving. Look at it', and handed the glasses to another gentleman. He in turn, after focussing the glasses on the object, emitted a low whistle of surprise and followed it up with the remark 'Well I'm dashed if I've ever seen anything like it before'. What he saw was certainly anything but a star, for although as bright as Venus, it moved in the firmament. 'It's gone now', he muttered. 'No, there it is again – and there's another', was his exclamation as a second object of the same character came into view in close proximity to the first. 'Ah! I can hear the engines now'. This came from the father, who had concentrated the glasses on the lights. Sure enough, the sound of aircraft engines could be heard, growing more audible each moment.

Then they realised that what they had been told about the preparedness of our Air Services was true, and remained out of doors, watching the tiny lights which represented our machines circling over the coast and far away across the sea. The monotony of waiting for something exciting to happen had driven many indoors by midnight, but others more patient who remained out, cheered lustily when word reached the town that at least one raider had been brought down in flames off the Essex coast. Several people in fact claimed to have seen the descent of the burning monster from points of vantage in Thanet, but there was disappointment by reason of the fact that the airmen guarding Thanet had not been given an opportunity of showing their prowess.

Just along the coast at the North Foreland observation post, the demise of L32 was also seen, the observers reporting that at 12.15am: 'We saw a pin point of red light high in the sky and far distant grow and grow and grow until it resembled a red pear drop – the point skyward – and so plunge to earth'.

Closer to home, Nell Tyrell, a schoolgirl in Brentwood, was keeping a diary. Of the destruction of L32, she wrote:

> … our Zeppelin was the most exciting of all. I call it ours, as it fell so near Brentwood and we saw it from beginning to end.
>
> We were first warned by a policeman at 9.15pm coming to say that our lights must be put out as Zeppelins were about. It was a Sunday evening, a very dark quiet evening, ideal in every way for a raid. We of course put out all lights and went upstairs to be in readiness to get the children up in case of Brentwood being bombed. At 10 o'c the maids came home and we all watched the searchlights from our window, trying to find the Raider or Raiders. She went up to the outskirts of London and we could hear bombs dropping and see the shrapnel bursting in the distance then quite suddenly we heard the loud throbbing of a Zeppelin's engines and knew that she was not a great way off. Then away in the distance a searchlight found her and in a flash searchlights from everywhere seemed to spring up and all converge to the spot. The Zeppelin looked like a large silver cigar shaped fish,

which wriggled and twisted to get out of the lights. She flew along right in front of the windows until she seemed to be just getting out of range of the searchlights and we thought we had lost her. At the same moment in a shaft of light we saw an aeroplane above the Zeppelin drop its little red signal light to stop firing and a moment after the airship showed a tiny red flame which spread wildly along the whole length and enveloped it in flames.

Shouts of delight and cheers were heard everywhere and no-one thought of the awful deaths of the crew of the doomed airship in the delight of getting her down. She took quite a long time to sink to earth, behind Wilson's Stores opposite. We all saw her drop except Frances who again slept through all the excitement. It is a sight never to be forgotten, and although awful was the most exciting moment I've ever experienced. After it was all over we tried to go to sleep, but the crowds of cars and cyclists, carts and carriages made such a noise that we none of us got any more sleep that night.

This is the BE2c aircraft in which Frederick Sowrey flew from Suttons Farm airfield when he brought down Zeppelin L32 near Billericay on the night of 23/24 September 1916. (*Imperial War Museum, H(AM) 2186*)

Half of a stereocard view showing the impression in the ground made by Oberleutnant Werner Peterson after he jumped from Zeppelin L32, which was brought down near Billericay by Frederick Sowrey on the night of 23/24 September 1916. (*Author's collection*)

One resident of Hornchurch sent a postcard to her friend in Sandy saying:

No doubt you have heard the good news about the Zepp's coming down, it was so very exciting to see them come down, we all fancyed our selves in France.

Evelyn Potter, in Stratford, saw this too and recorded in her diary:

A raid on tonight. 1.30am. After a terrible din of guns, then a silence, we heard people shouting and clapping. Rushing out we saw a great red glow, like a Chinese lantern in the sky, over towards Avenue Road and in the centre – voila – Monsieur Le Zepp, burning from end to end! Slowly it sank down, a burning shape. What a terrible fate for the men inside! Sirens going – shouting – people's feet – am going out to the front door again.

Scarcely a week later, Zeppelin L31, commanded by Heinrich Mathy and which had carried out the raid on Lea Bridge Road on 23/24 September 1916, was destroyed when shot down at Oakmere Park, Potters Bar on the night of Sunday 1/Monday 2 October by 2nd Lieutenant Wulstan Tempest[3] of No. 39 Squadron flying from North Weald airfield. Having crossed the coast near Lowestoft, at 9.45pm the airship was caught in the beam from the Kelvedon Hatch searchlight. Turning north-west, Mathy then approached from north of Waltham Abbey where L31 came under fire from two AA guns, one of which was probably at Monkham's Hall. Pursued by Tempest, in an effort to gain height Mathy released all of the airship's bombs, which fell on Cheshunt, damaging more than 340 houses and destroying all forty glasshouses, spread over nearly seven acres, belonging to Walnut Tree Nurseries. However, on his second approach, Tempest's bursts of incendiary gunfire set the airship ablaze.

Leyton resident Gladys Rowlands recalled:

… standing with my parents in the neighbours' next door, in the front of the flat looking across to Daniels' Field. Across Lea Bridge Road, up in the sky there was a balloon alight, it was the First World War, they sent it over and it caught fire, and it came down at Potters Bar, I think. I could only have been about four, but I remember they were all standing there looking up in the sky and talking about it.

Norman Russell was a young boy living in Highams Park during the war and he later recalled the destruction of L31:

The Zeppelin was slowly floating along, getting lower and lower, a long envelope of flames. It took some little time to finally come down, after it was set on fire. We thought, as boys, that the bits which were seen falling off it were members of the crew jumping out, but some people said it was bits breaking off the structure. However, I can remember a picture in the newspaper a day or two later, of where the commander of the Zeppelin fell in the soft mud and made an indentation, with his arms and legs spread out.[4] After it happened a few times, they gave up sending the Zeppelins over.

Charles Perfect, over in Hornchurch, remembered:

> On the night of Sunday, October 1st, 1916, there were evident signs of another Zeppelin raid. Just before 10 o'clock the first searchlight shot its piercing shaft of light across the sky, and about a quarter of an hour later we heard an aeroplane ascending from our Aerodrome. We then awaited events with a feeling akin to curiosity, as, after the bringing down of the two 'Zepps' already recorded, many people thought the Huns would try a safer hunting ground than Essex. However, soon after 11 o'clock the unmistakable sound of an approaching 'Zepp' was heard, but this time it was to the N.E. and apparently a considerable distance off, our searchlights failing to discover it, and it passed safely on its way to London. At about 11.40 we heard the distant sounds of guns and bombs, and we waited with some expectation for what would happen. Suddenly the now familiar red glare again illuminated the heavens to the N.W., and at the same moment a mighty shout rent the air, and we then saw the burning airship slowly descending to earth. At this further exploit by our aerial defence excitement knew no bounds, and, after this had to some extent subsided, we stood about the streets wondering where the airship had been brought down. When it became known that the wrecked Zepp was lying at Potters Bar, no one dared to hope that the splendid feat had been accomplished by one of our own airmen, but the news at last came through that Lieut. William [*sic*] J. Tempest was the hero of the night, and we almost danced for joy.

Out at Epping, Sidney Hills recalled:

> We watched the sight from our flat on the second floor of an Epping High Street garage; and afterwards with many more went out to the High Street to welcome back Lieutenant Tempest, as he rode in on his motorcycle combination, cheered by Epping folk.

A J. Hyde of nearby Coopersale remembered:

> The Zeppelin looked no larger than a cucumber. Suddenly what appeared to be a Very light[5] was seen. Immediately the guns stopped firing and the searchlights switched off. For several minutes nothing seemed to happen, then what looked like an orange glow appeared. Then suddenly we saw flames, small at first, then becoming like a gigantic bonfire. By this time we could see the whole of the Zeppelin being burned. It broke into two pieces and the impression one got was of two large flaming parrot cages. Many

people were heard cheering but I remember several people saying, 'Poor devils, they're being roasted alive – but that's war'.

Not everyone was so enthusiastic about the destruction of L31, however. Sybil Morrison,[6] an ambulance driver in London recalled:

> The Zeppelin made a big noise, its engines were pretty powerful. And we all heard the shouts. My friends had a balcony in their house in Harrow, and we all went out and saw this awful sight. It was like a big cigar and all of the back part, the gas part, had caught fire. It was soaring flames – blue, red, purple. And it seemed to come floating slowly down instead of falling with a 'bang!'. And we knew there were about sixteen people in it and that they were being roasted to death. Of course, you weren't supposed to feel any pity for your enemies, nevertheless, I was appalled to see the kind, good-hearted British people dancing about in the street at the sight of sixteen people being burned alive – clapping and singing and cheering. And my own friends delighted! When I said that I was appalled that anyone could be pleased to see such a terrible sight, they said, 'But they're German, they're the enemy. They're Germans, yes, Germans – not human beings'. And it was like a flash to me that this is what war did: it created utter inhumanity in perfectly nice, gentle, kindly people. I felt, 'It's not right, it is wrong, and I can't have any further part in it'.

Clearly visible from all over south-west Essex and further afield, the exploits of Robinson, Sowrey and Tempest in shooting down these airships gave a huge boost to public morale. Such was the impact of the three local pilots' achievements on the inhabitants of Hornchurch that between 2,000 and 3,000 of them subscribed from 1*d* to 2/6 for three silver cups to be presented to the pilots. On Saturday 14 October, at Grey Towers Park, Robinson and Sowrey received their gifts; Tempest was unable to attend as he was away on duty. Robinson's bore the following inscription:

> Presented by the residents of Hornchurch, Essex, as a token of admiration and gratitude to Lieutenant William Leefe Robinson, V.C., Worcestershire regiment and Royal Flying Corps. Lieut. Robinson with conspicuous bravery attacked and destroyed an enemy aeroplane under circumstances of great difficulty and danger during the night of September 2/3rd, 1916.

The cups for Sowrey and Tempest were similarly inscribed.

Chapter 7

'A huge hostile air fleet'

Gothas by day . . .

Aeroplane raiders are the final part in this story for, in the summer of 1917, a greater menace was to appear in the skies above south-west Essex – Gothas and Giants, two- and four-engine bombers capable of dropping bombs more accurately than the Zeppelins.

In the autumn of 1916, the German air forces were looking to rely on two new weapons – the G-type bombers and the R-planes – to carry on the campaign of aerial attacks on London. Germany had been working on the design of a long-range bomber to attack London, and several aircraft companies were given specifications for production. The requirements were finally met in September 1916 with the production of the Gotha GIV by Gothaer Waggonfabrik AG.

The Gotha GIV was a twin-engine biplane 41 feet long and with a wingspan of 77 feet, making it the largest aircraft in the German air forces up to that point. It was powered by two 260hp six-cylinder water-cooled Mercedes engines enabling it to fly at 80mph. Its weapons comprised three 7.92mm Parabellum machine-guns: one at the front and two at the tail end for the rear gunner, who could fire above the fuselage or through an open tunnel under the tail of the bomber using armour-piercing Mauser bullets.

Each Gotha GIV could carry up to 300kg of 12½kg or 50kg anti-personnel bombs. The 50kg was the more powerful weapon and could destroy a three-storey house with a direct hit, but its fuses were unreliable and nearly a third of all these bombs proved to be duds or exploded prematurely. The 12½kg was the more reliable, with 90 per cent detonating successfully. A Goerz bombsight enabled potentially greater accuracy than had been possible by the Zeppelins.

The Gothas each had a crew of three: a pilot, a rear-gunner and a commander who was also the navigator, bomb-releaser and front-gunner. Commanders were normally pre-war officers who also had some experience in fighting with infantry. The skill of the pilot was essential, especially after a six-hour flight when the plane was empty and low on fuel. Pilots were normally recruited from soldiers of all military ranks who had shown exceptional talent in flying these aircraft. The rear-gunner usually came from a lower rank.

London was to be approached from the north-east, the Gothas setting a course via Foulness, easily identified from the North Sea, then using Epping Forest and the Chingford reservoirs as a guide. The bombers were to fly in a tight formation, usually a 'V' or a diamond shape, to ensure a close defensive system, but would open out into different formations when the need arose, such as during intense AA fire. They would have to fly high to avoid the AA guns and defending fighters and they could reach 18,000 feet, although 12,500–16,000 feet was the normal flying height. Communication during flights was very limited; there was no intercom or telephone, only hand signals or shouting above the roar of the engines was possible. Contact between the planes was by light signals. There were several pathfinders in specially coloured aircraft flying directly in front of the flight and, by firing signals of different colours, these could transmit a new heading or cancel a raid. With no radio on board, two or three carrier pigeons accompanied each plane on its way to England. In the event of a crash, it was hoped that they would fly back to base with a note from the crew informing what had happened to them.

In early 1917, Kampfgeschwader der Obersten Heersleitung 3 (KG3), otherwise known as KAGOHL III or Englandgeschwader (England Squadron),[1] was formed under the command of 34-year-old Hauptmann Ernst Brandenburg. The operations against Britain were to be known as Turkenkreuz (Turk's Cross) and classified as top secret. Each assault would consist of at least eighteen Gotha aircraft with London the main target, although in the event of bad weather, military sites, communications and coastal towns could be hit. The main aim of the attacks remained the same: to force withdrawal of British forces from the Western Front to bolster home defences and create such panic amongst the civilian population that a peace settlement favourable to Germany would be brought about.

Four airfields were laid out for the Gothas in Belgium at Mariakerke, Melle-Gontrode, Oostacker, and St Denis-Westrem. On 18 May 1917, the squadron moved to an intermediate landing field at Nieuwmunster, but a period of bad weather forced the Gothas to return to their bases. Then, on 25 May, twenty-three bombers left two airfields in Belgium. Their target was London, but they were halted by heavy cloud. Despite these early setbacks, two daytime raids by the squadron did eventually reach the capital (with more elsewhere in England).

Wednesday 13 June 1917 was a fine day when fourteen Gothas led by Brandenburg flew over south-west Essex. No.39 Squadron had received warning of the incoming Gothas at 10.53am and Captain Trygve Gran, flying from Suttons Farm, attacked one of the raiders over Romford. Eleven AA

Gotha bombers of the 'Englandgeschwader' at a Belgian airfield before taking off to attack England. (*Imperial War Museum, Q 108845*)

guns in the area fired on the bombers; at 11.24am the 3-inch AA gun at Romford opened fire, followed by the gun at Rainham at 11.30am. One of the Gotha commanders later wrote:

Suddenly there stand, as if by magic here and there in our course, little clouds of cotton, the greetings of enemy guns. They multiply with astonishing rapidity. We fly through them and leave the suburbs behind us. It is the heart of London that must be hit.

On the ground at Hornchurch, Charles Perfect recalled this raid:

I was in my garden when I noticed unusual activity in the air, and looking upwards found that several British aeroplanes had ascended to a high altitude to the north of the village. They certainly appeared as if expecting visitors, and it was not many minutes before a huge hostile air fleet hove in sight, well away to the north, the drone of their engines creating a weird and impressive effect. Our airmen endeavoured to intercept them, but the whole flight proceeded on its way to London, apparently without mishap. The weather conditions were so favourable, and the visibility so good, that the passage to and from London was discernable all the time, the combined enemy and home forces looking like a large flock of birds, showing up bright and silvery in the strong sunlight, with incessant bursts of white puffs of smoke from anti-aircraft shells in their midst ...

The Gothas began dropping their bombs just before noon, first on an allotment in North Street, Barking, causing no casualties; then seven more on East Ham where two fell in Alexandra Road, killing four people, injuring eleven and damaging forty-two houses. At 11.35am, another fell on the Royal Albert Dock, killing eight dock workers and injuring nine. This bomb broke windows in the Seamen's Hospital and damaged other buildings, vehicles and a railway truck. A bomb dropped near Freemasons Road and the Custom House failed to explode; another at Canning Town damaged a tram and injured six people. More bombs were then dropped around Poplar, Liverpool Street station, Clerkenwell, Dalston and Stepney. The departing Gothas unloaded their final bombs on Bow and Stratford.

Two days after the raid, *The Ilford Recorder* reported:

Ilford was startled by the great air raid over the Metropolis on Wednesday morning. The first intimation was a loud droning apparently overhead, unlike that of our own aircraft but exactly resembling the noise of approaching Zeppelins. Many people rushed into the streets and gazed skyward, but nothing could be discerned through the haze. While the aerial roar was still clearly audible, a bomb exploded with a deafening, nerve-shaking bang, causing most people to run for cover. Other reports came in quick succession, one from a detonation much closer than the others, and thereafter the muffled displosions of the deadly enemy missiles alternated with the peppering of our own gun-fire. The bursting shrapnel was plainly seen in the distance, and fragments dropped in the neighbourhood. No warning whatever was given, and had a bomb fallen upon one of our crowded schools, there would have been an awful loss of child lives, whereas a warning would have enabled them to disperse and reach their homes.

The raid caused a great sensation, which was increased when news of the damage in east London and elsewhere began to filter through. For the most part, telephonic communication was cut off owing to pressure upon the lines in the City, and the utmost anxiety prevailed here as to the fate of many thousands of people who had gone to London to their daily duties an hour or two before ...

It was persistently rumoured that two bombs fell at Seven Kings, but this is said to be untrue. It is believed that not a single bomb exploded within the Ilford area, though numerous fragments of shrapnel have been picked up. A large piece of metal work, apparently part of a Taube,[2] fell in the playground of a Barking school.

Ilford was again startled just before eight o'clock yesterday (Thursday) morning by heavy gun-firing quite near the town, and it was thought to be associated with another raid, but no bombs were heard. It can scarcely have been gun practice, on the morrow of Wednesday's disquieting experience. Besides the dates and times of practice are regularly announced in the Press.

The newspaper report was correct that no bombs fell on Ilford and that there were no casualties in the town. However, as many Ilford residents travelled into the City for their employment, several of them there were victims of the bombs falling on London. The town itself had a narrow escape when the departing raiders were attacked over Loxford. A Bristol F2B Fighter from No. 35 (Training) Squadron at Northolt, piloted by Captain C.W.E. Cole-Hamilton with Captain C.H. Keevil as observer and gunner, caught up with three straggling Gothas and a machine-gun fight went on across Ilford Broadway and Cranbrook Road. Combat continued for more than thirty miles and, as the aircraft approached Southend-on-Sea, in an exchange of fire a bullet pierced Keevil's neck and killed him.

The Gothas' flight home across south-west Essex was viewed by Charles Perfect:

> Many of us at Hornchurch were watching the return from London fervently hoping our men would 'bag' some of the Huns. From the corner of Stanley Road, Suttons Lane, the flight was distinctly visible, and several of us watched there the oncoming of the Germans, until the gun in our close vicinity opened fire, and we then thought it prudent to shelter indoors. At that time the flight was apparently over Dagenham, heading straight towards us, but the heavy gunfire evidently decided the enemy to incline to the north-east, and in doing so they passed right over Suttons Lane. I came out of doors again just in time to observe the tail of the flight making towards the direction of Upminster.

Following the first daylight raid there was a great outcry from the public and politicians that nearly twenty aircraft could fly across Britain unimpeded and reach London. A meeting by some of Walthamstow's residents passed a resolution:

> That this meeting ... calls on the Government to institute immediately a policy of ceaseless air attacks on German towns and cities in order that

their population may experience the effects of such methods of warfare, and thus be induced to force the German authorities to cease this wanton destruction of life and property.

In Barking the tone was less fierce. There the council simply expressed 'the continued hope that the Government will immediately take effective measures to prevent a recurrence of the recent disastrous air raid'.

It was now clear to the War Office that the existing defence organization, built up to combat Zeppelins, was inadequate to cope with the new menace. One action taken to improve London's defences was to recall two RFC squadrons temporarily from the Western Front to boost Home Defence numbers. Another was to form three new fighter squadrons, including No. 44 Squadron based at Hainault Farm airfield.

The second daylight raid on London took place on 7 July 1917. On a bright and sunny Saturday morning, twenty-one Gothas approached London over Epping Forest. At 10.21am the AA gun at Higham Hill opened fire and the Wanstead battery did so two minutes later. The formation of bombers opened out and one dropped a bomb on Chingford before they all headed for Stoke Newington and the City of London.

Hilda Bazalgette recalled this raid:

I remember the daytime raid in July 1917 very clearly. It was one Saturday morning and my sister was out in the forest with her sketching class, so she had an uninterrupted view of the aircraft coming. There were more than a dozen planes, flying in a V-formation like a flock of geese. It was something tremendously bold on the part of the enemy, and it came as a great shock to the British that it was possible for them to come over and see their targets below.

Of the raid, one journalist wrote:

To the spectator, in the midst of a quiet orderly London suburb, busily engaged in its Saturday shopping, it seemed ludicrously incredible that this swarm of black specks moving across the summer sky was a squadron of enemy aircraft, laden with explosive bombs waiting to be dropped into 'the brown' of London's vast expanse of brick and mortar.

... and by night

In August 1917, daylight bombing raids on London came to an end, the raiders largely deterred by the capital's increasingly efficient defences, but on Tuesday 4/Wednesday 5 September night attacks on London began. From late summer 1917 to the spring of 1918 Gothas raided London on fifteen occasions at night.

During that first night raid, seven detachments, consisting of twenty-six aircraft, attacked the mouth of the Thames and London. As a result of harassment by fighters and guns only five Gothas reached London. At 11.25pm two bombs fell at Barking, and three more were dropped over West Ham: at the junction of Henniker Road and Leytonstone Road where it damaged shop fronts and broke a water main – one man was killed; in Gurney Road, Forest Gate, where a house was damaged; and at the rear of Ravenstone Road where it blew out the backs of three houses.

At Stratford, a 50kg HE bomb fell in Carpenters Road on the former factory of William Ritchie, a jute spinner and weaver. The factory had closed in 1904, but more recently had been used as an internment camp for German and Austrian aliens until June 1917; being empty, no casualties were caused. Another 50kg HE bomb was dropped at the rear of Gibbon Road, damaging several houses and injuring two men. At about 11.55pm six 12½kg bombs then fell in Wanstead Park. One bomb dropped on the ridge of the Temple roof and exploded between the tiles and the ceiling, doing considerable damage; four fell at the rear of the chalet and one fell close to the park boundary fence, these damaging the park's refreshment rooms.

During a raid on the night of 24 September, five incendiary bombs were dropped on Poplar and West Ham, but they did little damage; falling shells from AA guns injured one man at 77 Hampton Road, Forest Gate. The following night, a falling AA shell hit the SS *Stockwell* berthed in the Royal Albert Dock, killing three men and injuring one; twenty-four houses were also damaged. On Saturday 29 September, Gothas briefly reached south-west Essex, dropping an incendiary bomb and damaging a house in Forest Gate at 8.10pm. By 9.15pm the raiders were heard over Woodford.

The following night, Sunday 30 September, at least nine aircraft dropped bombs over a wide area of metropolitan Essex. At 7.40pm, an aircraft was heard at Ilford, which subsequently dropped a 50kg HE bomb on the MR sidings at Plaistow station and four 50kg HE bombs on the railway cleaning sheds in Durban Road, West Ham, and the nearby allotments: three locomotives and many houses were damaged. At 7.44pm, a 50kg HE bomb fell on the East London Cemetery in Plaistow, where it did no damage; and an incendiary hit Queens Road, Upton Park, which damaged the roadway. At 7.55pm an aircraft was heard at Wanstead, and thirty-five minutes later two 12½kg HE bombs were dropped there, injuring two people. At 8.15pm, a bomb fell on 3 Fairfoot Road, Bromley-by-Bow, demolishing the two-storey house, killing its 80-year-old inhabitant, and injuring a sailor home on leave,

These refreshment rooms and the nearby Temple in Wanstead Park were damaged in the first night raid by Gotha bombers on 4/5 September 1917. (*Author's collection*)

his wife, another woman and a child. It also damaged twelve other houses in the road. At 8.40pm, two 50kg HE bombs and eight incendiaries landed in fields near Movers Lane in Barking and adjoining streets, but they caused no damage or casualties. Other bombs that night included incendiaries in Silvertown; Victoria Dock Road, Custom House; and Fords Park Road, Canning Town, all of which caused no damage. An incendiary in Lichfield Road, East Ham, damaged a house, and two more incendiaries at East Ham Isolation Hospital in Roman Road damaged the roof. Just before 8.00pm, one raider had been attacked over Lambourne End by Captain W.H. Haynes of No. 44 Squadron flying from Hainault Farm airfield; this was possibly the same aircraft that was later heard at Waltham Abbey at 9.35pm, probably on its way home.

There was no let-up, for the next night, 1 October, raiders were heard at Romford at 7.43pm, at Noak Hill where one was caught in the searchlight at 7.46pm, and at Woodford at 7.50pm. By 8.47pm, aircraft were being heard at North Woolwich. At the end of the month, during the night of 31 October/ 1 November, three Gothas were heard at Upminster at 1.02am.

Constance Haggar, a 17-year-old girl living in Forest Gate when the war started, remembered one of the night raids:

They dropped a lot of bombs on Wanstead Flats – one made a hole big enough to put a bus in. There were lots of big guns mounted all over the Flats to shoot the German planes down. They had a very good view of the sky from that big open space. My cousin ran a coffee stall on the Flats for the men drilling there.

They dug a trench beside Centre Road, which runs through the middle of Wanstead Flats. It would have been about 10 feet deep, and if a raid started and you were walking across the Flats, you could drop down in there. I was engaged then, and one day my boyfriend and I were walking across the Flats when the warning went, so we ran home. When we got there my mother was at the bedroom window calling out 'Connie, where are you, where are you?', but we got home alright. Nobody liked to be caught out in an air raid.

Hilda Bazalgette recalled:

I remember an air raid one night when my father counted the sound of seventeen detonations as the bombs hit the ground. The next morning we went out and found the craters where some of the bombs had landed on the forest, at Leyton Flats. They weren't deep craters, but then they were only small aircraft bringing the bombs. My father came to the conclusion that the aircraft had jettisoned the bombs, possibly because they couldn't find the target.

Winifred Freeman also wrote about the night raids. Again undated, her letters from Leyton to her parents tell of her experiences:

Once again we are all safe & sound except for the dreadful shock & fright while the raid was on. To begin with Monday morning we all expected Air Raids as the weather was so suitable, nothing happened however. Monday night no Searchlights out, people were out till past 1 am but we went to bed 10.45 & dropped asleep just after 12 midnight tho, then the Searchlights were out. Last night the Searchlights were out 9.40 pm. Will was out at cadets so I went to bed 10.15, he came home about 10.45 & we were fast asleep, when at 11.20 we were woke up by a terrific crash. We dashed out of bed both together. I flew in & brought Joan in our bed & Will got Roy. I then started to dress, got on chemise & corsets but the bangs were so dreadful & were steadily coming closer, so we carried the kiddies down to the Dining room, placed them on the floor & got wraps for them & Will ran up & got clothes for himself & me, then I went & got more rugs. I crept to the window once or twice upstairs & the noise of the Aeroplanes was dreadful. It seemed as tho there were hundreds. I've never known a raid last so long. It seemed as tho the Gothas kept coming over one after the other. The guns & noise would die away & we peeped out, then we heard another coming & the noise they make, it came closer & closer, then the guns started to roar again & we could hear the hum of our aeroplanes as tho they were Massing it, these happened time after time & last from 11.20 till 1.20, then we put the kiddies to bed in our bed & Will got in with them, but I wouldn't lie down till <u>all clear</u> came through just before 2.00am.

And again:

Thought you would like to know we are all safe once again but I am feeling very tired out to-day & had dreadful neuralgia when the raid was over. To begin the tale – Roy went to bed 7.20 & kept calling out, seemed as tho he couldn't settle, about 7.35 Mrs Frankland & Cecil came along. I said to Mrs F how do you feel & she said, 'Oh I'm sure something is going to happen tonight,' then Roy called down 'I can hear an Aeroplane mama.' I said rubbish it's only a Motor, but I went out the front door & listened & could hear not one but many. I only just got inside & the guns started. We flew up & fetched the kiddies down. A strange lady knocked & asked for shelter. Gwenny Jones came running up as she was alone in their house, so we had quite a party camping out on the Dinning [*sic*] Room floor. The guns were dreadful. Two mobile guns were in the roads near us & they kept on without ceasing till it nearly drove you mad. Big guns kept sending shells & the whoo oo oo oo of them up & down the scale struck terror to your 'innards'. We heard something knock against the wall outside, & after it was over, Will picked up a bit of shell, only a small bit but enough to kill any one. It lasted from 7.50 till 9.45. The church bell was tolled three times, as soon as all was clear. Four different times Aeroplanes came over & the guns after them. I took the kiddies to bed about 11 pm & they soon dropped asleep. Will stayed with Gwenny Jones till her dad got back from night school about 11.30 & then he retired & we slept till morning. We all got up the usual time, & Roy & Joan went off to school quite cheerfully.

On 10 October 1917, Walthamstow UDC resolved:

We, the Members of the Walthamstow Council, note with satisfaction the statement publicly made by the Prime Minister that the systematic murder of the civilian population of England, by bombs dropped from German aircraft, should at once be punished by retaliatory raids on German towns. And we pledge ourselves by all means in our power to support the Government in their efforts by these means to protect our defenceless women and children.

On 3 November, Leyton UDC resolved to support this stance too.

A raid on London on the night of 31 October/1 November saw a departing Gotha drop bombs on Plaistow; and on 5/6 December, a falling AA shell killed a man in Wanstead.

The 'Giants'

There was another Zeppelin product, this time one of its heavier-than-air craft, which was also to terrorize the British population from September 1917. This was a strategic bomber aircraft called the Zeppelin-Staaken RVI (the 'R' stands for Riesenflugzeug – literally 'huge aircraft', or in common parlance 'Giant'). These were the largest aircraft to bomb Britain in either

One of the immense Zeppelin-Staaken RVI 'Giants' that bombed England in 1917 and 1918. On the night of 29/30 January 1918, such an aircraft was intercepted between Shenfield and Hainault and it then proceeded to drop twenty HE bombs on open fields around Wanstead before fleeing for the coast. (*Imperial War Museum, Q 67882*)

A photograph showing the comparative sizes of 12½kg, 50kg and 100kg bombs dropped from Gotha and Giant aircraft. (*Author's collection*)

the First or Second World War – the width of a Giant's tailplane alone was greater than the wingspan of a Sopwith Camel. The payloads of the Gothas paled when compared with the Giants, which could carry up to 1,950kg of bombs – similar to Hitler's principal bomber, the Heinkel He 111, a generation later. However, the Giant was extremely complex to manufacture and it became a considerable drain on the German aircraft industry as the Allied blockade tightened over time. Many of the airship crews were transferred to the Giant squadrons, particularly the mechanics whose knowledge of the Maybach engine was found very useful.

Sorties by about five different Giants were flown against the capital at night between September 1917 and May 1918. A total of eleven such raids took place during which nearly thirty tons of bombs were dropped. The aircraft flew individually to their targets on moonlit nights, requesting directional bearings by radio after take-off, then using the River Thames as a navigational landmark. Missions on the 340-mile round-trip lasted seven hours. None was lost in combat over Britain, but two aircraft crashed on returning to their home bases (compared to twenty-eight Gotha bombers and eighty of their crewmen shot down over England).

Into 1918

A large raid took place during the night of 28/29 January 1918. One aircraft was heard over Romford at 8.30pm and two more at Brentwood at 8.54pm. These two proceeded to Romford and Ilford where they separated, one flying on to Barking and then London; the other aircraft reached London and returned over East Ham at 9.33pm. Another Gotha was reported over Leyton then Romford just before 10.00pm; this was subsequently shot down by Captain G.H. Hackwill and 2nd Lieutenant C.C. Banks in Sopwith Camels of No. 44 Squadron who shared in its destruction after a running battle. The Gotha eventually crashed at Frund's Farm, Wickford, the two pilots making history with the first night victory in air combat between aircraft. This was also the first enemy bomber brought down by Home Defence aircraft on British soil, but it was to remain No. 44 Squadron's only victory. Hackwill and Banks both received the Military Cross (MC) for their endeavours. That same evening, one of the Giants was spotted over Harlow by 2nd Lieutenant Goodyear of No. 39 Squadron who was patrolling in his Bristol F2B between Suttons Farm and Sawbridgeworth. He fired 200 rounds at the aircraft but, in the return fire, his observer was hit and his fuel tank punctured so he called off the attack. The Giant went on to bomb London, passing over Loughton at 12.07am.

Evelyn Potter's diary recorded this raid:

Long raid last night. Lasted from 9.30pm to 1.15am. We heard the siren, then went into Aunt Hettie's house. Stood at her gate and saw the maroons go up – reports, then red stars which slowly sank. Like fireworks. Beattie played the piano all the barrage time so it kept things lively. At times the noise outside was deafening, drowning the playing inside. They had a mobile gun running up and down the road.

On Tuesday 29 January, heading for London, a damaged Giant was intercepted between Shenfield and Hainault by Major G.W. Murlis Green of No. 44 Squadron. Just after midnight (now on 30 January), with the Woodford balloon apron looming up, the bomber dropped its entire load of twenty HE bombs on open fields around Wanstead before escaping back over Rayleigh and the Essex coast. Another Giant was reported on the night of 7/8 March, appearing over Rainham at 11.40pm and later to the south of Ilford.

The last air raid of the war on Britain by aircraft took place on the night of Whit Sunday 19/Monday 20 May[3] and during that raid, at about 11.40pm, a Gotha dropped a 100kg bomb in Richard's Place, off Hoe Street, Walthamstow, behind *The Rose and Crown* pub. No-one was hurt, but damage was extensive. Miss H.C. Hawsher recalled:

I was staying with a friend in Pearl Road, Walthamstow, when the warning went in the early hours … We took a walk along Hoe Street … we saw all the windows broken in. They were saying it was a shell or an aerial torpedo that had been dropped.

At 11.45pm bombs fell on Manor Park and at midnight on Forest Gate and Stratford. It was during this raid that No. 39 Squadron achieved its first victory against the Gothas. Lieutenant Anthony Arkell, an experienced Home Defence pilot although aged only 19, and his gunner-observer First Air Mechanic Albert Stagg, flying in their Bristol F2B (floridly named 'Devil in the Dusk'), brought down a Gotha bomber. The two had taken off from their base at North Weald when, just after midnight, they spotted something suspicious below them at 10,000 feet, north of Hainault, and went to investigate. Arkell vividly recounted the ensuing melee in a letter to his father, the Reverend Arkell, written later the same day:

I dived down under it, as it was hazy, and then saw against the starlight the shape of a Gotha. What I thought were lights were the exhausts of the engines. I could see the two engines, and the long planes quite clearly. I

Bomb damage to property at Terb Road, Manor Park, caused by Gothas on the night of Whit Sunday 19/Monday 20 May 1918 during London's last air raid of the war. (*Imperial War Museum*)

soon caught it up. I was much faster and could climb better than it. After a little manoeuvring I got under its tail, about 150 yards behind. The observer Stagg fired 20 rounds, very scattered, and then stopped. I zoomed up level with its tail firing my front guns. Directly we started firing, it fired back. And when we weren't firing I could hear pop-pop-pop quite plainly. Stagg fired another drum of about 100 rounds; but, as his shooting wasn't very good, I decided the sooner we finished the Hun off the better, so got as close as I could underneath him. He was 3 times as big as we were. We were firing at point blank range, Stagg and I firing in turn. In the end Stagg fired the actual shot that set his right-hand petrol tank alight.

Arkell and Stagg between them had fired around 700 rounds by this time, with little damage in reply from the German. The Gotha had been gradually forced lower during the fight before it rolled over and crashed to the ground

A Bristol F2B Fighter similar to that flown by Anthony Arkell and Albert Stagg when they brought down a Gotha bomber at East Ham on the night of Whit Sunday 19/Monday 20 May 1918 during London's last air raid of the war. (*Imperial War Museum, Q 69892*)

at East Ham at 12.20am. It came down in a bean field off Roman Road, 200 yards from the Royal Albert Dock, by the north bank of the River Thames, the wreckage spread over 100 yards. All three of the crew leapt to their deaths, their bodies being found on an allotment in Brooks Avenue, a good half-mile north-east of the Gotha; in a ditch some 300 yards south of the aircraft; and a quarter-mile south in the next field.

In its edition of Tuesday 21 May, *The Times* reported that the burning aeroplane was seen for miles around and:

> Sirens, near and far, sounded a shrill note of victory, and from the watching people came a long and satisfied roll of cheering ... A bomb which dropped a little distance away from the spot where the raider fell caused little damage and there were no casualties. Broken windows in cottages were the only signs of the explosion. The occupiers, standing in the little gardens before their homes were kept busy yesterday afternoon telling the story of the bringing down of the German machine to a swarm of holidaymakers,

who made pilgrimage to the bean field their Whit Monday excursion. Among the visitors who were permitted a close inspection of the wreckage of the Gotha were half-a-dozen American naval men. They were openly delighted at the success of the Royal Air Force. 'That's the first German machine I've seen. It looks good – there', one of the party remarked as he walked towards the heap of burned fragments.

The next morning Arkell visited the wreckage, which was less burnt than he expected – only the rear and part of the fuselage had caught fire, the rest was just crashed, with the engines buried in the earth. His letter to his father continued:

It had eight wheels, all more or less intact. The planes were a dark blue camouflage. I brought back a small bit of canvas, a bit of charred wood, and 1 german cartridge case as small souvenirs, but it will be topping if I can get that prop. I also got a three ply box that contained the belt of ammunition for the Hun machine gun, slightly charred. I didn't get to bed till 3.30 last night and was up again at 7.00, so feel pretty sleepy and not too bright. We hear five Gothas are down for certain last night, and two more possibly …

Understandably, Arkell was delighted with his feat, for which he received the MC, and Stagg the Military Medal (MM). But he also had a sense of compassion towards the enemy crew, as he said in his letter:

I couldn't help feeling sorry for the poor fellows. For after all they were only acting under orders, and it must take very brave men to come all that way at night over the sea and hostile country.

The raid also featured another Giant, this one observed over Barking at 12.20am, which subsequently dropped a 50kg HE bomb on Kings Road, causing no damage but some injuries. At 12.38am, it dropped another 50kg HE bomb on waste ground near Saxon Road, East Ham, close to the wreck of the Gotha shot down by Arkell and Stagg, but probably aimed at the Beckton searchlight. Another 50kg HE bomb fell on Grange Road Elementary School in West Ham, where there was damage but no casualties; and a 50kg HE bomb at the junction of Balaam Street and Whitwell Road, Plaistow, damaged 100 houses and the West Ham Public Baths. A 100kg HE bomb landed on allotments at Prince Regent Place, Plaistow, and a 50kg HE bomb fell into the garden of 21 Saxon Road, Bow, causing some damage but injuring no-one. A 100kg HE bomb was dropped on 12 Ladysmith Road, Canning Town, where it killed one person and injured three more.

Chapter 8

'Attendance this week has suffered considerably'

Children's education and their attendance at schools in south-west Essex were significantly affected by air raids. Amidst notes about male staff members leaving for the services and female teachers temporarily replacing them, collections for the Sick and Wounded Horses' Fund, and local Tank Days (the tank 'Julian' was displayed outside Walthamstow town hall at the County Cricket Ground in Leyton in March 1918), school logbooks contain a wealth of information about how many children came to school after a night-time air raid and what happened if a daytime raid occurred during school hours. Leyton UDC minutes also help to fill out the details of how the war intruded into daily life at school.

1915

An entry in the Harrow Green Boys' School logbook for 1 June 1915 noted that owing to the excitement caused by the Zeppelin raid the previous night many boys had had no sleep and consequently did not attend school that day. After the raid on Leyton on 17/18 August of that year, the logbook recorded:

> 23 August 1915. School was re-opened this morning after the summer vacation with a diminished Attendance for the corresponding date of last year – 339 against 344. Several boys were absent owing to their homes being demolished in the Zeppelin raid of Tuesday evening last.

Leyton High Road Mixed School recorded:

> 23rd August: The attendance was poor, obviously due to the effects of air raid on 17th inst, when two scholars, Emily Forrest and Sidney Smee, were injured.

There were some lighter moments in a school day, as the logbook for Harrow Green Boys' School reported for 8 September:

> An army aeroplane having alighted on The Flats, the pilot having lost his bearing, in the morning mist, I sent Classes I, II, III and IV to see it this afternoon, the ordinary Time Table work being suspended in their absence.

Pupils from Cobbold Road School also went to see the aeroplane on the Flats that day.

The following day, 9 September, Canterbury Road Girls' School logbook noted that fifty children were absent in the morning following the previous night's air raid. Harrow Green Boys' School logbook noted that the Zeppelin raids that week had very materially affected the attendance of scholars, only forty being present and below that of the previous week. On Friday 10 September, Leyton High Road Mixed School's logbook also noted that, as a result of air raids on the previous Tuesday and Wednesday nights, attendance for the week had suffered considerably, falling to 83.8 per cent. Canterbury Road Girls' School also reported very low attendance at 85 per cent. Lea Bridge Road School recorded low attendance since Wednesday owing to air raids. Church Road School's logbook noted that, owing to the air raids, many children had been kept up until early morning and then allowed to sleep on – this caused a drop in attendance. At Kirkdale Road School in Leytonstone, the logbook for the week ending 17 September recorded that several families had left or were leaving the district owing to recent air raids, but that attendance had otherwise improved that week.

In September, Leyton UDC reported that Mr E. Gringer, on behalf of residents in the neighbourhood of Norlington Road School, had requested permission to use the school's basement as a shelter during air raids – the council refused this request.

On 14 October, Church Road School's logbook reported that the air raid of the previous night had caused a considerable drop in attendance that day. Reduced street lighting also affected schools. On 18 November, the logbook for Downsell Road Girls' School recorded that, for the afternoon sessions, the school would assemble at 1.30pm and close at 3.35pm from that date to the end of March owing to the darkened streets.

1916

On 3 April 1916, Harrow Green Boys' School attendance was badly affected in the morning by the previous night's air raid following on those of Friday and Saturday evenings.

The night of 23/24 September saw a heavy air raid on Leyton and, on 25 September, the logbook of Leyton High Road Mixed School recorded that attendance was very low as a result. At the end of that week, on 29 September, the headmaster of Kirkdale Road School in Leytonstone noted:

> The attendance this week has suffered considerably owing to the Zeppelin Raid over this district on Sunday morning last. The average attendance for the week = 349.4 as against 377 for the corresponding week last year.

At Canterbury Road Girls' School, the logbook for 29 September reported:

> Percentage of attendance this week only 79, owing to a Zeppelin Raid on 23rd inst., which damaged many houses on this Estate. Sixty panes of glass were broken here.

Leyton UDC minutes recorded that, in addition, some tiles on the school roof had been broken and part of one ceiling had fallen down during that raid.

On the same day, the head teacher at Benyon County Primary School in South Ockendon recorded in his school's logbook:

> The recent Zeppelin raid has had an effect on children. Many of parishioners, after the terrifying affect [*sic*] of week end, have refused to go to bed in case of another visit, and consequently some are suffering from shock and sleeplessness. Exam papers have been prepared for half-year exams but owing to disturbed state of children's minds and absence of staff, it will have to be deferred for a few days.

On 2 October, the logbook of Leyton High Road Mixed School recorded that, owing to an air raid the previous night, attendance was again very low. At Church Road School attendance was very poor in the morning owing to many children being up most of the night. At Canterbury Road Girls' School it was down to 49 per cent but up to 80 per cent by 6 October.

At Creekmouth School, Barking, on 1 November, of seventy-six pupils only nineteen attended school after the previous night's raid. At the end of the month, on 30 November, Harrow Green Boys' School was closed for the morning session at 11.45am owing to an air raid scare and parents coming and asking to be allowed to take their children home. Church Road School reported attendance slightly affected. At Harrow Green Infants' School an aircraft scare in the morning caused many parents to come and ask for their children to be allowed to leave school and so the school closed at 11.45am; only 176 out of 262 were present in the afternoon.

By this stage of the war some schools were carrying out regular air raid drills. At Creekmouth, the entire school was expected to be in 'safety positions' as soon as possible, and on 29 November, it took just twenty seconds to achieve this. The pupils at Westbury County School in Barking took three and a half minutes. Students at Becontree Heath Boys' School held daily drills in the summer of 1917. There the children marched to the fields at the back of the school, where they sheltered in prepared ditches.

1917

Schools were particularly vulnerable to aeroplane raiders because when they came by day it was at times when schools would normally be full. The daylight raid of Wednesday 13 June 1917 inflicted a grave loss of life at one LCC school[1] and this caused significant concern at many schools across south-west Essex.

On the day of the raid, the Beckton School logbook recorded:

13th June: Air raid 11.15 to 11.45. No warning given. The children behaved well. The teachers calm and holding classes well in hand. Some few parents came. These added to the anxiety of the staff. In the afternoon, 33% of the scholars were present.

Harrow Green Boys' School logbook noted:

Noise of hostile engines was very plainly heard about 11.20. This continued about thirty minutes interrupted more or less by sound of guns (machine & otherwise) & exploding bombs. Children were placed away from windows under the desks and sent home at 12.00 when noises had ceased for 10 minutes.

The logbook of Harrow Green Infants' School reported:

Air Raid in Neighbourhood. At 11.20 sounds of what seemed to be hostile aircraft were very distinctively heard, & shortly afterwards there was loud firing, as the children were told to take cover under their desks. A few parents came up while the firing was in progress, and two or three claimed their children, while the others, realizing that the children were safe & being well looked after, went away. At twelve o'clock the danger seemed to be over, and many parents then came for the scholars, so the school was dismissed at the usual time.

278 scholars were present this morning, and 50 less this afternoon.

At Cann Hall Road School the logbook recorded:

In consequence of the Air Raid being very severe over the district about 11.30am, the whole of the upper school was transferred to the lower corridors, where they remained till able to go home in safety at 12.5 noon. In the afternoon the attendance fell to 325 being 135 less than in the morning.

Acting on a special message sent by Detective Inspector Casalton, saying that a raid was on, the boys were dismissed for the day, at 3.30pm.

The head teacher at Church Road School noted in the logbook:

Notice of Air Raid received this morning at 11.35 a.m.

Went round school & warned teachers & also suggested that classes were to be as clear as possible from windows. Matters having cleared I allowed classes to leave at intervals & assisted at Infants' School afterwards.

78 scholars were absent in the afternoon, i.e. a.m. 361, p.m. 283.

Ruckholt Road School in Leyton was closed at 11.40 that morning and attendance in the afternoon was low. The adjacent Girls' School was dismissed at 11.45am owing to parents coming to ask for their children following rumours of air raids. The school was dismissed again at 3.00pm after official notice from the Town Hall that another air raid was impending. At Lea Bridge Road School attendance was down in the afternoon, only 159 children turning up out of 309 on the school roll. At Downsell Road Girls' School, 204 children were present in the afternoon. Kirkdale Road School had dismissed its pupils at 12.15pm and only 257 came back in the afternoon – 346 having been present in the morning. Canterbury Road Girls' School was also dismissed at 12.15pm and there were 86 absences for the afternoon session.

The logbook of Leyton High Road Mixed School recorded:

Air raid on London. At 11.30am gunfire, aircraft, and machine gunfire were heard in the neighbourhood. Official warning was received at 11.40. Arrangements for the safety of the children were carried out according to pre-arranged plan. Children were dismissed at 12.15. The behaviour of both teachers and scholars was excellent.

Evelyn Potter was at school in Stratford and this extract from her diary shows that there was no panic at her school:

About 11.30am at school heard a buzzing noise like aeroplanes. Then thuds and guns. Got nearer till it was overhead. A raid, I felt sure. We went on with the lesson, though the noise was dreadful. Miss Graydon advised getting away from windows.

The following day, 14 June, Leyton High Road Mixed School's log book recorded:

Children were sent home at 11.45am owing to information being received indirectly through the police that aircraft were expected. School was closed at 3.00pm owing to receipt of official warning that hostile aircraft were expected. Owing to the unusual causes, the attendances of the scholars were not cancelled on 13th and 14th June.

At Harrow Green Infants' School it was reported:

Rumour of an Air Raid at 10.25. Parents came for their children and 130 were withdrawn. Almost immediately 31 returned to their classes, the police having assured the people that nothing was the matter. The attendance marks of 99 who did not return were accordingly cancelled.

Just before three in the afternoon, there was another rumour, & by 3.10 nearly all the scholars had been withdrawn, & on the advice of the Head Master, the remainder were dismissed, and all Attendances for the afternoon cancelled.

School closed at 3.10.

Lea Bridge Road School was dismissed at 3.00pm, Ruckholt Road School and Kirkdale Road School at 3.15pm, and the girls' schools in Downsell Road and Canterbury Road at 3.20pm following notice from the fire station of an anticipated air raid. Harrow Green Boys' School was closed at 3.05pm following similar notice and so many parents coming to withdraw their children; all attendance marks were cancelled. Cobbold Road School was also closed that afternoon, and its logbook the following day noted that attendance that week had been seriously affected by enemy air raids.

Entries for the rest of that week in the Beckton School logbook noted:

June 14th: A great many parents came to the school in response to a rumour of an air raid. They were allowed to take their children home with them this morning and again this afternoon.

June 18th: Head Teacher left school at 3.50 in order to attend a meeting of local head teachers called by the Chairman of the Education Committee at 4.30. Discussion to be held upon the steps to be taken in future air raids.

Following the 13 June raid, some authorities on the eastern side of London set up their own warning systems. Barking UDC had three motorcycle messengers permanently on duty, with two of them in communication with the fire station. When an alert was declared, warnings written on cards were taken by boys to all the local schools with instructions to show them to the first teacher they saw. Headmasters were given permission to dismiss all pupils when the siren in Woolwich (on the other side of the Thames) was heard.

On 15 June, Leyton UDC reported that it had appointed an Air Raid Sub-Committee to make arrangements for notifying schools simultaneously of impending air raids, supplying bandages for each school and of the general course of action to be followed in schools. The sub-committee subsequently issued instructions that Boy Scouts, or other reliable scholars, from each school should be in attendance in relays at the nearest fire station or fire box from 8.45am to 1.00pm and from 1.00pm to 4.15pm. When the fire brigade received warning, a scout would run to each school and inform the head teacher. He would then run back to the fire station and later return to the school with news of the 'All clear'. Scouts were to be based as below:

- Town Hall, covering Ruckholt Road, Goodall Road, Downsell Road and Newport Road schools.
- Leytonstone fire box,[2] covering Kirkdale Road, Davies Lane, Norlington Road, Connaught Road and Colworth Road schools.
- Harrow Green fire station, covering Cobbold Road, Trumpington Road, Cann Hall Road, Mayville Road, and Harrow Green schools.
- Leyton fire station, covering Church Road, Farmer Road, St Joseph's, Sybourn Street and Lea Bridge Road schools.
- *The Bakers' Arms* fire box, covering Capworth Street, High Road and Canterbury Road schools.

A boy would also be appointed at each school to communicate with the fire brigade if a fire occurred or other assistance was needed.

The sub-committee determined that if notice of an air raid was received before the AA guns were heard or bombs fell, schools should be dismissed (this was changed in October 1917). If a raid was in progress, pupils were to move to the lower floors. Teachers with 'expertise and tact' were to deal with parents who came to schools, and children should be released on the demand of a parent. If schools were dismissed after a warning or 'All clear' they would not re-open that day.

The sub-committee also considered connecting schools to fire stations by telephone, but as the only method available would be by bell signals, would take time to install, would break down and would cost £500, the sub-committee did not recommend doing so. It did, however, suggest installing a siren at the electricity works, but this too was not carried out.

The 18 June entry in the logbook for Church Road School reported that, in accordance with instructions from the Town Hall, the head teacher had arranged for a Boy Scout to be in attendance at the fire station each morning and afternoon.

On 18 June, the Ilford Education Committee met and considered what lessons could be learnt from the raid of 13 June:

The secretary also intimated that he had received a petition from a number of parents of children attending the Valentines School asking that their children be released from school in case of future air raids.

A discussion took place upon the subject and it was ultimately agreed that every endeavour would be made for the safety of the children in the future as in the past, and that the children, if it was thought advisable and in the interests of safety and time permitted after sufficient warning had been received, would be allowed to return home. It was pointed out that in the recent raid no warning whatever was obtained of the intended raid, the first intimation received being the actual raid itself, at which time it would have been most detrimental to the safety of the children to turn them out into the streets. At all the schools perfect discipline was maintained during the raid, and not the slightest panic occurred among either the teachers or the children.

The secretary presented the following report:- As members are aware, a flotilla of hostile aircraft passed over the town on Wednesday morning last, and during the end of the morning school session. The enemy presumably passed either immediately over or in close proximity to all the large public elementary schools of the town. No warning was received of their on-coming; and the air battle was in actual progress when the problem was realised. Pre-arranged air raid precautions were thereupon immediately adopted in the whole of the schools. The committee will doubtless remember that the possibility of daylight air raids was fully realised in the early stages of the war, with the result that the best possible arrangements were brought into practice on Wednesday last, and depend on the basic principle that, in the event of daylight air raids during school time, and occurring without warning, the children should, generally speaking, remain in school under cover in extended order in the class-rooms, and as far removed as possible from outer walls and windows. All the authorities that we have been able to approach agree that this is the best policy to adopt under the conditions mentioned, and well calculated to minimise the danger to life. In the event of a timely and reliable warning coming to hand, the children would, of course, be dispersed: and Lord French has been appealed to with a view to ascertaining whether, failing the institution of a warning of a general character, a direct-special warning to Educational Offices cannot be arranged. Meanwhile, through the courtesy of the surveyor and through the willing co-operation of the fire superintendant, arrangements have been made for our own Education Offices to be indirectly advised through the Fire Station as soon as possible.

I beg to take this opportunity of reporting, with pleasure, the total absence of anything approaching panic in the schools, during the actual time of the raid. The children were quite bright and cheerful, the staff cool and collected. This fact, coupled with the circumstance that the schools are now principally staffed with ladies, will no doubt be particularly gratifying to the Committee. I was personally in touch with many hundreds of the children at the time, and have since received full reports from all departments; and I find that the calmness of the children and the control of the teaching staff was magnificent. The same remark applies to the working of the schools on the following day (Thursday), when air raid action was again taken: and the orderliness and effectiveness of the arrangements was then commented upon by one of His Majesty's Inspectors (a lady) who happened to be upon certain school premises at the time and saw the children concerned respond smartly to pre-arranged plans under adverse circumstances. A number of mothers came to the school gates for individual children both on Wednesday and Thursday. The number was relatively small, but was more marked on Thursday. Every sympathy was extended to the callers, and their wishes were met as far as possible without disturbing the effectiveness of the general arrangements.

On Saturday I called a conference of head teachers to review our arrangements in the light of actual experience. It was unanimously felt that the existing arrangements, which were first issued in January, 1916, should stand. There is, of course, great scope for individual discretion on matters of detail, and such points were very carefully considered, subject to the maintenance of guiding principles. The conference accepted the suggestion that parents, particularly mothers, and more especially those affected by the operation of the war, should be invited to the schools on an early date or dates with a view to their being advised directly and verbally and sympathetically, of the arrangements which are made for the general safety of their children during actual raids. In this way, it is hoped that the parents as a whole will fully appreciate the fact that this matter of affording all possible protection to the school children has been, and will continue to be, carefully safeguarded. The great point desired in this connection is to establish a feeling of confidence between the home and the school, and a mutual agreement that certain lines of action should and will be naturally taken under understood conditions.

Following the head teachers' conference, back in Beckton action was being taken as the school logbook for 22 June recorded that notices were sent out to parents regarding conduct during air raids. Lea Bridge Road School again recorded a low attendance percentage as a result of the previous week's air raid.

The next month, on 4 July, Leyton High Road Mixed School's logbook recorded that the scholars were dismissed and the school closed at 10.40am for the remainder of the day as the result of the probability of an air raid. The air raid was actually at Harwich at 7.15am, but an alarm was also given in Leyton which caused poor attendance at Kirkdale Road School. At Harrow Green Boys' School several boys were absent or late during the morning session. Canterbury Road Girls' School was also closed owing to this air raid alarm. At Harrow Green Infants' School only 234 pupils turned up (compared with 281 the previous day) and one boy was withdrawn by his mother shortly before 10.00am on account of some loud firing being heard; 264 were present in the afternoon.

Of the second daylight raid, on 7 July, Norman Russell remembered:

When I was a boy I went to school at Warner College, a small private school in The Avenue, Highams Park. Towards the end of the war the Germans made a daylight raid on London and the principal said we were all to get under our desks. So all the children got under their desks – except me. I crawled out on my hands and knees, with all the shrapnel falling about, and went into the conservatory. I looked up and I could see about twenty planes dodging about in the sky. The Germans had been intercepted by our fighters, and even in those days of biplanes they were having a dog-fight. The guns were blazing away, and I was in this glasshouse watching it all. I got a terrible wigging from the principal over that!

At the end of that week, on 13 July, the logbook at Harrow Green Infants' School recorded that week's attendance as 82 per cent, the lowest since 15 June; several children were suffering from fright after the raid of 7 July and had been absent all week.

Night raids on London by aircraft began in September 1917 and from that point on the number of entries about air raids rapidly rises. On 5 September, Leyton High Road Mixed School and Cann Hall Road School both recorded low attendances owing to an air raid the previous night, and at Harrow Green Boys' School forty fewer pupils attended than on the previous day; attendance at Canterbury Road Girls' School and at Church Road School was very low in the morning. At Harrow Green Infants' School only 137 out of 220 pupils were present in the morning. On 6 September, after a raid the previous night, only 70 per cent of the pupils at Barking's North Street Girls' School attended. On 7 September, Cobbold Road School's logbook noted that attendance that week had been seriously affected by that Wednesday's air raid.

On 25 September, Leyton UDC reported that Boy Scouts were damaging the fixtures and fittings at the fire stations. The council resolved that the scouts be withdrawn and other arrangements would have to be made for warning of air raids. That same day, Kirkdale Road School noted very poor attendance in the morning on account of an air raid the previous night; the logbook also noted that many families were leaving the district. Lea Bridge Road School recorded only 165 children present out of 264, and the next day the school was dismissed at 8.55am following receipt of an air raid warning.

On 26 September, the Beckton School logbook recorded:

> Several parents came to the school at 10.30 this morning and asked for their children as a rumour of an impending air raid was afloat. The children asked for were allowed to go. With those remaining, air-raid drill was taken and school dismissed at the usual time.

Harrow Green Boys' School logbook entry for 27 September reported that air raids on moonlit evenings that week had caused several families to move away from the district for the time being and the school's attendance had suffered somewhat. The next day, Leyton High Road Mixed School logbook mentioned that owing to air raids on 24 and 25 September and the consequent effect on the children, the head teacher had instructed teachers to allow a reasonable relaxation in their work. On 28 September, the Canterbury Road Girls' School logbook recorded that week's attendance as 75 per cent, owing to air raids on the nights of 24 and 25 September.

Also in September, Leyton UDC considered a request from Mr B. Tuchschneider to be allowed to take cover in Mayville Road School during air raids. The council refused his request due to the need to have regard to the arrangements in place for the safety of scholars.

A raid on the night of 30 September/1 October caused very low attendance at Leyton High Road Mixed School and the children who did turn up were described as 'unfit for normal work'. At Kirkdale Road Schools fewer than 50 per cent of the children were present. At Downsell Road Girls' School 227 out of 470 attended and an air raid drill was practised upstairs. At Canterbury Road Girls' School only 50 per cent of pupils were present in the morning. At Harrow Green Infants' School only 118 out of 225 pupils attended. The same raid led to a low attendance at Beckton School, and the next day the logbook noted:

> October 2nd: This afternoon 30% only of the children came in answer to the bell. These were dismissed at 2.30. An air-raid was given during the dinner hour – hence the low attendance.

That same day, Canterbury Road Girls' School noted only 42 per cent attendance in the morning and at Harrow Green Infants' School only 118 were there; both schools closed in the afternoon following a dinner hour air raid warning. At Harrow Green the staff stayed at their posts until the 'All clear' came at 2.00pm. Church Road School received its air raid warning at 12.58pm and the school did not re-open in the afternoon. Leyton High Road Mixed School was closed for the afternoon at 1.00pm, and Kirkdale Road School at 1.15pm following receipt of an official warning of an impending air raid. Downsell Road Girls' School had only 207 children present, and the school closed in the afternoon due to an air raid warning during the dinner hour. Lea Bridge Road School received its air raid warning at 1.15pm and no children attended after dinner. Ruckholt Road Girls' School and Cann Hall Road School were also closed that afternoon.

Harrow Green Boys' School logbook recorded:

> In consequence of warning of an approaching attack by hostile air-craft at about 1.10pm I had the yards cleared, children in them sent home and gates locked. The 'All Clear' notice did not reach here until just before 2.00pm so school was not opened for the afternoon session.

On 5 October, Cann Hall Road School recorded another very low attendance owing to air raid effects. At the end of that week the weekly attendance at Leyton High Road Mixed School was down to 70 per cent, at Downsell Road Girls' School it was 59 per cent, and Church Road School recorded 77 per cent.

On 1 November, after an air raid the previous night when gunfire had been heard at Leyton for several hours, attendance at Ruckholt Road Girls' School was down to 37 per cent compared with 84 per cent the day before. At Canterbury Road Girls' School it was down to 40 per cent, and Kirkdale Road School saw only 35 per cent of pupils attend. At Harrow Green Infants' School attendance was down to 85 in the morning and 154 in the afternoon, out of 229 on the school roll. At Leyton High Road Mixed School attendance was also low and the children present were unable to do much work. Cann Hall Road School noted very low attendance and at Lea Bridge Road School only 106 children out of 253 were present in the morning. Harrow Green Boys' School recorded 'very small' attendance figures of 206 in the morning and 78 more in the afternoon. Following another raid that night, attendance at North Street Girls' School in Barking fell to 40 per cent on 2 November, and after three other raids in 1917/1918 attendances were never more than 69 per cent.

In that month, Leyton UDC received a letter from thirteen mothers of children at Murchison Road School asking if it could be arranged to close schools on the morning after a night air raid as their children were not then fit to receive instruction. The Air Raid Sub-Committee was not able to recommend approval.

At Creekmouth School an air raid on 5 December resulted in only forty-three of the seventy-five pupils being present. The next day, Leyton High Road Mixed School and Harrow Green Infants' School both recorded very low attendance in the morning owing to an air raid. At Kirkdale Road School attendance was 239 out of 366, and at Canterbury Road Girls' School it was down to 65 per cent. On 7 December, Lea Bridge Road School recorded a considerable fall in attendance caused by the Thursday morning air raid.

On 19 December, Lea Bridge Road School and Harrow Green Infants' School recorded poor attendance owing to the previous night's air raid. The Leyton High Road Mixed School logbook noted:

> Owing to Air raid last evening the attendance this day is very low and as a raid is anticipated this evening Standards I & II started their party at 3.00pm instead of 5 o'clock.

Reviewing the term as a whole, on 20 December, the head teacher at Harrow Green Boys' School noted that 'Air raids with their consequent loss of rest do not tend to keep up our high percentage of attendance as in the two previous years'.

In December, Leyton UDC reported that earlier in the year it had asked the Board of Education not to inspect schools in session after an air raid. It had now heard that the Board was unable to comply, but said that in such cases it would not inspect in the usual sense, but the inspector would give advice and assistance.

Also in the final month of the year, Leyton UDC's architect had been asked to consider what could be done to protect single-storey school buildings in air raids. In January 1918, he reported that:

> As regards the flying missiles from explosion in the air, these fall more or less vertically, they are rarely of sufficient size and weight to penetrate the roofs and ceilings, and where they strike the outer walls they usually strike a glancing blow, and do not as a rule penetrate the windows. Probably the greatest danger from these to anyone under cover is when they hit a skylight, and the danger in that case is mostly from falling glass. A certain amount of protection in these cases can be afforded by the use of blinds or flexible screens ...
>
> I consider that in the Schools the greatest danger is to be looked for from the flying splinters of glass and debris, and apart from sandbagging up the entire window openings which is not practicable, and still retain the Schools for Educational purposes, I believe the most effective protection is

afforded by stout canvas blinds or screens, secured at top and bottom, and not stretched tight, but left somewhat loose.

The architect reported that this could be done at a cost of £50–60 per school.

1918

As the war entered its last year, air raids or the fear of them were still disrupting school days. Leyton UDC decided it was now time to dismiss the schools at Canterbury Road, Church Road, Cobbold Road, Harrow Green, High Road and Lea Bridge Road immediately on receipt of an air raid warning. On 10 January 1918, Harrow Green Boys' School logbook recorded:

> An Air Raid Drill was again carried out this morning but Classes 2 and 3 did not join in as their quarters are handy and well known. The object was to acquaint Mrs Murphy and Miss Turner with the arrangements and positions for their classes as these ladies have not been present on previous drill occasions.

On 18 January, the Church Road School logbook noted that attendance for the week was down to 84 per cent on account of bad weather and air raids. On 29 January attendance at Harrow Green Infants' School fell to 98 in the morning after a very prolonged air raid the previous night. At Leyton High Road Mixed School attendance was very low; at Lea Bridge Road School only 103 children out of 266 (38 per cent) turned up in the morning; at Kirkdale Road School there were 149 attending. At Downsell Road Girls' School the morning attendance was also low – 206 out of 450, which was 160 fewer than the same day the previous year. At Canterbury Road Girls' School a very low attendance of 42 per cent was recorded in the morning. The same raid brought attendance at Beckton School down to 55 per cent. Not only were pupils having trouble getting to school, so were the staff, as Beckton School's logbook for the next day, 30 January, showed when the head teachers and five assistants were late that morning owing to trams being delayed. An air raid the previous night also meant that attendance there was low in the morning. Leyton High Road Mixed School also had a very low attendance that day, and Lea Bridge Road School had only 112 (42 per cent) attending. Harrow Green Infants' School reported only 102 children attending in the morning and Harrow Green Boys' School also reported adversely affected attendance; Downsell Road Girls' School had only 200 present in the morning.

The following month, on 1 February, Cann Hall Road School's logbook recorded very low attendance owing to air raids and bad weather. On 15 February, Leyton UDC reported that, during the last air raid, Cann Hall Road

School was damaged by an unexploded AA shell (the school logbook makes no mention of this); and at Goodhall Road School panes of glass had been cracked by the concussion of AA gunfire. On 18 February, Lea Bridge Road School had only 147 children present (out of 276 on the school roll) due to an air raid the previous night; Harrow Green Infants' School had 108 children there in the morning. Leyton High Road Mixed School's logbook also recorded another low attendance, and Ruckholt Road School logbook also recorded that attendance was not good owing to an air raid. At Cann Hall Road School the logbook noted very low attendance again owing to air raids of the previous two nights. That same day, all schools in Leyton received notice from the Education Committee instructing that, following a night air raid the official opening time should be changed to 9.45am (i.e. three-quarters of an hour later than normal); registers were to be marked and closed straightaway.

There was an air raid that same night, and only 281 children were present at Kirkdale Road School on 19 February. At Harrow Green Infants' School 152 turned up and, on 22 February, the logbook reported that owing to sickness and air raids the attendance that week had been only 63 per cent. In that same month, Leyton's education committee published figures showing that following two air raid alerts only 9,000 of the borough's 20,000 pupils attended school the next day.

On 6 March, Wanstead Flats were once more the site of an aircraft landing and the head teacher at Harrow Green Boys' School again sent a group of boys there to see it that afternoon (instead of going on their usual nature ramble).

Two days later Beckton School's logbook noted:

March 8th: School opened at 9.30 this morning after last night's air raid in accordance with the council's instructions. Attendance 76%.

The entry in the logbook for Kirkdale Road School on St George's Day noted:

23 April 1918. Head Mistress attended Meeting at Town Hall – called by Mr Vincent to discuss cancellation of marks after an air raid, if numbers were substantially reduced – If only 75% of the children were in attendance after a Raid, it was decided to cancel attendances.

On 3 May, Kirkdale Road School practised its air raid drill, and at the end of the month the logbook recorded:

30 May 1918. The girls from the High School were dismissed at 10.30am, & told that the first warning of an Air Raid had been given. The

consequence was that several parents came to inquire about their children, and nine (9) were withdrawn before having received two hours secular instruction. Consequently their marks were cancelled, & attendance for this day = 313.5, the average for the first three days being 330.

On 11 November, the head teacher at Harrow Green Boys' School recorded in the logbook:

At 11.00am this morning the maroons, blank firing from the Flats Anti-Air-Craft guns and hooting of sirens gave warning of the signing of the Armi-stice by the German plenipotentiaries. At 11.40 the boys were assembled in the playground, I addressed a few sentences to them and they sang a verse of the National Anthem, after which they were dismissed for the morning. Our attendance this morning was much improved, but this afternoon many of the boys were allowed by their parents to take a holiday.

Chapter 9

'The bomber will always get through'

Robert Graves' autobiography, *Goodbye to All That,* mentions the effect of the Zeppelin raids on England. Graves was in London on leave in the summer of 1915:

> The Zeppelin scare had just begun. Some friends of the family came in one night, and began telling me of the Zeppelin air-raids, of bombs dropped only three streets off.
>
> 'Well, do you know,' I said, 'the other day I was asleep in a house and in the early morning a bomb dropped next door and killed three soldiers who were billeted there, a woman, and a child.'
>
> 'Good gracious,' they cried, 'what did you do then?'
>
> 'It was at a place called Beuvry, about four miles behind the trenches,' I explained, 'and I was tired out, so I went to sleep again.' 'Oh,' they said, 'but that happened in France!' and the look of interest faded from their faces as though I had taken them in with a stupid catch. 'Yes,' I agreed, 'and it was only an aeroplane that dropped the bomb'.

In these few sentences, Graves covers the fear in Britain of the Zeppelin, the frightfulness of civilians being attacked, and the gulf in experiences and attitudes between soldiers and civilians. On the ground, the effects of the aerial bombing were minimal compared to the carnage experienced on the Western Front, but unlike the fields of northern France and Flanders, this was the heart of the British Empire. Britons had not experienced great conflicts with foreigners involving civilians or fought in populated areas and now, for the first time since the Dutch naval raids of 1667, London had been subject to bombardment. Furthermore, not only was it the first time in more than 150 years that Britain had experienced a major conflict at home (the last being the Jacobite rebellions in 1715 and 1745), but it was also the first time that British civilians were targeted by their enemy in their own homes. As *The Times* wrote, this brought about:

> ... the realisation that they were no longer immune from war ... they too, like their soldiers, were in the firing line ... while armed airships might be the proper means of attacking armies and navies, it was an entirely new and

barbarous practice to use them as weapons of aggression against defence-less civilians.

For two years, in 1915 and 1916, the Zeppelin was the premier long-range assault aircraft. It was a formidable weapon that briefly terrified some of the population of south-west Essex. By bringing civilians into a war, the German High Command believed that air raids would cause such terror that Britons would demand their government make peace on German terms. *The Times* wrote, 'It takes little to throw civilians into a panic in peace; it was natural, therefore, to expect that bomb dropping would throw them into a panic in war'. But it is equally certain that the air raid campaign failed to spread the panic that the German government hoped it would.

Zeppelins came to symbolize German technology and prowess in the early years of the war, before there was an adequate response to combat the raids and the first of the airships was shot down. But, in purely military terms, Zeppelins were a costly experiment, incapable of targeting positions accurately. Doubtless the airships' objectives had been London, not Leyton or Ilford or the nearby Essex countryside. The Germans might have aimed for factories, docks and transport arteries, but any damage caused was more by luck than judgement. Instead, bombs were dropped almost at random, as one former Zeppelin crew member later acknowledged:

> So-called targets were no targets. They thought they were over, say, the estuary of the Thames, and in reality they were near Portsmouth. It is rubbish to say that this was the so-and-so building and we dropped our bombs over that building. You were happy enough if you found London, and you were even happier if you could drop your bombs and go home as soon as possible.

Wishful thinking and consistent exaggeration in the German reporting of bombing successes, and the heavy censorship of British newspapers that prevented the Germans from learning the true nature of the damage inflicted by their bombs, meant that Germany remained convinced that the Zeppelin was helping it win the war. In truth, the Zeppelins were facing increasing losses for diminishing returns and they must be considered a failure as a weapon of war. In fifty-four raids on Britain, Zeppelins dropped an estimated 196 tons of bombs (compared with 13,000 tons dropped on London alone by the Luftwaffe in the 1940–41 Blitz), injuring 1,358 people, and killing 577 (of the nearly 10 million killed in the war). Only nine Zeppelin raids actually reached the capital, killing 181 people and injuring 504 people, with German losses in those nine being six Zeppelins and about 130 personnel.

For all the drama of the raids, Zeppelins did little to influence the outcome of the war and they did not weaken the resolve of the British people to fight. In fact, they probably hardened their resolve, as the raids were used to vilify the Germans as 'murderers', 'Huns', 'baby killers' and 'sky pirates', and Zeppelins were depicted on recruiting posters to spur men to fight. With hindsight, the 'First Blitz' was neither as potent nor as destructive as contemporary accounts on both sides proclaimed – the Zeppelin raiders inflicted only £1,527,585 of damage on the United Kingdom – about the cost of ten airships; over the same period, rats destroyed crops and other material worth nearly fifty times as much. Perhaps the Zeppelins' main achievement was in tying down British soldiers and diverting guns and aircraft from the Western Front. In January 1917, 17,341 officers and men and 110 aircraft were retained in Britain exclusively for defence against the Zeppelins.

Gothas and Giants proved to be weapons of greater precision than the Zeppelins, and they mostly passed over south-west Essex before dropping the bulk of their bombs. They carried out twenty-seven raids on Britain, dropping 74 tons of bombs which killed 835 people and injured 1,973; damage caused was estimated at £1,418,274. Of these raids, seventeen were on London, two in the daytime and fifteen at night, where they inflicted more casualties than the Zeppelins – 486 people were killed and 1,432 injured. But these raids also failed to achieve their purpose of crushing British morale on the home front. Although the activities of these aircraft led to the formation of LADA and the RAF, ultimately the end of major aeroplane raids owed more to the needs of the German army in France than anything else.

Conversely, despite the numerous sorties made by German airships and aircraft across the English coast on raids, only forty-five were destroyed (including thirteen by AA guns, and twenty by fighters). So it is easy to see how, in the long run, the most enduring consequence of the raids was probably a psychological one. 'The scars of World War I air raids were never healed in the British mind', wrote Hanson Baldwin, a military analyst for *The New York Times*, half a century later; 'People's thoughts instinctively fly upwards', wrote historian Liddell Hart. The air raids had made an indelible impression in the collective mind, according to Hart: 'The tendency, whenever they think of war, is for the thought to be associated with the idea of being bombed from the air'. Additionally, the immunity of the Giants to the British air defences did cause much concern to the authorities, and ultimately spawned the slogan 'The bomber will always get through', which remained firmly fixed in the mind of some British military men and politicians for many years after the war.

The defence of London

Flight, 22 October 1915:

MPs in Parliament asked a series of questions relating to October's raid and London's defences. Reflecting the thoughts of many London civilians, questions included: 'Have the military authorities permission to fire at hostile aircraft? Does the Admiralty consider that three aeroplanes are an adequate defence against as many, or more, Zeppelins? Is the Home Secretary aware that during the last raid many motorcars with powerful lamps were observed in the main streets on the night of attack?' Answered mostly by Prime Minister Stanley Baldwin and Home Secretary Sir John Simon, their overall response was that all possible strictness would continue to be enforced and that both gun crews and searchlight crews would continue working how they had. Stating that no headlights were permitted, save in cases of certain military or naval cars on urgent duty, Simon concluded that the public's observance of the raids regulations was of great importance. Balfour also continued that, '... under no circumstances will the authorities consider that an adequate defence against night attack by Zeppelins could be provided by aeroplanes'. Trying to assure the public by explaining that officers were on training courses at Chatham Gunnery School, the response was sarcastic: 'When is it considered probable that these gunners will be able to attack the Zeppelins?'

Flight, 29 October 1915:

The question of the defence of London was raised in the House of Lords on 21 October 1915 when Lord Strachie addressed the following questions to the Civil Lord of the Admiralty:

1. Whether the anti-aircraft guns were of any more effect on October 13th than they were during the previous Zeppelin raid on London?
2. Whether the great reduction of the lighting of London was of any real value during the last raid in comparison with the previous one?
3. Whether any steps have been taken to give London as far as possible the same protection from aircraft which Paris enjoys and if not, why not?

4. Whether the anti-aircraft guns here were not used effectively against the Zeppelins as they might have been for fear of doing damage to persons or buildings?

He also said that he was informed that there was no landing place for aeroplanes nearer to London than Hendon; surely Hyde Park was large enough for that purpose, and if the trees were said to be an obstacle, some of them could easily be removed. The Earl of Portsmouth urged that when a raid was anticipated an official warning to the public should be issued by the Admiralty. He also asked for an assurance that the valuable treasures housed in public buildings in London would be removed to a place of safety.

Lord Sydenham said the great difficulties of obtaining protection against aircraft bombs had not been appreciated. The Zeppelin must first be found by the searchlights, the range of which was often considerably less than that of the guns, and was influenced by the atmospheric conditions. The gunner must know the range within very narrow limits of accuracy, and the time fuse of the shell must be set very accurately in order that the shell should burst at a proper distance from the object. The sighting of guns, too, was calculated upon terrestrial targets, and, therefore, it was wrong when one began to shoot in the air.

Unless all these and other conditions were remembered, it would be seen that to put untrained and unpractised men in charge of guns like those was very much like expecting a man who has never fired a gun before to bring down driven grouse. His own impression from watching the shooting last week was that there was a good deal of random shooting, some of the shells bursting nowhere near the Zeppelin. If the men using the guns had come from the trenches, where they had been able to get actual practice, very different results might have been obtained.

The danger to our own population from using anti-aircraft guns was very small provided a time-fuse was used. The fragments of the burst shell were very small, and they would fall at low velocities, so that except for the small risk of hitting an individual in the street there was nothing to fear. Buildings would be entirely immune.

The question of the illumination of London was a very difficult one. On clear nights it was impossible to prevent a Zeppelin crew knowing they were over a city of the size of London, but they must be prevented from accurately locating themselves so as to be able to select a target. If the illumination was kept so low as to prevent the identification of special objects, nothing more would be gained by decreasing it. The lower the illumination the more prominent became our searchlights, which helped to guide the Zeppelins, and the more easy it would be for the crew to see signals which any aliens in our midst might be flashing.

He thought we had gone a little further than was necessary in the low illumination of the town. When the fogs come traffic in the streets will be extremely difficult and dangerous, though, if the fogs spread far into the country around London, then a Zeppelin, being entirely navigated by dead reckoning, would be entirely baffled.

The suggestion that aeroplanes should cruise about London when Zeppelins were expected was useless. In the only two cases in which Zeppelins had been brought down by aeroplanes bombs were used. Lieutenant Warneford[1] had to drop five or six bombs before he effected his object, and if a contest of that kind went on over London our own bombs would be added to the danger of the Zeppelin bombs. We had already lost some lives and damaged a great many aeroplanes by sending them up on wild-goose chases in the dark.

The real chance of the aeroplane is to find the Zeppelin when it strikes the coast before the light fails or when it passes some point on its course which it must pass before dark comes.

The conditions in Paris were very different from those in London. Paris was surrounded by a chain of forts, heavily armed, and no doubt provided with a large number of anti-aircraft guns. One legitimate cause of complaint, he thought, was the long delay that occurred before there was anything like a proper organisation for defence against air raids. It was only lately the whole question was taken in hand, and he was not sure even now that there was not divided responsibility.

He was strongly opposed to reprisals, but he believed that with proper organisation and proper handling of the guns by men who know how to use them we could soon assure ourselves that these raids will never be attempted again.

The Duke of Devonshire (Civil Lord of the Admiralty) replied that the speech of Lord Sydenham had, to a large extent, answered the question on the paper.

He had heard the question of giving warning of the approach of Zeppelins discussed, but he thought the probable effect of such a course would be to bring a larger number of people on to the street than now. It was anticipated that any such warning would probably lead to the emptying of theatres and the collection of large crowds.

With regard to the question on the paper he had to say:

1. There is no evidence in the possession of the Admiralty to show that any Zeppelin was brought down by gun-fire in either of the two raids on London.
2. This clearly must be a matter more or less of speculation, but the information of the departments concerned is that the reduction of the lighting in London was of value.
3. The cases of Paris and London are not exactly on all fours. We are thoroughly cognisant of what is done in Paris, and we are making every effort, with the means at our disposal, for the protection of London.
4. I am in a position to state that there is no foundation for the suggestion contained therein.

He could give the assurance that the Admiralty would not rest content until every step had been taken to render the protection of the Metropolis as efficient as they possibly could. The problem was by no means simple. It required great consideration. They had availed themselves of the best information they had got. No effort had been spared to get the best material, and he hoped they would be in a position to make the defence of London satisfactory.

The matter was raised in the House of Commons on 21 October, when, in reply to questions by Mr Annan Bryce, Mr Balfour (First Lord of the Admiralty) said the degree to which it is desirable to use aeroplanes for night defence against Zeppelins is a difficult matter, and cannot properly be dealt with in answer to a question, but under no circumstances do the authorities consider that adequate defence against night attacks by Zeppelins can be provided by aeroplanes. As regards the action of aeroplanes on the 13th inst., the weather conditions in London rendered it impossible for any large number to go up.

In reply to further questions as to the anti-aircraft corps, Mr Balfour said there had been no change in the personnel. The guns' crews work for 24 hours every other day, and are paid 4s 2d a day, finding their own food and lodgings. Searchlight crews work from dark to daylight every other night. Two crews divide the night, and they are paid 2s 1d per day, finding their own food and lodgings. The officers go through a short course at a gunnery school, and the men are being sent to the Chatham gunnery school. Arrangements are also being made for men to be sent for training to the British Army in France. Experienced naval ratings are attached to the guns and searchlights.

Questioned by Mr Anderson as to the possibility of giving warnings of Zeppelin raids, Sir John Simon, the Home Secretary, said: The question whether public warning should be issued by the authorities in advance of the arrival of the Zeppelins in the London area was a question which has been more than once most carefully considered by the authorities responsible. Indeed, the last occasion when it was minutely examined was so lately as that morning, when he had the advantage of hearing in detail the views of the department at the Admiralty which answered for the gun defence of London. There was really no confusion between the responsibilities of one department or another. The defence of London from Zeppelin attack was in charge of the Admiralty. The way in which the Home Office came into the matter was this – that as a consequence of such attacks there might very well be special and most urgent action to be taken by the police, and there was also the question of the regulation of lights. These were necessarily police matters, and it was those matters of a non-military character which the Home Office endeavour to administer, but always subject to the advice of the anti-aircraft department of the Admiralty. How did this matter of warning the public as to the approach of Zeppelins stand? He would say at once that his anxiety in it was not that London would become panic stricken. Nothing was more remarkable, nothing was more worthy of praise than the consistent coolness with which the population of the Metropolis had taken the visits of these aerial strangers when they happened to drop in. That was not really the difficulty.

The difficulty was a twofold one, and he would like to put it quite plainly to the House. First of all, it must not be supposed that when the authorities first had reason to think that there might be a Zeppelin attack on a given night they were in a position to assert that there was going to be a Zeppelin raid in the London area. The first news, of course, which the authorities were able to collect, was news of the passage of these Zeppelins, it may be across the North Sea, or across what some people used to call the German Ocean. It had constantly happened that Zeppelins had been out for a nocturnal airing, and had never got inland at all, and it had constantly happened that, although they did touch some portion of the coast of this land, they had wandered about in a perfectly aimless way and dropped destructive bombs on various agricultural areas, or sometimes, whether by accident or design, on perfectly innocent people in various provincial towns and villages. The House would see, therefore, that when one spoke of the authorities knowing there was going to be a Zeppelin attack, the first thing that was known was nothing more than that there were some of these visitors on the way; but whether they would ever get here, or whether, if they did get to England, they would succeed in making their way to this particular area of London, was a thing no one could possibly prophesy with confidence. Therefore, if you were going to give warnings to the public, you must face this, that nine times out of ten – choosing a round figure – he did not know whether he should express it rightly when he said the public would be disappointed. That was the first difficulty, and it was its connection with that fact, of course, that arrangements were made to protect, not only London, but other parts of the country, as rapidly as the information at the command of the authorities permitted. He did not think this was a matter on which public interest required that one should preserve complete silence, and he was most anxious that the public should understand how very thoroughly and systematically this problem was being studied and attempts at a satisfactory solution were being made. It was a matter of the greatest importance that we should not ourselves, by foolish gossip, and indiscreet statements, assist these invaders in the slightest degree to identify the part to which they had come.

But there was not the slightest reason why the public should not understand the sort of way in which this invasion was sought to be dealt with. As soon as it was known that there might be such an attempt, and long before it was known with any certainty that London was going to be the objective, of course steps were taken in order that all possible observation should be kept by those whose duty it is to keep that observation on the different areas of the coast. If they reached the coast steps were at once taken so as to control the railway traffic in the area affected in order to reduce to a minimum the risk of trains acting as guides to this place or that. That did not mean, of course, that at a moment and in a flash all the trains coming to and from London were stopped, but it meant that the traffic was controlled. The most careful arrangements were made in advance to secure that this was effectively done. Arrangements were made in advance to do this in such areas as were material to the purpose for checkmating the invader. It might be that at a later stage some better and more certain judgment could be formed as to whether the London area was likely to be reached. That sometimes happens, and sometimes it does not. Of course there were some things which obviously ought to be done and are done as a precaution forthwith. At a suitable moment the special constables were warned. The system by which is secured the service of doctors in London at different suitable points was also put in motion. You could not tell what portion of the London area was likely to be attacked, for the best of all reasons, that the Zeppelin itself had not the remotest idea, and there were strong reasons for believing that it had not only no idea in advance but a very hazy idea after the event. Consequently you had to arrange in the London area that a series of precautions of that sort were quietly taken.

But it had been thought, after the most careful consideration, that it was better not to make a preliminary announcement at large to the public, for instance, by the ringing of church bells or the sounding of a hooter. A better guide could not be imagined for a Zeppelin wandering about the flats in Essex or about Epping Forest than suddenly hearing the unanimous chorus of all the church bells and steam whistles of the Metropolis. That was the first difficulty they had endeavoured to face, and that was the conclusion to which they had come. But there was a second point. He had said that it was not panic which disturbed them. After all, if you do tell the men and the women and children of the Metropolis that it may be that in the course of an hour or two hours' time they would be honoured with a visit from a Zeppelin, what is it exactly which the men, women, and children are expected to do? Of course, if those who conduct these invasions were careful to do no damage to civilian life, if they really were prepared and were able to take precautions not to strike private property, it would be a very reasonable thing to secure that everybody went home. But their own experience went to show that the Zeppelin did not pay the slightest attention to things of that sort. Supposing you tell the population of London that there might be a Zeppelin coming, he could not help suspecting that what most of them would do would be to go out into the streets and have a look at it, and experience had really confirmed that. It was an instance of the coolness and courage and of the contempt with which the Londoner regarded these dastardly outrages. But that did not assist to protect the lives of Londoners. He asked the other day that the papers should be analysed in order that he might know in regard to the different casualties in the London area whether they had occurred in the open air or in the houses, and the House might be interested to know that a very substantial proportion of the casualties, both fatal and otherwise, had occurred in the streets, and they would observe that all these attacks occurred at night and at a time when the larger part of the population would naturally be under cover. That went to show that the probable consequence of telling everybody that there might be a Zeppelin to-night would not reduce the number of people suffering injury.

He would say frankly that there had been one or two cases in which he had been much puzzled as to what would be the better course to take. It might happen before they had done with these invaders that a theatre got struck, and the people assembled there for perfectly peaceful and innocent enjoyment might suddenly find a bomb dropped among them. If unfortunately that did happen, it might do damage to a number of innocent people, and, great as the coolness of the Londoner is, that might create some sort of local panic. He thought at one time that it might be desirable that they should arrange with the theatres that in certain events they should be warned of this possibility. But he asked the House to consider the arguments the other way. In the first place, it was questionable what the effect would be on a theatre audience. He heard of a case at a cinema where there was some such intimation given, and he believed the proceedings were stopped, and afterwards one or two persons present bitterly complained that, having paid their money, they wanted their money's worth. A great many more people thought the alternative attraction was too good to be missed, and promptly went into the streets. Perhaps these people might be urged to go home, but a large number of them go home by train. If there was any immediate risk of a Zeppelin attack on the London area the trains are stopped, and the result would be that if you were able to warn the peaceful population, a large proportion of them would assemble at the termini of the railway stations. The trains could not run out, and the consequence would be that you would have a great collection of people under another roof which, if the enemy paid any regard to ordinary military considerations, would be a more suitable object for his attention than a theatre or a music hall. There were all sorts of other assemblies. He was glad of the opportunity of telling hon. members publicly that the view which was presented by the Admiralty and which they had felt it right to adopt, always subject of course to consideration in the light of further and greater experience, was that, on the whole, it was better not to attempt to warn people of the suggested approach of the Zeppelins. The people must therefore understand that if they felt, as some of them very naturally might do, that this left them in more than one sense in the dark, they must really take their own risk if they choose to go to places where a number of people are assembled together at night, and they would be able to estimate the extent of that risk, and he had no doubt that they would act in the matter reasonably and fairly. This was a matter in which the man in the street was very naturally and closely concerned. He (Sir J. Simon) was anxious to show to the House that it had not been some deliberate policy of the Government to conceal from the people of England the truth. It was a deliberate policy adopted as a practical decision after most carefully weighing the pros and cons of the matter.

He might say in conclusion that he believed there were some areas and towns in England where the alternative policy had been tried. He had not had any representations from members representing those areas as to how it was worked, but in one such area he had reason to know, the number of false alarms that had been given had produced a very great deal of consternation and disappointment, and the total result, to say the least of it, was extremely doubtful from the point of view of promoting public security and safety.

The truth was that in this and other matters, since we were at war and since our enemy chose to adopt these devices, we had to show him that it was not an idle boast, but a genuine fact, that English men and women, Londoners no less than others, were prepared to face even the tragic incidents of war with courage, calmness, and resolution. Londoners and others might be perfectly satisfied that everything that could be done would be done in order to minimise any risk to which they may be put. Nobody could feel more keenly than the Government did the seriousness of the individual tragedies which had been created by these horrible attacks, but just as it was the determination of our people to carry this war to a victorious conclusion, so this was, after all, an incident, though a very grave incident, which we at home had got to bear, and which was small in comparison with the daily and nightly risks run by our heroes on the field of battle.

Replying to Sir H. Dalziel and others on Tuesday, Mr Balfour said the Admiralty are responsible for the defence against aircraft of both London and most parts of the country. There are however, certain places – for example, fortified ports – for the defence of which responsibility rests with the Army. He need hardly say that this division of responsibility did not imply that the Navy and Army do not endeavour by wholehearted co-operation each to assist the other in their respective tasks.

The Army co-operates so far as its means permit, but the primary responsibility for London, under an arrangement made last year rests with the Admiralty.

No attempt has been made to increase the number of aeroplanes in consequence of the last raid, but there has been a steady and rapid increase in the number of aeroplanes, and that increase is going on quite irrespective of the defence of London or of any other part of the United Kingdom. It is part of the general policy of the Government.

The Admiralty are quite ready to state, so far as the public interest permits, what had occurred on the day of the raid but all subsequent statements, he thought, should be made by some other office directly connected with facts. For instance, the public were naturally anxious to know the number of casualties. The Admiralty have no information as to that except what they get from the Home Office. It would be better for the Home Office to supply that information direct.

Appendix B

The German view

This account is of a raid on London on the night of 8/9 September 1915. Mathy also commanded L31 when it bombed Leyton and Leytonstone later that month on 23/24 September. He was killed in the destruction of L31 at Potters Bar on 1/2 October 1916 (a year to the day after the date of publication of the article in *Flight* magazine).

Flight, 1 October 1915:

THE ZEPPELIN CAPTAIN'S STORY

The following narrative has been published in the *New York World*, and is the version given by Commander Mathy, who was in charge of the airship which recently visited London and scattered promiscuous murder around amongst women, children and non-combatants, to Mr Karl von Wiegand, the *World*'s correspondent in Germany. We reprint the story, as a picturesque account of what the narrator thinks (or the contrary) occurred. As a journalistic effort it has considerable merit. As a recital of facts anything more ludicrous can hardly be imagined. We are prepared to accept the details of what happened in the Zeppelin. If they are not facts, at least they are painted with the brush of a consummate artist; but if they are as accurate as the rest of the story, well after reading the note of the Home Office which prefaces Commander Mathy's little effort, let the Zeppelin pilot speak for himself and be judged by facts as we know them.

The following is passed by the Home Office for publication, with the comment that it contains numerous statements which are quite untrue, and one (to the effect that an anti-aircraft gun has been placed under cover of St Paul's) which can only he characterised as a falsehood apparently invented to excuse what German aircraft are attempting to do.

'London is a vast military centre and military-defended city in every sense of the laws of war, written or unwritten, as applicable to aerial warfare. Therefore property, from point of aerial attack, so far concerns everything usable for military purposes, such as big railway stations, banks, docks, shipyards, and industrial establishments. If anyone believes London is not 'defended', and pretty well defended at that, he should have stood by my side in the front gondola of my Zeppelin in my last attack on London a few nights ago, and seen the red, angry flashes of scores of cannon belching shrapnel at my craft'. So spoke Lieut-Commander Mathy, of the Zeppelin aerial cruiser squadron of the German Navy.

'The day of battles in the air and attacks from the air, of which romance writers have long dreamed prophetic, though, perhaps, somewhat fantastic dreams, has come to stay. Only the future can tell how much of the futuristic, impressionistic visions in the air pictured by fictionists in their romances on the subject may come true. Years ago anyone who would have believed Jules Verne's dreams would become more or less a reality would have been regarded as being not entirely normal. Two years' training and service in the big Zeppelin cruisers of Germany's airship fleet attached to our Navy convinces me we are only at the dawn of day of war in the air and from the air, and only at the beginning of a great era of development of aerial crafts which will have great bearing on future Wars'.

To-day I was so fortunate as to have an opportunity to talk with the man in command of the latest aerial attack on London. Mathy is commander of the L , one of Count Zeppelin's latest, biggest, and fastest cruisers of Germany's aerial fleet, the value of which as scouting craft for the navy has been much underestimated abroad, and as fighting craft have, as Count Zeppelin told me in February, by no means reached their final development. That, despite their size, they are not so easily hit and brought down as has been the general impression is evident from the fact that the Germans lost no Zeppelins in any of the numerous attacks on England. Attacking under the cover of night, coming and going with great speed, and disappearing within a few minutes, they are like a vision in the night. The aeroplanes of England's flying corps have so far proved no defence against the Zeppelin raids.

Mathy is a man of perhaps thirty-four years, with closely-cropped hair, which gives him the appearance of an entirely bald, smooth-faced figure, slender and supple as a young woman. He was formerly commander of a destroyer in the torpedo flotilla. Like officers of German submarines I have met, he made the impression of being all nerves, and those nerves of steel. Mathy and his Zeppelin have participated in every attack made on England from the air. His last, which was on the downtown City of London, was his 'century Zeppelin run', or hundredth voyage in the air, counting his training and trial trips, he told me.

'What I call luck has played a big part with me', he declared. And Mathy has been lucky. Despite something which I cannot mention, but which every superstitious believer in omens and signs would regard as a very magnet of disaster and ill-luck, Mathy has been lucky. The day before its destruction he was on a Zeppelin which I saw burned and destroyed in the air above Johannisthal[1] two years ago, and only missed that trip by some manie. He was on a navy Zeppelin the day before the craft was wrecked in a storm on the North Sea off Denmark two years ago, and in some way missed the voyage on the fatal day. As nothing in this war has appealed more to the popular imagination or awakened greater interest than the war under sea and in the air, I asked Mathy to tell me about his last attack on London. I will go so far as I can without disclosing what might touch upon military secrets, and that is pretty much everything about a Zeppelin. Even the secrets of Germany's famous submarines are not guarded as closely or jealously as the Zeppelins. I have been aboard one of the largest U boats and looked through the periscopes, went through from stem to stern, but have never been able to get within gunshot of one of the Zeppelin harbours. Even the officers and crew of war Zeppelins have been carefully kept away from correspondents, or, rather, the correspondents away from them. I promised Mathy I wouldn't ask him any questions that would get him into trouble with the Admiralty.

'It was my hundredth Zeppelin cruise, counting my training trips, and I was much interested in it because of that, and wondered whether I would safely round out my century', said the commander of the L . 'I had taken my Zeppelin in safety to England and back several times, and learned something of value each trip applicable to the next time. The first time I took my Zeppelin to England it was something akin to discovering a new country, and my impressions were much more vivid than now. It and some of the following were more or less experimental. We had much to learn, despite all our practice and training. It was a new sort of warfare, in which we had, more or less, to feel our way and study aerial strategy, aerial tactics, and to learn to locate in darkness the military points and objects we desired to attack'.

'We had to study the aerial currents above the North Sea and England. What we have done to England so far is by no means all that we can do now that we have learned many things we did not know and are necessary to know. The Zeppelins had to be their own scouts and information gatherers. Now, for the first time, my instructions were to attack certain points in the downtown City of London, such as railway stations, bridges, industrial establishments. Strict orders to do everything possible to avoid hitting St Paul's and other churches, museums, Buckingham Palace, Westminster Abbey, Parliament, and, of course, residential districts'.

'I want to say there's not an officer or man in the aerial fleet who doesn't feel it as deeply when he learns that women and children and other non-combatants are killed, as does a gunner or commander of big guns when he hears his shell didn't strike exactly where he wanted it to, and resulted in the death and injury of non-combatants. In fact, I would much rather stand on the bridge of a torpedo-boat, fighting ship against ship, than attack a city from the air, although not because the danger to me is much greater in the latter'.

'Let me say that a Zeppelin voyage to England and back depends largely on the weather and wind conditions. If very favourable it can be made in less time with our new fast cruisers. But you want to know about my last attack on London. The weather stations and meteorological balloons attached to the aerial service reported favourable conditions. The colder the weather the more we can carry. The temperature was quite cool when we started, with full magazine bombs which constitute Zeppelin ammunition, and not much unlike shells fired from a ship or siege artillery, which, after all, come through the air, too'.

'Soon we were out over the North Sea and moving upon England through the air at a lively speed with a favourable wind. Back of us were the receding shores of Germany, below us the white-capped billows of the North Sea like a watery desert in motion stretching out as far as we can see, without a sign of life except a single fishing craft'.

'What was the principal emotion or impression up there on the bridge of your Zeppelin?' I asked the man who makes war from the air.

'My chief impression was speed, and we get very cold. Our new Zeppelins are very much faster than a ship, and I always think of the great difference in wind pressure as compared when I stood on the bridge of my ship. Formerly when commanders' gondolas on older Zeppelins were entirely open this was even more marked. Our new ones have somewhat of a protection in the form of a windbreak. But it's intensely cold 3,000 to 5,000 or more feet in the air, moving at the speed. There is no chance to move about much, of course; no way of warming pilots of aeroplanes, and wearing thick felt boots. Despite that we get cold, very cold, especially on the last trip. We ate before we started, then occasionally took a pull at a Thermos bottle of hot coffee or tea'.

'Nothing stronger, commander?' I broke in.

'No, absolutely nothing stronger. Zeppelins have neither bar, kitchen nor dining-room. Zeppelins are teetotalers. We have got to have clear heads up there, and cool steady nerves, the nerves which spirits don't necessarily furnish. And we can't while away our time between firing – for we call it firing, too – and dodging shrapnel by smoking. A Zeppelin is the strictest Sunday School institution; there is no drink nor smoke. Each man's pockets are his pantry, for he carries a snack. I take a bottle of cognac, along with some first aid material, in case someone gets hit'.

'No doctor?'

'No, we carry no doctor. If a shrapnel ball hits any of us we bandage the wounded man as best we can, and give him a drink of cognac, and he has to wait until we get back. If we were brought down I guess there would be doctors there, if we needed any, which would be unlikely. But to return to my narrative'.

In short, terse, staccato-like sentences Mathy told the story of the attack. 'As the sun sank in the west we were still a considerable distance out over the North Sea. Below us it was rapidly getting dark, but was still light up where we were. On one side or the other was a Zeppelin, in grey war paint, like that of my craft, visible in the waning light against the clear sky, gliding majestically through the air. A low, mist-like fog hung over the spot in the distance where England was. Stars came out and it grew colder. We took another pull at our Thermos bottles and ate something. As we neared the coast I set the elevating planes to go still higher in order that our motors might not disclose our presence too soon'.

'I cannot tell you exactly the time or place we crossed the coast-line, as that might be an advantage to the enemy. Men went to the guns which fight off airmen should we be attacked, and the others were each at his post. My lieutenant took his place at the 'firing apparatus', which releases bombs and controls the speed or rapidity with which they are dropped according to my orders from the bridge on the front gondola. It is a cold, clear, star-lit night, with no moon – one of those nights when distances and objects in looking toward the sky are illusive, and it is difficult to get the range on rapidly-moving objects, while our instruments tell us exactly how high we are'.

'The mist disappeared, and in the distance we can see the Thames river, which points the way to London. It is an indestructible guide-post, and a sure road to the great city. The English can darken London as much as they like, they can never eradicate or cover up the Thames. It is our great orientation point from which we can always get our bearings and pick up any point in London we desire. That doesn't mean that we always come up along the Thames, by any means. London is darkened, but was so sufficiently lighted that on this night I saw a reflected glow in the sky sixty kilometres away shortly before ten o'clock. I headed straight for the glow in the sky, and then a point on the Thames, to get my bearings for my objective attacks'.

'Soon the city was outlined, still and silent, below in the distance. There were dark spots which stood out from the blur of lights in the well-lit portions. The residential sections were not much darkened. It was the dark spots I was after, and I bore down upon them, as they marked the downtown portion of the city. A large city seen at night from a great height is a fairy-like picture. We were too high to see human beings in the streets below. There was no sign of life, except in the distance moving lights, which were probably railroad trains. All seems still and quiet; no noise ascends from below that penetrates the sputtering motors and whirring propellers. As if in the twinkling of an eye all this changes. There is a sudden flash, and a narrow band of brilliant light reaches out from below, and begins to feel around the sky, a second, a third, a fourth, a fifth, until soon there are more than a score of criss-crossing ribbons. As viewed from a Zeppelin, it looks as if the city had suddenly come to life, waving its arms around the sky, and sending out feelers for the danger that threatens. But our impression was more, that they are tentacles seeking to drag us to destruction'.

'London keeps a good watch on the sky. Our motors and propellers soon revealed our presence. First one, then another and another of those ribbons shooting out from the glaring, eye-like searchlights, pick us up. Now from below comes an ominous sound that penetrates the noise of our motors and propellers. There are little red flashes and short bursts of fire which stand out prominently against the black background. From north, from south, from right, from left they appear, and following the flashes rolls up from below the sound of guns'.

'It is a beautiful, impressive, but fleeting picture as seen from above, probably no less interesting from below, the greyish, dim outline of the Zeppelins gliding through the waving ribbons of light and shrapnel cloud-lets which hang thick. We can see thousands of small lamps, and amidst these, especially in the black spots, the baleful, gleaming, great eye-like searchlights, and constant red flashes from many guns. But we have no time to admire; our eyes and mind must be concentrated on our work, for any moment we may be plunged below a shapeless mass of wreckage and human bodies shattered beyond recognition. You saw it at Johannisthal two years ago. I had so little time to register impressions that I have to think back now to give you a descriptive word picture of the scene. When first the searchlight picks you up you see the first flash of guns from below: your nerves get a little shock, but then you steady down, and put your mind on what you are there for. I picked up St Paul's, and with that point of orientation laid a course for the Bank of England'.

'There was a big searchlight in the immediate vicinity of St Paul's, and the English had placed a battery of guns under cover of that church, as I could plainly see from the flashes as they belched shrapnel at us. Perhaps from a military standpoint I would, under the circumstances, have been justified in dropping bombs on the battery, which was very near St Paul's, but had neither the desire nor the intention to do so, for fear possibly of damaging the church. However, I don't think the English should use churches, museums and similar buildings as a cover or protection for their guns. Although we had been fired upon from all sides we had not yet dropped a bomb. Above the Bank of England I shouted through the speaking-tube connecting me with my lieutenant at the firing apparatus, 'Fire slowly'. Now, mingling with the dim thunder and vivid flash of the guns below, came the explosions and burst of flames from our bombs. With the mind solely concentrated on picking out places previously on the program for attack as being factors having a military bearing on the preparation, concentration or transportation of troops, or places of other military use, and on stopping the Zeppelin and directing the firing, the comparatively short time above London appeared much longer than it actually was. We soon observed flames bursting forth from several places. Over Holborn Viaduct, in the vicinity of Holborn station, we dropped several bombs. From the Bank of England to the Tower was a short distance. I tried to hit the bridge, and believe I was successful'.

'To what extent damage was done I could not determine. Flashes from the Tower showed guns placed there which I had already observed on a previous attack. They were keeping up a lively fire. Maneuvring and arriving directly over Liverpool Street Station, I shouted 'Rapid fire' through the tube, and bombs rained down. There were a succession of detonations and bursts of fire, and I could see that we had hit well and apparently done great damage, which has been confirmed by reliable reports we have since received. Flames burst forth from several places in that vicinity'.

'Having dropped all my bombs I turned my ship for home. My orders had been carried out, and carried out quickly. Despite the bombardment of the sky we had not been hit. Several times I leaned out and looked up and back at the dark outlines of my Zeppelin, but she had no hole in her grey sides. In point of damage done, and hitting objects which I had received instructions to attack, it was my most successful trip in London or the vicinity. Ascending or descending until we found a favourable wind current we made a quick return'.

'How long were you over London?' I asked the Lieutenantcommander, or captain-lieutenant, as is that title in German, and upon whose left breast was the Iron Cross of the First Class.

'The main attack was from 10.50 to 11, just ten minutes'.

'Then the Zeppelin tactics of attack are to make a dash to points to be bombarded and quickly get away?'

'Yes; attacks must be short and quick'.

The carefulness with which the plans of attack are studied beforehand developed during our talk. Mathy mentioned figures and seemed to know to a yard how far it was from St Paul's to the Bank of England, thence the Tower and the different railway stations, and how long it took his Zeppelin, given the velocity of the wind and the revolutions of the propellers, to cover those distances. He often referred to new instruments and apparatus in use in Zeppelins for navigation, locating and measuring objects below, and controlling dropping bombs. This gave me the impression that there has been much research, experimenting and considerable progress along those lines in recent months. There are a number of interesting facts in connection with Zeppelins which, for obvious reasons, I cannot include in this story, among others the number of hours it now takes to make a dash to London and return. There is good reason for assuming that in the latest Zeppelins there are many improvements, that they are much faster, can carry more, and go higher than formerly. Count Zeppelin told me in February that those were three things he was working on.

Asked from what height he attacked London on the last raid, the Zeppelin commander replied, 'Sorry, but I don't want you to give the English their range. They are doing well enough as it is, and learning fast'.

'Balfour said London was not a fortified city, and that its defences against aerial attack were poor', I ventured.

'We know there are several forts and batteries around the City and outside, and had he stood by my side a few nights ago and looked into those flashing guns, all over, he wouldn't say London was not a militarily defended city, and perhaps not think so poorly of its aerial defence'.

When I asked how many bombs he carried and their size, Mathy remarked that, much as he would like to oblige me, that was a military question. 'We carry two kinds of explosive bombs, and similar shells and fire bombs for destruction by fire. I cannot tell you their size, but they are of tremendous destructive force, as probably you could convince yourself if you could see around Liverpool Street Station. The number we carry depends largely on the distance we intend covering, and the quantity of benzine for the motors it is necessary to take'.

Mathy intimated that the new Zeppelins have a considerably greater radius of action than London and back. I asked the Zeppelin commander if he had ever been attacked by aeroplanes on any of his raids on England. 'I have never experienced a fight with an aeroplane; in fact, have never been bothered by them. Men are always at my guns watching for them, but so far none has attempted an attack. We are pretty well prepared for them'. He remarked, significantly: 'I am not afraid of them, and think I could make it interesting and take care of them unless, perhaps, there was a regular swarm. So far as aeroplane corps for the defence of London could be effective, it must be remembered that it takes some time for an aeroplane to screw itself up as high as we are, and by the time it gets there we are gone. Then, too, a great difficulty is for the aeroplane to land at night, while we can stay up all night and longer, if need be'.

In my trips to and from Denmark I have observed Zeppelins out as far as Copenhagen scouting for enemy ships. My impression is that they have been of valuable service to the German Navy as scouts, and this is confirmed by some things Mathy said. 'What could a fleet of twenty-five or more Zeppelins do in an attack on London?' was my parting question to the commander. 'If you mean an attack without consideration for anything or anyone, that would be terrible, awful. Zeppelins then could stay much higher than now, when we have to pick out certain points. Such a fleet could probably cause more than a thousand fires, and would mean the destruction of the greater part of London; but I don't think there is any danger of that. We have no wish to destroy indiscriminately or to injure and kill women, children and other non combatants'.

Appendix C

On the ground

How did an air raid look to those defending London on the ground? Some idea is given here by Frank Heap, of No. 6 London Anti-Aircraft Company, based at the searchlight station at Little Heath, Potters Bar. He wrote the following to his wife on Sunday 3 September 1916:

My dearest Ada,

I am going to describe to you my experiences of last night (Saturday) not with any intention of causing you any worry about me, because in that case I should tell you nothing. My experiences of Saturday are quite unique so far and I don't expect that such circumstances will ever occur again and I hope not. You will have seen from the newspapers that a great Zeppelin raid occurred last night over London and the Eastern Counties.

It was a calm night with a rather heavy ground fog – a suitable night for a raid.

At 9 o'clock we had the order to stand by and test light under cover and to cover all lights on the station. I was an observer – required to get well out in the field and look out for Zepps or anything unusual and to report same.

At 11 o'clock we got the first information that Zepps had approached the coast and 5 mins later we were told to sweep and search the sky for aircraft. This is always an anxious time as any second we may pick up something unusual.

At 11.15 a Zeppelin was reported 35 miles away and travelling West.

At 11.30 another Zepp was reported to be 30 miles away travelling S West.

10 minutes later another (or perhaps the same) was reported to be 38 miles away and also travelling S West. Then came more orders about airships (German) being 40 miles away and sounds of Zepps heard elsewhere.

Just after midnight a Zepp was reported to be 17 miles away – here it was getting exciting – the Zepp was getting near and the carbons in the lamp were almost burnt out. However we were given permission to change carbons quickly and immediately after Woolwich guns were reported (and heard) to be in action as the Zeppelin was over a place called Bickley. And then the whereabouts of another Zepp were unknown – and the only information was that it was making for London from the North (that is through Little Heath district) and then it was as I stood alone observing our beam from the field that I got my first sounds of my first Zeppelin approaching us from the West. The noise was to begin with, like a whistle of a steam engine and the tone about G (key C). There was a gradual crescendo of sound until a time when you could hear the throb of the engines and then as it got overhead a rapid whir-r-r of sound – passing quickly like a flash of light. Just before reaching our station it dropped a bomb the explosions being quite distinct. The Zepp passed quickly over us and travelled South East. All the time we directed our beam on it as far as possible from the sound – the fog prevented us from seeing her. That was at 1.30 am. It was not a very pleasant sensation to hear your enemy passing overhead and yet not be able to spot her. Twenty minutes later the sounds of another Zepp were heard this time from the West and approaching us very rapidly. To hear that peculiar <u>whir-r</u> approaching you is not very pleasant I can tell you. A man in a trench has a chance in a dug out or behind the parapet – with us it meant show your light all the time and so give yourself away.

Quicker than any aeroplane and like a <u>double</u> express train the Zepp rushed over us to the East and her home dropping three bombs in quick succession.

I cannot describe to you the feeling when we were actually under fire. You can distinctly hear the fall of the bombs through the air (like one long scream) terminating in a violent explosion and then a thud. As I said early on it was a foggy night here and the result was that most of our light from the beam did not penetrate the fog but was reflected as from a mirror down again to the earth so that the little district around was illuminated and stood out in the intense darkness. I think the Zepp took the lights we made to be the lights of a town or factory and so we got the bombs quite near. On the approach of the Zepp overhead all the dogs in the district began barking and there was a regular stampede of about twenty horses across one field immediately the explosions occurred. I was observing when they stampeded and they passed in the dark within a foot or two of me.

Looking in the opposite direction and having heard for some time the rap-rap-rap of a Gatling Gun on an aeroplane (British) I saw a tremendous sight.

A Zepp on fire! The luminous mass lit up the sky for miles. It was like a huge torch red with flames and for several seconds it grew brighter and brighter. It descended slowly first in a horizontal position and then turned nose down and slowly dived to earth, a bright red mass. Oh a wonderful sight and one which I shall never forget. We had the pleasure of following it to earth with our beam. That was at 2.37am.

Nothing more happened only occasional sweeping for a Zepp believed to be about on the North at 3.15 am. At 4.15 we were shut down and breathed again.

Three of us resolved to find out what damage had been done and if near. The first thing noticed was an incendiary bomb burning itself out in the corner of the field 400yds from us – no damage.

A little further beyond and in the village of Little Heath (say 800yds direct line from us) a bomb had dropped strange to say in the <u>middle</u> of the road and with the exception of a few windows broken and the water main burst absolutely no real military damage and no casualties. Really it was marvellous as on both sides of the road where the bomb fell were inhabited houses. All the occupants got was a shaking.[1]

The police and the specials were on the scene and some were discussing the situation in the parlour of the nearest house. To this discussion we were invited – every one was complementing every one else on escaping. <u>That</u> bomb of course was a try for our light but turned out a miss.

Some time later a policeman reported that a Zepp had been brought down – the flame we saw[2] was later thought to be one of our aeroplanes and <u>not</u> a Zepp 3 miles away in the direction we had noted the falling flame. Dawn was breaking and it was suggested that a Mr So and So should motor us over to see the supposed Zepp. We had some time to wait and I looked round the great hole made in the road for any shell pieces to keep as souvenirs – and at last I found the nose-cap of the actual bomb. I am keeping it safely and wouldn't part with it for any amount of money.

To make a long story short we reached Cuffley, near here, where the Zepp had been brought down and which we had observed to fall. We found a great smouldering heap of wire, metal, the charred bodies of Germans and woodwork. Oh what a sight – what if the Kaiser could see it! I saw about ten bodies, baked brown and broken, recovered from the wreckage – parts of the engine, petrol tank, maxim gun and propeller were saved and put on one side.

I managed to obtain some 'bits' of the Zepp which I am keeping as souvenirs. I will send all to you later.

Two other bombs were dropped near us (⅓ mile away) and I have managed to get some pieces of the bombs from the huge craters made by the explosions.

I am very proud of all the 'tit bits' of Zepps that I have got and wouldn't part with them now.

Frank

The Zeppelins' fates

All three airships that dropped bombs on Leyton met with fiery ends. Several others that flew over south-west Essex also met similar fates.

LZ38 (bombed Leyton on 31 May/1 June 1915)

LZ38, commanded by Hauptmann Erich Linnarz, was the army's most successful airship. It flew on five operations against England in April and May 1915 before being destroyed in its shed at Brussels-Evere by RNAS bombing on 7 June 1915.

L10 (bombed Leyton on 17/18 August 1915)

L10, commanded by Oberleutnant Friedrich Wenke, was destroyed on 3 September 1915 in a thunderstorm over the North Sea; it exploded and burned near Neuwerk Island off Cuxhaven, when hydrogen gas being vented was ignited by lightning; all nineteen crew were killed.

SL11 (shooting down witnessed across south-west Essex on 2/3 September 1916)

On the night of 2/3 September 1916, 2nd Lieutenant William Leefe Robinson, of No. 39 (Home Defence) Squadron, RFC, flying a BE2c from Suttons Farm, shot down German army Schütte-Lanz airship SL11, commanded by Hauptmann Wilhelm Schramm, at Cuffley, Hertfordshire. This was the first Zeppelin to be shot down by another aircraft over England. SL11 was brought down from 11,500 feet, bursting into flames and crashing in a field behind *The Plough* inn at Cuffley, Hertfordshire. The airship was approaching central London when the AA gun based in Finsbury Park opened fire. More guns joined in the attack and SL11 veered away over Haringey towards Tottenham then dropped a number of bombs on Edmonton, Ponders End and Enfield Highway. The airship deposited one bomb on Crews Hill Golf Club, in Cattlegate Road, Enfield, nine bombs on a stud farm, in Clay Hill, Enfield, and others near the Enfield Isolation Hospital, in Worlds End Lane, Winchmore Hill, and on Oak Lodge Farm in Chase Road, Oakwood. As the crew released twelve more bombs on Forty Hill and Turkey Street, the Cuffley searchlight caught the airship, which came under fire from Robinson eventually falling in flames. Robinson was awarded the Victoria Cross for his bravery, and the report below records his exploits:

From:
   Lieutenant Robinson
   Suttons Farm
To:
   The Officer Commanding
   39 HD Squadron
Sir,

I have the honour to make the following report on Night Patrol made by me on the night of the 2nd–3rd instant. I went up at about 2308 hours with instructions to patrol between Suttons Farm and Joyce Green.

I climbed to 10,000 feet in 53 minutes and I counted what I thought were ten sets of flares – there were a few clouds below me but on the whole it was a beautifully clear night.

I saw nothing till 0110 hours when two searchlights picked up a Zeppelin south-east of Woolwich. The clouds had collected in this quarter, and the searchlights had some difficulty in keeping on the aircraft.

By this time I had managed to climb to 12,000 feet, and I made in the direction of the Zeppelin which was being fired on by a few anti-aircraft guns – hoping to cut it off on its way eastward. I very slowly gained on it for about ten minutes – I judged it to be about 800 feet below me, and I sacrificed my speed in order to keep the height. It went behind some clouds, avoided the searchlights, and I lost sight of it. After 15 minutes fruitless search I returned to my patrol.

I managed to pick up and distinguish my flares again.

At about 0150 hours I noticed a red glow in north-east London. Taking it to be an outbreak of fire I went in that direction.

At 0205 hours a Zeppelin was picked up by the searchlights over north-north-east London (as far as I could judge).

Remembering my last failure I sacrificed height (I was still at 12,900 feet) for speed and made nose down in the direction of the Zeppelin. I saw shells bursting and night tracer shells bursting and flying around it. When I drew closer I noticed the anti-aircraft aim was too high or too low; also a good many some 800 feet behind – a few tracers went right over. I could hear the bursts when about 3,000 feet from the Zeppelin.

I flew about 800 feet below it from bow to stern and distributed one drum along it (alternate New Brock and Pomeroy. It seemed to have no effect; I therefore moved to one side and gave it another drum distributed along its side – without apparent effect. I then got behind it (by this time I was very close – 50 feet or less below) and concentrated one drum on one part (underneath rear). I was then at a height of 11,500 feet when attacking the Zeppelin.

I hardly finished the drum before I saw the part fired at glow. In a few seconds the whole rear part was blazing.

When the third drum was fired there were no searchlights on the Zeppelin and no anti-aircraft guns were firing.

I quickly got out of the way of the falling blazing Zeppelin and, being very excited, fired off a few red Very's lights and dropped a parachute flare.

Having very little oil and petrol left I returned to Suttons Farm, landing at 0245 hours.

On landing I found I had shot away the machine gun wire guard, the rear part of the centre section, and had pierced the rear main spar several times.

I have the honour to be, Sir,
Your obedient servant
(Signed) W.L. Robinson, Lieutenant
No. 39 Squadron RFC

The following morning *The Star* reported:

A member of the staff of 'The Daily News' who was at Cuffley yesterday thus describes the wreckage of the Zeppelin: It is a tangled mess that at the moment occupies not more than a space 30 feet square. Several bodies laid neatly by the wreckage is the only clue to the size of the giant that a few hours earlier had set out to work its frightfulness on the women and children of the Metropolis. One of them – probably the skipper, for, like the machine, the bodies are unrecognisable – still wears the Iron Cross.

The time the raider was brought to earth can be fixed by a wrist-watch picked up in the field to-day. Like its owner, it is terribly charred. Its white face is blackened and the numerals are gone, but the position of the hands shows 3.20.[1]

The commander's clean-shaven face, with high cheekbones that suggested a Mongolian, his square head, and his hair had not been touched by the flames, says another correspondent. His sheepskin coat and all the upper part of his clothing hung on him, all scorched.

The 'Daily Sketch' was told at Enfield yesterday that the shrieks of the occupants of the cars could be distinctly heard as the Zeppelin fell.

The airship itself, to a near view, came down only slowly, and the impression was general among the observers that some of the men threw themselves out of the gondolas.

Tens of thousands left London to go and see the crash site, one of whom was Robinson himself. Of Robinson's visit, one newspaper reported:

> Early on Sunday morning he motored over to Cuffley to view his 'bag'. By that time a number of troops were on the spot, and they gave him a splendid reception, climbing into his car to shake his hand. He was presented with several interesting souvenirs of the exploit, among them being an Iron Cross found among the debris, a gold watch thought to have been that of the commander, a revolver, and also the log of the Zeppelin, its leaves somewhat scorched, but still largely decipherable. His latest souvenir is the Victoria Cross.
>
> When he returned here for the second time that morning his was truly a triumphal progress. Crowds of villagers and soldiers – among them many Colonials – lined the roads and crowded round his car. The rest of the day he spent in civilian dress in London, endeavouring to avoid recognition and avoid congratulation.

L32 (shooting down witnessed across south-west Essex on 23/24 September 1916)

On the night of 23/24 September, Zeppelin L32 commanded by Oberleutnant Werner Peterson, was shot down over Great Burstead, near Billericay in Essex by 2nd Lieutenant Frederick Sowrey of No. 39 (Home Defence) Squadron flying BE2c 4112 from Suttons Farm. L32 had reached London on the same raid as L31, which caused so much damage along the Lea Bridge Road that night. Sowrey's report read:

> To:
>   Officer Commanding
>   No. 39 HD Squadron
>   Royal Flying Corps
>   Woodford Green
> From:
>   Second-Lieutenant F. Sowrey
>   B Flight, 39 HD Squadron, RFC
>   Suttons Farm
> Sir,
> I have the honour to report the following on my action during the night of September 23/24, 1916. At 2325 hours I received orders to patrol between Suttons Farm and Joyce Green and at 2330 hours I left the aerodrome. The weather was clear with a few thin clouds at 3,000 feet. At 4,000 feet I passed

another machine proceeding in a northerly direction. I was then flying due south. I continued climbing as hard as possible and at 0010 hours I noticed an enemy airship in a southerly direction. It appeared to be over Woolwich. I made for the airship at once, but before I could reach it, the searchlights lost it. I was at this time at 8,000 feet. There was a certain amount of gun fire but it was not intense.

I continued to climb and reached a height of 13,000 feet. I was still patrolling between Suttons Farm and Joyce Green. At 0045 hours I noticed an enemy airship in an easterly direction. I at once made in this direction and manoeuvred into a position underneath. The airship was well lighted by searchlights but there was not a sign of any gun fire. I could distinctly see the propellers revolving and the airship was manoeuvring to avoid the searchlight beams. I fired at it.

The first two drums of ammunition had apparently no effect but the third one caused the envelope to catch on fire in several places; in the centre and front. All firing was traversing fire along the envelope. The drums were loaded with a mixture of Brock, Pomeroy and tracer ammunition. I watched the burning airship strike the ground and then proceeded to find my flares. I landed at Suttons Farm at 0140 hours, 24th instant.

My machine was BE2c 4112.

After seeing the Zeppelin had caught on fire, I fired a red Very's light.

I have the honour to be, Sir,
Your obedient servant,
(Signed) F. Sowrey
Second-Lieutenant, RFC

The aftermath of the crash is described by Henry Williamson, at the end of *The Golden Virgin*:

They made their way to Snail's Hall Farm, where the Zeppelin's empty frame lay glittering like part of the Crystal Palace in the bright sunlight of the hot day as it straddled two burnt fields across a scorched hedge, broken in the middle where it had sunk down upon an oak tree. It was 700 feet long ... Approaching the buckled frame, they saw the white corrosion of fire on the aluminium girders and cross members, and the oak tree, 40 feet high, with all its branches crushed around the trunk.

Two rows of bodies lay [in a barn] on straw. Their faces looked to have been tarred, and the tar to have cracked, revealing old red paint beneath. Their thick greatcoats were frizzled, their long felt boots grew black lichen. The arms and legs were those of dummies, ready to dangle loose about skulled faces with stubbed ears and noses, and flat eyes. He counted twenty-one. The twenty-second corpse, lying apart, was not burned. Grass stuck to the Iron Cross in the buttonhole of the reefer jacket. 'He's the commander, sir', said the sergeant. 'He was picked up in the field, some way off the airship. There's the impression, six inches deep in the ground, where he was plonked down'.

The police had difficulty in keeping sightseers and looters away. Many attempted, successfully, to take away souvenirs, particularly pieces of the air-ship's aluminium superstructure as these were light and easy to carry off. The penalty for absconding with items of potential military importance was a fine of £100 or six months hard labour, but this proved no deterrent. Nell Tyrell, from Brentwood, recorded in her diary:

> Next day we went over to Billericay to see the wreck and had to stop about half a mile away and walk to the spot, where the huge carcase lay, of twisted aluminium framework. She had fallen on a British oak which had broken her in half and she lay all along the side of a turnip field about 200 yards from a farm house. All the dead and burnt crew had been removed to a shed belonging to a farm and we were lucky enough to just miss the removal of the bodies. While we were there an aeroplane flew around and landed in the field and some people say that F.W. Sowrey the airman who wrecked her was in it – but I didn't see him …
>
> For weeks after this, motor lorries of the Navy and Army full of Zeppelin remains passed through Brentwood. At first it attracted crowds of people, all clamouring for pieces of souvenirs, but the novelty soon wore off.

L33 (bombed Stratford on 23/24 September 1916)

L33, commanded by Alois Böcker, was shot down on its return journey over Essex on the night of 23/24 September 1916. AA guns at Beckton or on Wanstead Flats scored a direct hit on the six-engine craft, damaging one of the propellers, its steering mechanism and gas cells, and it began to lose height. The stricken airship unloaded large amounts of its 2,000 gallons of fuel over Woodham Ferrers and appeared to be following the course of the GER line to Maldon. It only just managed to clear the rooftops of Maldon and it was supposed that the commander was attempting to drop into the Ray Channel (off West Mersea), but a gust of wind blew it over the sea wall. It hovered for some time over the Tiptree jam factory and the crew threw out a machine-gun, two cases of machine-gun cartridges, a machine-gun belt, an electric battery in a leather case, an instrument box, a celluloid screen, two packages of aluminium sheeting, two portions of maps, a metal tube and a canvas bag to try to gain height, but to no avail. The Zeppelin eventually came down intact between 1.00am and 2.00am on 24 September at Little Wigborough, partly in Knapps Field and Glebe Field and across Copt Hall Lane, within 30 feet of two farm cottages, one occupied by Thomas Lewis and his family and the other by Frederick Choat; both men were workers at nearby New Hall Farm.

Here Böcker's crew set light to the airship to ensure it did not fall into British hands. Prior to setting light to the Zeppelin, the crew attempted to warn the occupants of the two cottages, but they refused to open their doors. The crew returned to the airship and promptly set it on fire, leaving just the skeletal wreckage looking like 'a beached whale' or 'a Crystal Palace without its glass'. The countryside was lit up for miles around and a local dog was killed in the conflagration. The only damage to the cottages was a few broken windows and burnt paintwork.

Alfred Wright, a 45-year-old seedsman from nearby Grove Farm was passing and, seeing the Zeppelin but unsure if any of the crew were armed, set out on his motorcycle for West Mersea to tell the military authorities there. In the darkness he was hit by a car and his leg was badly injured; he died in hospital two months later. A baby girl born that night at Abbots Hall Cottages, Great Wigborough, was named Zeppelina Clark.

Police Constable Charles Smith was quickly on the scene to arrest the twenty-one enemy airmen – he was subsequently promoted to Sergeant for his efforts and thereafter known as 'Zepp' Smith. Special Constables Edgar Nicholas and Elijah Traylor, and Special Sergeant Ernest Edwards, were already there and were awarded silver half-hunter pocket watches inscribed inside the back 'Essex Constabulary. Presented to E.W. Traylor [and E. Nicholas] for good services when Zeppelin L33 was brought down in Essex on 24.9.16'. The Germans were marched to Mersea Island where they were handed over to the vicar of West Mersea, the Reverend Pierrepont Edwards, himself a military hero with an MC to his name. They were locked up in a barn (some say a church hall) before eventually being transferred to the Colchester Military Garrison.

Meanwhile, the wreckage of L33 was guarded by armed men of the Lancashire Fusiliers, but not before souvenir hunters had taken their share. At a later stage, items were sold off to visiting spectators – and there were a lot of them, 250,000 over the following months – who were charged the sum of 2*d* a time for a glimpse of the scene. Having been examined by Admiralty engineers and draftsmen, the Zeppelin's remains were finally dismantled and removed some fourteen weeks later.

L31 (bombed Leyton on 23/24 September 1916)

On 1 October 1916, 2nd Lieutenant Wulstan Tempest was visiting Epping and dining with friends at a doctor's house in the High Street when he was summoned to North Weald airfield. He took off at 10.00pm in BE2c 4577, but soon his engine-driven fuel pump failed. Consequently Tempest had to use the hand pump, but at 15,000 feet this was very exhausting; furthermore, it meant that he had one fewer hand with which to fly the plane and fire his Lewis gun. Despite these difficulties, just before midnight, Tempest found and shot down German navy Zeppelin L31, commanded by Kapitänleutnant Heinrich Mathy, over Oakmere Park, near Potters Bar in Hertfordshire. Tempest crashed his aircraft on landing back at North Weald, but was fit enough to return to Epping in triumph in his motorcycle combination. His short report stated:

From:
  Second-Lieutenant Tempest
  'B' Flight
  No. 39 HD Squadron, RFC
To:
  Adjutant
  No. 39 HD Squadron
Sir,
I have the honour to report that on October 1, at 2200 hours I left the ground in BE2c 4577 to patrol between Joyce Green and Hainault. Approximately at 2340 hours I first sighted a Zeppelin. I immediately made for her and fired one drum which took effect at once and set her on fire at about 12,700 feet. I then proceeded to North Weald to land and wrecked the machine on the aerodrome without hurting myself at 0210 hours.
  I have the honour to be, Sir,
  Your obedient servant,
  (Signed) Second-Lieutenant W.J. Tempest

Tempest was awarded the Distinguished Service Order (DSO) for his Zeppelin-hunting. All the crew of L31 perished. Several, including Mathy – the most respected and successful of the Zeppelin commanders – jumped to their deaths rather than burn alive.

The wreckage of L31 was an attraction for spectators and souvenir hunters for several days after the event. Newspapers gave guidance on how to get to the site, and thousands turned out, including the band of the French *Garde Republicane*, which was on a concert tour of the UK at the time. Huge numbers of sightseers descended on Potters Bar, but the army had got there first, placing a cordon of soldiers around the whole area so that no-one could get too close. The owner of the field in which the wreckage lay got permission from the local army commander to charge a shilling a head to allow visitors to enter his land for the best view, the proceeds being promised to the Red Cross after deductions to put right the damage to his land.

Notes

Foreword

1. Situated to the east of the River Lea, Leyton and Ilford both lie within the boundaries of the traditional county of Essex. Ilford Urban District Council was formed in 1894, and Leyton Urban District Council in 1895; these were elected councils, which shared some responsibilities for local government with Essex County Council. These arrangements continued when Leyton and Ilford both became municipal boroughs in 1926. Neither Leyton nor Ilford was ever part of the London County Council area, but they both became part of Greater London in 1965 when the London boroughs of Waltham Forest and Redbridge were created. Essex County Cricket Club had its headquarters in Leyton until 1933 and played matches there until 1977; it also played matches in Ilford until 2002.

Chapter 1: 'Peril from above'

1. Playwright Guy du Maurier was the son of the writer George du Maurier and the brother of the actor Gerald du Maurier. *An Englishman's Home* tells the story of the Brown family under invasion by an unnamed foreign power. When the play was staged in Germany, it caused an outrage, as the German press saw clear references to their homeland. In 1940, it was made into a propaganda film entitled *Mad Men of Europe*.
2. Founded in 1909 as the Aerial League of the British Empire, the League's intention was to counter 'the backwardness and apathy' shown by Britain in the face of emerging aeronautical developments and to stress 'the vital importance from a commercial and national defence point of view of this new means of communication'.
3. Launched in 1906, the Royal Navy's HMS *Dreadnought* had two revolutionary features: an unprecedented number of heavy-calibre guns; and steam turbine propulsion. This design made such a strong impression on people's minds that similar battleships built subsequently were referred to generically as dreadnoughts. They became a crucial symbol of national power and renewed the naval arms race between Britain and Germany.
4. German spy mania predates even this. Erskine Childers' *The Riddle of the Sands* was written on this theme and was published in 1903. The prolific author William Le Queux also wrote popular novels of espionage, identifying Germany as the principal threat. His works include *England's Peril* (1899), *The Invasion of 1910* (1905) and *Spies of the Kaiser* (1909).
5. William Heath Robinson was an artist, cartoonist and illustrator of books. These eleven cartoons in *The Sketch* began on 20 April 1910, appearing one per week, up to the sixth on 1 June 1910. The last five cartoons appeared in sequence in the issue for 22 June 1910.
6. With the growing recognition of the potential for aircraft as a cost-effective method of reconnaissance and artillery observation, the Committee of Imperial Defence looked

at the question of military aviation in November 1911. In the following February its findings recommended that a flying corps be formed consisting of a naval wing, a military wing, a central flying school and an aircraft factory. The recommendations were accepted and the Royal Flying Corps was formed in 1912 and the Royal Naval Air Service in 1914.

Chapter 2: 'Our nerves are on edge'

1. When the time came, on the night of 1/2 October 1916, as fire spread rapidly through Zeppelin L31, Mathy chose to jump to his death.

Chapter 3: 'The Zeppelins were able to escape'

1. Winston Spencer Churchill (1874–1965) was President of the Board of Trade, Home Secretary, and First Lord of the Admiralty as part of Herbert Asquith's pre-war Liberal government. During the war, he continued as First Lord of the Admiralty until the Gallipoli campaign caused his departure from government. He then briefly resumed active army service on the Western Front as commander of the 6th Battalion of the Royal Scots Fusiliers. He returned to join David Lloyd George's Coalition government as Minister of Munitions, Secretary of State for War, and Secretary of State for Air.

2. Field Marshal John Denton Pinkstone French, 1st Earl of Ypres (1852–1925), known as The Viscount French between 1916 and 1922, was an Anglo-Irish officer in the British Army. He distinguished himself commanding the Cavalry Division during the Second Boer War, became Chief of the Imperial General Staff in 1912. He resigned over the Curragh incident and then served as Commander-in-Chief of the British Expeditionary Force for the first two years of the First World War before serving as Commander-in-Chief, Home Forces. He became Lord Lieutenant of Ireland in 1918, a position which he held throughout much of the Irish War of Independence.

3. Edward Bailey Ashmore (1872–1953) was an artillery officer who had also been a pilot and had commanded an RFC unit in France.

4. Sir (Toby) Alfred Rawlinson, 3rd Baronet (1867–1934) was a pioneer motorist and aviator, soldier, intelligence officer and sportsman. In 1914 he volunteered for active service, and became a chauffeur; he was then transferred to a staff position with IV Corps of the British Expeditionary Force. On 9 May 1915, he was injured by a German heavy shell at the Battle of Aubers Ridge and returned to England.

5. At the end of the war, the two generators from the tramcars were the subject of much hard bargaining between Ilford UDC and the War Office. The council offered £50; the War Office wanted £100; the two parties finally settled for £75. The generators were fitted up in the council's works depot and were used to charge the batteries of some 'Orwell' dustcarts.

6. Wanstead Flats are part of Epping Forest and are managed by the City of London Corporation.

7. In pre-war days, the site at Pole Hill had been used as a Boy Scout and school cadet camp by Vyvyan Richards, a history teacher at Bancroft School in Woodford Green. His friend, T.E. Lawrence (later 'Lawrence of Arabia'), was also involved with this camp and after the war purchased eighteen acres of land on the western side of the hill. Richards continued the camp and built himself a small wooden dwelling there (named 'The Cloister' and replacing an earlier hut burnt down in 1921). He also stored a lot of

Lawrence's books in one of the former AA huts which remained standing. Arabia Close is nearby and is named after Lawrence.

8. Some of the barrage names were probably standard military terms: Union Jack, Mercury, Kingfisher, Polygon; but where did Mary Jane, Cold Feet, No Trumps, Noisy Norah, Charley's Aunt or Dandy Dick come from? The last two appear to be the names of popular farces at the time; perhaps the gun crews chose them, or maybe they were named on the whim of a junior officer.

9. Claybury asylum was a psychiatric hospital opened in 1893. It was the final hospital to be built by Middlesex County Council before London County Council was formed. The Middlesex authorities chose the site of Claybury Hall at Woodford Bridge, which was situated on the top of a hill and within a 250-acre estate including ancient woodland and open parkland, ponds, pasture and historic gardens. Claybury was one of the first hospitals in the country to incorporate a laboratory to try to determine the pathology of mental illness. By 1896, the hospital had reached its total capacity of 2,500 patients. The hospital workshops housed a munitions factory during the First World War. The hospital closed in 1997.

10. At the time of the 1911 census, Robert Stroud was a 55-year-old builder, brickmaker and farmer living at Barley Hall, Goodmayes, in Ilford UDC's Hainault South ward. Robert lived with his wife, Charlotte, their four sons, all of whom helped in the business, and their two daughters, both of whom were at school. They also had one servant and a housekeeper and his wife living there. Barley Hall was rather grand, with eleven rooms including the kitchen, but excluding the scullery, lobby, halls and bathroom; there were three more rooms in the housekeeper's cottage. Over the period 1891–1911, Ilford had grown in population from about 11,000 to 78,000. Many of these people commuted by train to London and lived in new suburban housing, the chief developer of which was Archibald Cameron Corbett, a Liberal MP. Robert Stroud was Corbett's major contractor; he was also a Justice of the Peace for Essex and a retiring Essex County Councillor in 1913. At his death in 1925, his assets were reckoned to be worth £55,000.

11. Arthur George Morrison (1863–1945) was an author, playwright and authority on Japanese prints. He lived at 'Arabin House', High Beach. He was also an inspector in the Special Constabulary during the war.

12. This would be Joyce Green, an RFC Home Defence airfield on the Kent marshes near Dartford.

13. Jan Christiaan Smuts (1870–1950) was a prominent South African and British statesman, military leader and philosopher. In addition to holding various British cabinet posts, he served as Prime Minister of the Union of South Africa from 1919–1924 and 1939–1948. During the Great War, he led the armies of South Africa against Germany, capturing German South-West Africa and commanding the British army in east Africa. From 1917–1919, he was also one of the members of David Lloyd George's War Cabinet. He was the only person to sign both of the peace treaties ending the First and Second World Wars.

14. Also at High Beach, the War Office had commandeered Riggs Retreat early in the war for use as a training centre. The retreat was a popular place of refreshment on Wellington Hill used by thousands of visitors to Epping Forest. The War Office relinquished the building in 1916. Jubilee Retreat nearby, in Bury Road, Chingford,

was occupied by pilots of the Royal Canadian Flying Corps while training at RNAS Chingford.

15. The Royal Air Force was formed on 1 April 1918 by the merger of the Royal Flying Corps and the Royal Naval Air Service.

16. These Giants were so large that the crew included a mechanic in each engine nacelle.

17. Ilford also had another link with First World War aviation. In December 1916, the roller-skating rink on Ilford Hill was taken over by Oakley & Co Ltd to build twenty-five Sopwith Triplanes for the RFC (the original order had been for the same number of 1½ Strutters). Although having no experience of building aeroplanes, the firm's woodworking skill was considered sufficient. However, the inexperience of Oakley & Co in aeroplane manufacturing was evident in the inordinate length of time before its products began to appear. By October 1917, only the first three of its Triplanes had been completed and the balance of its order was then cancelled.

18. In pre-war days the first aeroplane flight across London took off from Fairlop, when Edward Petre flew to Brooklands in a Handley Page Type E monoplane on 27 July 1912. At that time, Frederick Handley Page rented a shed at Creekmouth where he ran a small aircraft factory. However, the land around the site proved unsuitable for test flying and so he used the playing fields at Fairlop for this purpose. In September 1912, Handley Page moved his factory from Creekmouth to larger premises at Cricklewood, close by the established aerodrome at Hendon.

19. Hainault station was on the GER loop line between Ilford and Woodford. This line opened in 1903 and was intended to stimulate suburban growth. However, so remote was the station at Hainault that due to a lack of custom it closed to passenger and goods traffic on 1 October 1908 and did not reopen until 2 March 1930. In 1915, Arthur Hughes purchased land in New North Road, 200 yards west of Hainault station. Two years later he opened a factory there to meet the demand of the RFC for compasses, sextants, semaphores and other navigational aids. Originally known as Henry Hughes & Sons, the firm later became Kelvin Hughes. The factory closed in 2012 when the firm re-located to Enfield.

20. Stow Maries airfield remains largely intact today and is one of only a few near-complete First World War airfields anywhere in Europe. Many buildings survive, including technical buildings used for maintenance and repair, such as the smithy and workshops, and messes and accommodation for airmen and officers, plus separate women's accommodation for the few female RFC staff.

21. The squadron's HQ was initially at Hounslow and it had detachments of two BE2c aircraft each at Hainault Farm and Suttons Farm. When the HQ moved to Woodford Green, it was at 'Salway Lodge', originally the home of Richard Salway, an eighteenth-century merchant and, from 1900 to about 1910, the home of Joseph Malaby Dent (1849–1926), publisher of the Everyman's Library, a large collection of the great books of the world in a handsome affordable edition.

22. Arthur Travers Harris, 1st Baronet, (1892–1984) emigrated to Southern Rhodesia at the age of 17, but he returned to England in 1915 to fight in the European theatre of the First World War. He joined the RFC, with which he remained until the formation of the RAF in 1918. He remained in the RAF through the 1920s and 1930s, serving in India, Mesopotamia, Persia, Egypt, Palestine, and elsewhere. At the outbreak of the Second World War, Harris took command of No. 5 Group RAF in England. In

February 1942, he was appointed head of Bomber Command. He retained that position for the rest of the war.

23. Cecil Arthur Lewis (1898–1997) went on to co-found the British Broadcasting Company and enjoy a long career as a writer, notably of the aviation classic *Sagittarius Rising*.

24. By this time, pilots stood by for night raids in relays, so they were able to take it in turns to go into London. Lieutenant Ronald Adam recalled that London was less than an hour's drive away, and that a box at the Vaudeville Theatre was permanently reserved for the squadron's pilots.

25. Le Prieur rockets were a type of incendiary air-to-air rockets used against observation balloons and airships. They were invented by the French Lieutenant Yves Le Prieur and were first used in the Battle of Verdun in 1916. Due to great inaccuracy their range was limited to about 125 yards. The rockets comprised a cardboard tube filled with 200 grammes of black powder with a wooden conical head attached (by doped paper or linen tape) and a triangular knife blade inserted in a slot across the apex forming a spear point. A square-sectioned wooden stick was taped to the rocket with about five feet extending back from the base, and fitted snugly into a launch tube attached to the aircraft's interplane struts. The rockets were fired electrically via a cockpit switch, which would launch all the rockets consecutively.

26. Until 1918, there were no radio/telephone communications to guide pilots so, in the absence of electronic aids, a crude system of ground signals was developed – which was not much use at night.

Chapter 4: 'Take cover'

1. The GER ran most of the lines in the area, except for those of the Midland Railway out of Fenchurch Street station and between Tottenham and Forest Gate, and the Port of London Authority's internal system within the docks. Leyton, Leytonstone and Walthamstow had stations on both the GER and Midland Railway lines.

2. The Railway Executive was a central body which took directions from military authorities and liaised with the various railway companies.

3. In London, 24 civilians were killed and 196 injured by 'friendly' anti-aircraft fire during the war.

4. Herbert Henry Asquith, 1st Earl of Oxford and Asquith, (1852–1928) served as Liberal Prime Minister from 1908 to 1916. Following a Cabinet split on 25 May 1915, caused by the Shell Crisis and the failed offensive at Gallipoli, Asquith became head of a new coalition government. On 5 December 1916, no longer enjoying the support of the press or of leading Conservatives, he resigned and David Lloyd George became head of the coalition two days later. Asquith, along with most leading Liberals, refused to serve in the new government. He remained Leader of the Liberal party, but found it hard to conduct an official opposition in wartime.

5. William Wedgwood Benn, 1st Viscount Stansgate, (1877–1960) was a Liberal politician for the St George's Division of Tower Hamlets in east London, a seat he held until 1918. He served under Asquith as a Lord of the Treasury between 1910 and 1915.

6. David Lloyd George, 1st Earl Lloyd-George of Dwyfor, (1863–1945) was a Liberal politician and statesman. As Chancellor of the Exchequer (1908–1915), he was a key figure in the introduction of many reforms which laid the foundations of the modern

welfare state. His most important role came as Prime Minister of the wartime Coalition government (1916–22). He was a major player at the Paris Peace Conference of 1919.

7. A D-Notice, or Defence Notice, was an official request from the Government to news editors not to publish or broadcast particular items of news.

8. At least one other inquiry was held in London the same day, and others had taken place elsewhere in England after the first Zeppelin attacks in January. Coroners' inquests into air raid deaths were common features in the British press in the First World War.

Chapter 5: 'Knocking the chimneys down'

1. The Kaiser initially excluded London as a target and demanded that no attacks be made on historic or government buildings or museums.

2. Germans were one of the oldest immigrant communities in London and were some 4,000 strong as far back as the reign of James I. There was a rapid increase from 1850 onwards with many settling in what was already known as Little Germany – the area bounded by Whitechapel Road, Cannon Street Road, the Highway, and Leman Street. German influence became so great that West Ham council provided information in both English and German for people wishing to set up in business in the area. It was not long before there was a backlash. Fears of a loss of British identity were largely expressed as resentment that 'they' were taking 'our' jobs and the result was the Aliens Act of 1905.

3. On Saturday 24 April 1915, the last match of the season before suspension due to the war, all the Clapton Orient players and staff took a final farewell parade around the Millfields Road pitch. Forty-one players and officials from Clapton Orient joined the 17th (Footballers) Battalion of the Middlesex Regiment. The Admiralty, and then the army, took over the Millfields ground site for the duration of the war, with an anti-aircraft gun and searchlight positioned on the 'Spion Kop' to ward off German raiders.

4. This was Mr M. Meyers, a night-watchman for Leyton UDC. His widow subsequently applied to the council for assistance and she was granted a gratuity of £10. The road-roller that he was guarding cost the council £108 to repair.

5. The Carnegie Hero Fund Trust was established in 1908 as a British extension of the Carnegie Hero Fund Commission, which had been created four years earlier in Pittsburgh, USA. The Trust was founded upon a financial endowment from the Scottish philanthropist and steel magnate, Andrew Carnegie. The purpose of the Trust is to provide payments to individuals who have been injured or financially disadvantaged as a result of undertaking an act of heroism or in fatal cases to provide for the family or other dependants.

6. As a consequence, St Augustine's church remained closed until it was restored and re-dedicated in 1920. The original church, around the corner in Mayville Road and then in use as the church hall, temporarily came back into use for worship until restoration was completed.

7. Lieutenant General Sir Francis Lloyd (1853–1926) rose to become Major-General commanding the Brigade of Guards and General Officer Commanding London District. He became known as 'The Man Who Ran London during the Great War' following a comment made by a journalist about him when he was given delegated powers over hospitals and trains during the war.

8. West Ham Infirmary opened in 1903 with 672 beds in 24 wards housed in four blocks. In 1917, the name was changed to Whipps Cross Hospital. In October 1917, the War Office took over the adjacent Forest House as a war hospital catering for 180 acute and 160 convalescent patients.

9. Sir John Simon was first elected as Liberal MP in the election of 1906. He was Home Secretary from May 1915 to January 1916, when he resigned in protest against the introduction of conscription to the armed forces. He remained an MP until he lost his seat in the election of 1918. As a Liberal nationalist, Simon was not well regarded by the pro-war and pro-conscription Liberals of the day.

10. Tests by the RFC on what was visible at night from an aeroplane at various heights showed that, despite numerous tram flashes being visible across London, it was impossible for them to serve any useful purpose in guiding a Zeppelin to a target.

11. Dr Pace studied medicine at the London Hospital, qualifying in 1893. He held posts there as house surgeon and house physician, and passed his MB degree in 1897. He served as civil surgeon with the African Field Force during the Second Boer War and was district medical officer to Essex County Council and public vaccinator. Apart from that, his whole career was spent in general practice in Leyton, where he was known to two generations of Leytonians. He retired from general practice in 1933 and moved to Goring-on-Sea, where he died in 1939.

12. Alfred de Bathe Brandon was born in Wellington, New Zealand, and was educated in England, reading law at Trinity College, Cambridge, before being called to the bar at the Middle Temple in 1906. Returning to New Zealand, he joined the family law practice in Wellington. With Britain's entry into the war, Brandon sailed for England at the end of April 1915 to become a pilot in the RNAS – whereupon the Admiralty rejected him! A fellow New Zealander, serving with the RNAS at Chingford, suggested to Brandon that several civilian flying instructors were still giving lessons at Hendon aerodrome. Following up this suggestion, Brandon qualified for his pilot's licence on 17 October 1915 and volunteered for the RFC where he was accepted.

Chapter 6: 'A big cigar in front of the moon'

1. In April 1917, William Leefe Robinson (1895–1918) was posted to France as a Flight Commander with No. 48 Squadron. On the first patrol over the lines, Robinson's formation of six aircraft encountered fighters led by Manfred von Richthofen, and four were shot down; Robinson was wounded and captured. Following the Armistice and his release, Robinson died on 31 December 1918 at the Stanmore home of his sister, Baroness Heyking, from the effects of the Spanish flu pandemic. He was buried at All Saints' churchyard extension in Harrow Weald. A memorial to him was later erected near the spot where the airship crashed. Robinson Close is named after him in Hornchurch, on the site of the former Suttons Farm airfield.

2. Frederick Sowrey (1893–1968) rose rapidly in rank during the First World War. He remained in the RFC and RAF until 1940.

3. Wulstan Joseph Tempest (1891–1966) was born in Blackburn and after leaving school joined the Merchant Navy. On the outbreak of the First World War, he enlisted in the King's Own Yorkshire Light Infantry and served in Flanders. In October 1914, Tempest was wounded at the first Battle of Ypres and returned to England to recover from his injuries. After learning to fly, he joined the RFC being posted to No. 39 Squadron. Here Tempest became firm friends with his fellow pilots William Leefe

Robinson and Frederick Sowrey. Like Robinson and Sowrey, Tempest's success won him national admiration and public accolades. In Oakmere Park, Potters Bar two streets are named after him: Tempest Avenue and Wulstan Park; Tempest Mead at North Weald commemorates him too.

4. This photograph was actually of Oberleutnant Werner Peterson, commander of L32 shot down near Billericay on the night of 23/24 September 1916.

5. A 'Very' light was a pyrotechnic signal using white or coloured balls of fire projected from a special pistol. It was named after Edward W. Very, an American naval officer.

6. Sybil Morrison (1893–1984) was a suffragist and later a pacifist too. In 1916, she began to drive ambulances in London, and attributed her decision to become a pacifist to the sight of a Zeppelin being shot down over Potters Bar.

Chapter 7: 'A huge hostile air fleet'

1. In December 1917, it was renamed Bombengeschwader der Obersten Heersleitung, or BOGOHL III.

2. Although a Taube was a specific make of aircraft, British troops and the press frequently referred to all German aircraft as 'Taubes'.

3. The very last air raid of all took place on 5 August 1918, when five Zeppelins approached the Norfolk coast. On board L70 was Fregattenkapitän Peter Strasser, Chief of the Zeppelin Service. At 10.20pm, L70 was shot down into the sea 40 miles off Great Yarmouth by a De Havilland DH4 from the RAF's No. 4 Group at Denes airfield piloted by Lieutenant E. Cadbury with Lieutenant R. Leckie in the gunner's seat; Strasser died in the inferno.

Chapter 8: 'Attendance this week has suffered considerably'

1. At Upper North Street School, Poplar, there had been a girls' class on the top floor, a boys' class on the middle floor and an infants' class on the ground floor. A 50kg bomb had crashed through the roof then through the top two floors and exploded on the ground floor amongst the infants. Fifteen children had been killed outright, three fatally injured and twenty-seven maimed for life. Of those who died, sixteen had been aged from four to six years old. On 20 June, at All Saints' church, Poplar, one of the biggest funerals in London was held for these children. After the service, the funeral procession consisting of seven hearses, private carriages and motor cars, made its way through crowds lining the route. It first went west along East India Dock Road for some distance before doubling back on itself and then headed for the East London Cemetery. There 16 of the children were buried in a mass grave and the other two in private graves. A memorial in Poplar Recreation Ground, unveiled in June 1919, bears the names of the 18 pupils who lost their lives in the first daylight air raid on London.

2. This was originally near *The Green Man*, but was moved from Epping Forest land to a new location by the disused cab rank in Kirkdale Road; the cab shelter there became a fireman's box.

Appendix A: The defence of London

1. On 7 June 1915 at Ghent, Belgium, 2nd Lieutenant Reginald Warneford, RNAS, flying a Morane-Saulnier Type L, attacked German army airship LZ37. He chased the airship from the coast near Ostend and, despite its defensive machine-gun fire, succeeded in dropping his bombs on it, the last of which set the airship on fire. LZ37

subsequently crashed in Sint-Amandsberg. The explosion overturned Warneford's aircraft and stopped its engine. Having no alternative, Warneford had to land behind enemy lines, but after 35 minutes spent on repairs, he managed to restart the engine and returned to base. Warneford received the Victoria Cross for his exploits. Less than two weeks later he was involved in a flying accident, following which he died of his injuries on the way to hospital. He was buried at Brompton Cemetery on 21 June 1915 in a ceremony attended by thousands of mourners.

Appendix B: The German view

1. Johannisthal airfield, 10 miles south-east of Berlin, was Germany's first airfield. It opened on 26 September 1909, a few weeks after the world's first airfield at Rheims, France. The Johannisthal air disaster was one of the first multiple-fatality air disasters and involved the test flight of the German navy's L2 airship (manufactured by Luftschiffbau-Zeppelin as LZ18). On 17 October 1913, at approximately 10.30am, hydrogen gas which was being vented was sucked into the forward engine and ignited causing the airship to explode and burn. It crashed near Johannisthal airfield, resulting in the deaths of all twenty-eight passengers and crew on board.

Appendix C: On the ground

1. This was an HE bomb, which had exploded outside a house named 'Kerdistone', making a crater 30 feet wide in the road. The bomb severed water mains and damaged the roofs of two adjoining houses.
2. This flame was possibly that of the burning Glasgow Stud Farm, owned by Admiral of the Fleet the Hon Sir Hedworth Meux of Theobalds Park, near Cheshunt, where incendiaries had set alight a row of stables.

Appendix D: The Zeppelins' fates

1. German time was one hour ahead of that in Britain.

Sources and Bibliography

Primary sources

The National Archives, Kew, Surrey
AIR 1/543/16/15/4, Reports on air raids, various districts: Zeppelin or aircraft, April–June 1915 and June–November 1917.
AIR 1/552/16/15/38, Police reports and correspondence: air raids on England, January–June 1915.
AIR 1/563/16/15/69, British and foreign press cuttings about Zeppelins, April 1915–December 1916.
AIR 1/567/16/15/120, Record of Zeppelin attacks on England, carried out before 9.30pm, January 1915–November 1916.
AIR 1/605/16/15/247, Miscellaneous reports on various air raids, 1915.
AIR 1/633/17/122/89, Report of Zeppelin raid on London, 23/24 September 1916.
AIR 1/1259/204/9/1, Home Defence: action against Zeppelin raids, October 1915–April 1916.
AIR 1/1259/204/9/1A, Home Defence: reports on Zeppelin raids, October 1915.
AIR 1/1363/204/22/16, Zeppelin attack reports, May–June 1915.
AIR 1/2148/209/3/171, Four maps showing tracks of Zeppelins when raiding England, August–October 1915.
MEPO 2/1650, Zeppelin Raid on London: May 31 Divisional reports, 1915.
MPI 1/604/2a–2b, Report by the London Fire Brigade on air raid damages 23/24 September 1916.
MPI 1/604/3–4, Two maps showing the courses of Zeppelins during an air raid 23/24 September 1916.
MPI 1/604/5, North-east London. Map showing the routes of Zeppelins during an air raid 23/24 September 1916. Guns, lights on the ground and times of sightings are also shown.
MPI 1/605/1, Essex: Leyton (now in the London Borough of Waltham Forest). Map showing the location of bombs dropped by Zeppelin L31 during an air raid 23/24 September 1916.
MPI 1/605/4, Essex. Part of Ordnance Survey quarter-inch Third Edition England and Wales sheet 7 with coloured, MS additions illustrating an air raid 23–24 September 1916 and showing bombs dropped, objects dropped and direction of movements reported.

Waltham Forest Archives and Local Studies Library, Vestry House Museum, Walthamstow, London
Leyton Urban District Council minutes 1914–1919.
Leyton school logbooks 1914–1919.

Redbridge Information and Heritage Service, Central Library, Ilford, Essex
Ilford Urban District Council minutes 1914–1919.

Imperial War Museum, Lambeth, London
8153 Misc 208 (3020), Letter describing the Zeppelin Raid on London 17 August 1915.
79/15/1, Three typescript letters, nd [c.1916/1917/1918], from [Annie] Winifred Freeman, née Saunders, Leyton, to her parents.

Royal Air Force Museum, Hendon, London
X003-0322, Diary of Zeppelin raids in 1916 kept by a Brentwood schoolgirl, Nell Tyrrell.

Contemporary newspapers and magazines
Flight
The Leytonstone Express & Independent
The Ilford Recorder
The Times
The Walthamstow, Leyton & Chingford Guardian
The Walthamstow Sentinel
The War Illustrated: A Pictorial Record of the Conflict of Nations

Books and articles
ASHMORE, Major-General E.B., *Air Defence* (Longmans, Green & Co., 1929).

BARBER, Mark, *Royal Naval Air Service Pilot 1914–18* (Osprey Publishing, 2010).

BARFOOT, John, *Essex Airmen 1910–1918* (Tempus Publishing, 2006).

BARFOOT, John, *Over Here and Over There: Ilford's Aerodromes and Airmen in the Great War* (Ian Henry Publications, 1998).

BLAZICH, Frank A. Jr, 'The Enemy Above: British Reactions to German Zeppelin Raids in the Great War', *Stand To!*, No. 86 (August/September), 2009.

BOSTLE, Eileen, *Enfield's Night to Remember: the Airship Raid of 2nd/3rd September 1916* (Enfield Museum Service, 2014).

BOWYER, Chaz, *Bristol F2B Fighter* (Ian Allan, 1985).

BOWYER, Chaz, 'Home Defence 1914–18', *Aircraft Illustrated Extra*, No. 1 (August), 1969.

CASTLE, Ian, *London 1914–17: The Zeppelin Menace* (Osprey Publishing, 2008)

CASTLE, Ian, *London 1917–18: The Bomber Blitz* (Osprey, 2010).

CHORLTON, Martyn, 'Royal Aircraft Factory BE1 to BE12', *Aeroplane*, Vol. 42, No. 8 (August), 2014.

COLE, Christopher & CHEESMAN, E.F., *The Air Defence of Britain 1914–1918* (Putman, 1984).

COOKSLEY, Peter, *BE2 in Action* (Squadron/Signal Publications, 1992).

COOKSLEY, Peter G., *The Home Front. Civilian Life in World War One* (Tempus Publishing, 2006).

COOKSLEY, Peter G., *The RFC/RNAS Handbook 1914–18* (Sutton Publishing, 2000).

CROOKS, Nora, *The Road to Jeremy's Ferry: An Oral History of Lea Bridge Road* (Waltham Forest Oral History Workshop, 2003).

DAVIS, Leonard, *Chingfliers & Chingboys. The Story of Chingford Aerodrome 1915–1918* (Chingford Historical Society, 1996 (reprinted 2013)).

DAVIS, Mick, '6 Brigade RAF and its Predecessors – Some Further Aspects', *Cross & Cockade International*, Vol. 30, No. 2 (Summer), 1999.

DAVIS, Mick, *Sopwith Aircraft* (Crowood Press, 1999).

DAVIS, Mick & MORGAN, Bill, 'Gazetteer of Flying Sites in the UK and Ireland 1912–1920', *Cross & Cockade International*, 2010–2015.

DOBINSON, Colin, *AA Command* (Methuen, 2001).

EADE, David, *RAF North Weald. A Pictorial History* (Ad Hoc Publications, 2010).

EASDOWN, Martin & GENTH, Thomas, *A Glint in the Sky* (Pen & Sword, 2004).

van EMDEN, Richard & HUMPHRIES, Steve, *All Quiet on the Home Front: An Oral History of Life in Britain during the First World War* (Headline, 2003).

FARMER, Jack, *Woodford as I Knew It* (1986).

FAULKNER, Neil & DURRANI, Nadia, *In Search of the Zeppelin War: The Archaeology of the First Blitz* (Tempus Publishing, 2008).

FEGAN, Thomas, *The Baby Killers: German Air Raids on Britain in the First World War* (Pen & Sword, 2002).

FLETCHER, David, *War Cars. British Armoured Cars in the First World War* (HMSO, 1987).

FOLEY, Michael, *Essex in the First World War* (History Press, 2009).

FOWKES, Reginald L., *Woodford Then and Now* (Battle of Britain Prints International, 1981).

FREDETTE, Raymond H., *The Sky on Fire: The First Battle of Britain 1917–1918 and the Birth of the Royal Air Force* (Smithsonian Institution Press, 1966).

GARRISON, Air Commodore A.D., 'The First Battle of Britain', *Australian Defence Force Journal*, No. 91 (November/December), 1991.

GRAYZEL, Susan R., *At Home and Under Fire: Air Raids and Culture in Britain from the Great War to the Blitz* (Cambridge University Press, 2012).

GREEN, Georgina, *Keepers, Cockneys and Kitchen Maids. Memories of Epping Forest 1900–1925*, (1987).

GRIEHL, Manfred & DRESSEL, Joachim, *Zeppelin! The German Airship Story* (Arms & Armour Press, 1990).

GUNBY, Norman, *A Potted History of Ilford*, 2nd edn, 1997.

HADDOW, G.W. & GROSZ, Peter M., *The German Giants. The German R-Planes 1914–1918* (Putnam, 1988).

HALPENNY, Bruce Barrymore, *Action Stations. Vol. 8: Military Airfields of Greater London* (Patrick Stephens Ltd, 1984).

HANSON, Neil, *The First Blitz* (Doubleday, 2008).

HOLMAN, Brett, *The Next War in the Air: Britain's Fear of the Bomber, 1908–1941* (Ashgate, 2014).

HOON, John, *They Come, They Come! The Air Raids on London during the 1914–1918 War*, (1987).

JONES, H.A., *The War in the Air: Being the Story of the Part Played in the Great War by the Royal Air Force. Volume Three* (Clarendon Press, 1931; Naval & Military Press, 2002).

JONES, H.A., *The War in the Air: Being the Story of the Part Played in the Great War by the Royal Air Force. Volume Five* (Clarendon Press, 1931; Naval & Military Press, 2002).

LAYTON, R, 'Epping Forest and the Military during the Great War', *Essex Journal*, Vol. 23, No. 1 (Spring), 1988.

LEWIS, Jim, *London's Lea Valley and the Great War* (Libri Publishing, 2014).

LEWIS, Jim, *Weapons, Wireless and World Wars. The Vital Role of the Lea Valley* (Libri Publishing, 2010).

LINNARZ, Erich, 'I Was London's First Zepp Raider', *The Great War … I Was There!, Part 11*, nd [1938].

LONGMATE, Norman, *Island Fortress. The Defence of Great Britain 1603–1945* (Hutchinson, 1991).

MARWICK, Arthur, *The Deluge: British Society and the First World War* (Macmillan, 1965).

MONSON, Edward C.P. & MARSLAND, Ellis, *Air Raid Damage in London* (British Fire Prevention Committee, 1923).

MOOR, Anthony J., *Kent's Forgotten Airfield. Throwley 1917–1919* (Tempus Publishing, 2007).

MORRIS, A.J.A., *The Scaremongers. The Advocacy of War and Rearmament 1896–1914* (Routledge & Kegan Paul, 1984).

MORRIS, Joseph, *German Air Raids on Britain 1914–1918* (Sampson Low, Marston & Co, 1925; Nonsuch Publishing, 2007).

MORRIS, Richard, *The Man Who Ran London during the Great War* (Pen & Sword, 2010).

MUIR, Gerald T., 'A Home Defence Competition', *Cross & Cockade International*, Vol. 9, No. 4 (Winter), 1978.

Notes and Orders for Officers. Anti-Aircraft Corps of the Royal Naval Air Service. London Division (Royal Navy, 1914; Naval & Military Press, n.d.).

OAK-RHIND, Edwin Scoby, *The North Foreland Lookout Post in the Great War 1915–1917* (Michaels Bookshop [Ramsgate], 2005).

OSBORNE, Mike, *Defending London* (History Press, 2012).

OSBORNE, Mike, *20th Century Defences in Britain: The London Area* (Concrete Publications, 2006).

PENROSE, Harald, *British Aviation. The Great War and Armistice* (Putnam, 1969).

PERFECT, Charles Thomas, *Hornchurch during the Great War* (Benham, 1920).

PLUCK, A.R., *Stow Maries Great War Aerodrome* (Friends of Stow Maries Aerodrome, 2014).

POWERS, Barry D., *Strategy without Slide-Rule: British Air Strategy 1914–1939* (Croom Helm, 1976).

RAMSEY, Winston G., *The East End Then and Now* (Battle of Britain Prints International, 1997).

RAMSEY, Winston G. & FOWKES, Reginald L., *Epping Forest End Then and Now* (Battle of Britain Prints International, 1986).

RAWLINSON, Alfred, *The Defence of London 1915–1918* (A. Melrose, 1923; BiblioLife, 2010).

REAY, Colonel W.T.L., *The Specials: How They Served London. The Story of the Metropolitan Special Constabulary* (Heinemann, 1919).

RICHARDS, Peter G., 'Local Authorities and Civil Defence', *Public Administration Journal*, Vol. 30, No. 4 (December), 1952.

ROUTLEDGE, Brigadier N.W., *History of the Royal Regiment of Artillery: Anti-Aircraft Artillery 1914–55* (Brassey, 1994).

RUSIECKI, Paul, *The Impact of Catastrophe: The People of Essex and the First World War* (Essex Record Office, 2008).

SADLER, Nigel & COXON, Victoria, *Alfred Hitchcock: From Leytonstone to Hollywood* (Vestry House Museum, nd [c.2000])

SMITH, Eric, *First Things First. RAF Hornchurch and RAF Suttons Farm 1915–1962* (Ian Henry Publications, 1992).

SMITH, Graham, *Essex and its Race for the Skies 1900–1939* (Countryside Books, 2007).

SPOTO, Donald, *The Life of Alfred Hitchcock: The Dark Side of Genius* (Plexus Publishing Ltd, 1994).

STEPHENSON, Charles, *Zeppelins: German Airships 1900–40* (Osprey Publishing, 2004).

SUTHERLAND, Jonathan & CANWELL, Diane, *Battle of Britain 1917* (Pen & Sword, 2006).

TASKER, George E., *Country Rambles around Ilford* (South Essex Recorders Ltd, 1910).

TASKER, George E., *Country Rambles around Romford, Hornchurch and Upminster* (South Essex Recorders Ltd, 1911).

TAYLOR, John W.R., *Jane's Fighting Aircraft of World War I* (Studio, 1990).

THOMPSON, L.A., 'Trams and Trolleybuses in Ilford', *Ilford & District Historical Society*, Transaction No. 2, 1979.

WESTON, W.H., *The Story of Leyton and Leytonstone* (A. Wheaton & Co., 1921).

WARD, Bernard T., 'Lawrence of Arabia & Pole Hill, Chingford', *Essex Journal*, Vol. 9, No. 3 (Autumn), 1974.

WHITE, C.M., *The Gotha Summer: The German Daytime Raids on England May–August 1917* (Robert Hale, 1986).

WILLIAMS, Geoffrey, *Wings over Westgate* (Margate Civic Society, 1985) (reprinted 2014).

Websites

Airminded (http://airminded.org).

BARTHRAM, Adrienne, 'How did London civilians respond to the German airship raids of 1915?' (http://www.londonairshipraids1915.co.uk/zep_c.htm).

EVANS, J., 'The Dragon Slayers' (http://steemrok.com/features/Zepp.pdf).

Flight (http://www.flightglobal.com/pdfarchive/index.html).

FREEDMAN, Ariela, 'Zeppelin Fictions and the British Home Front' (http://www.jstor.org/stable/3831939).

Great War Forum (http://1914-1918.invisionzone.com/forums).

Hainault Farm airfield (http://www.prcraig.com/index.htm).

HOLMAN, Brett, 'The airship panic of 1913: the birth of aerial theatre and the British fear of Germany on the eve of the Great War' (http://airminded.org/downloads/download-info/the-airship-panic-of-1913-the-birth-of-aerial-theatre-and-the-british-fear-of-germany-on-the-eve-of-the-great-war).

West Essex Aviation (http://www.northwealdairfieldmuseum.com/West-Essex-Aviation-.html).

Zeppelin raids, Gothas and 'Giants' (http://www.iancastlezeppelin.co.uk/).

Index